THE
SOUTHERN ESSAYS
OF
Richard M. Weaver

Richard M. Weaver

THE

SOUTHERN ESSAYS

OF

Richard M. Weaver

EDITED BY GEORGE M. CURTIS, III

AND JAMES J. THOMPSON, JR.

Liberty*Press*

INDIANAPOLIS

Liberty*Press* is a publishing imprint of Liberty Fund, Inc., a foundation established to encourage study of the ideal of a society of free and responsible individuals.

The cuneiform inscription that serves as the design motif for our endpapers is the earliest-known written appearance of the word "freedom" (*ama-gi*), or "liberty." It is taken from a clay document written about 2300 B.C. in the Sumerian city-state of Lagash.

Cover photo from Black Star Publishing Co., Inc., New York, N.Y. Frontispiece photo courtesy of Mrs. Polly Weaver Beaton.

Library of Congress Cataloging-in-Publication Data

Weaver, Richard M., 1910–1963.
  The Southern essays of Richard M. Weaver.

  Includes index.
    1. Southern States—Civilization.   I. Curtis,
George M., 1935–   .   II. Thompson, James J.,
1944–   .   III. Title.
F209.5.W42   1987   975   87–2624

ISBN 0–86597–057–2
ISBN 0–86597–058–0 (pbk.)

10 9 8 7 6 5 4 3 2 1

So face with calm that heritage
And earn contempt before the age.

Allen Tate, "Brief Message" (1932)

CONTENTS

O N E

"Work with the Word":
Southern Literature and Thought

T W O

"The Contemplation of These Images":
The South in American History

T   H   R   E   E

"Discipline in Tragedy":
The Southern Tradition for an American Future

FOREWORD

The fact that it has clung to its belief in the supernatural, that it has never abandoned the idea that man is a special creation, that it persists in seeing life as a drama . . . in which creatures of free will make choices and are saved or damned, and that it has never accepted a simple equalitarianism is very closely related to its present literary renascence, as well as to its conservation of certain values that have been pretty well leached out of other societies. . . . The South remains, despite some terrible pounding from the outside and a good bit of betrayal within, a stronghold of humanism.

Richard M. Weaver
"The Land and the Literature" (1956)

Richard Weaver's career embodied the many strong recurring patterns revealed in the publications that record his mature thought from 1943 until his death in 1963, but none is more obvious and significant than his commitment to the American South and its civilization.

The first book that Weaver wrote was the study that would be published many years later as *The Southern Tradition at Bay* (1969); the present collection of his essays, long overdue, purports to be his last book. From the early 1940s until his sudden death, Weaver wrote regularly about Southern manners and mores, rhetoric and history, literature and religion.

Weaver explored what Allen Tate called the lower myth, which is "based upon ascertainable history," and the higher myth, which depends upon the religious imagination. The lower myth tends toward being literal and factual, the higher toward being symbolic; these views of the South meet, as Weaver has implied, in the idea and practice of chivalry, a secular religion.

Few critics of the South rival Richard Weaver in comprehensiveness of vision and depth of thought, and perhaps only Tate stands as clearly superior to him. The best Southern literary historian today, Lewis P. Simpson, may have been influenced by Weaver; and a similar indebtedness may apply to some of the work published by the best Southern historian of our time, C. Vann Woodward, whose "Irony of Southern History" was anticipated by Weaver in his commentaries on the Civil War.

These acutely written and closely argued pieces slightly overlap, since they were presented not for a book but for disparate occasions and purposes during the course of twenty years. Even so, over the two decades since Weaver's death, the essays have demonstrated marked originality and continuing vitality. "The Older Religiousness in the South," "Aspects of the Southern Philosophy," and "The South and the American Union" are profound and trenchant syntheses. "Agrarianism in Exile" (which is complemented here by "The Southern Phoenix") may well be the finest essay ever forged about the Vanderbilt group and *I'll Take My Stand.* "Contemporary Southern Literature," which belies its bland title, is among the strongest general essays written about the Southern renascence. And the essay on Randolph and Thoreau shows how good Weaver's comparative study of the minds of the South and New England would have been, had he lived to complete it.

Most of these pieces have been out of print for many years. To have them together, newly published, is more than a matter of convenience for readers seriously interested in the South, and the editors have accomplished far more than an act of piety toward the author and his native region: they have given us a singular testament of rare and enduring value.

George Core

George Core, who succeeded Andrew Lytle as editor of *The Sewanee Review* in 1973, is a frequent contributor to the periodical press. He has edited several books about the South, among them (with M. E. Bradford) Richard Weaver's *The Southern Tradition at Bay.*

PREFACE

Richard Weaver's name does not evoke instant recognition in most circles. Ideas, like the width of neckties and the length of hemlines, change with the seasons, and no one wants to be caught wearing yesterday's fashions. Few reputations endure in the realm of ideas. New thinkers constantly elbow their way to the fore, only to find themselves quickly relegated to the backwaters; the proverbial dustbin of history brims with long-forgotten thinkers and their moldering books. From 1948, when he published his first book, until his untimely death fifteen years later, Richard Weaver won substantial acclaim. His name continues to crop up from time to time, and a few devoted readers thumb his writings for their learning, clarity, and sagacity. One suspects, however, that even among conservatives Weaver, his importance acknowledged but his ideas no longer compellingly influential, is more mentioned than read. That is a distressing turn of events, for few American thinkers of the past half-century can match Weaver's keen perception.

The particulars of Weaver's life reveal nothing especially memorable. Born in 1910 in the western North Carolina town of Weaverville, he spent his adult years in the confines of academia. Having earned a bachelor's degree in English from the University of Kentucky in 1932, he entered Vanderbilt University and left two years later with an M.A. degree. After a brief stint of teaching, mainly at Texas A & M, he resumed graduate study, this time at Louisiana State University, which awarded him a doctorate in English in 1943. The University of Chicago then hired him to teach in its undergraduate college; he remained there until his death. In the 1940s his essays began to appear in literary quarterlies, and during his career he published several books, the most important of which were *Ideas Have Consequences* and *The Ethics of Rhetoric.* From his fugitive essays and unpublished manuscripts editors culled material for four more books: *Visions of Order, Life Without Prejudice, The Southern Tradition at Bay,* and *Language Is Sermonic.*

Weaver arrived at Vanderbilt during the high tide of Agrarianism, the intellectual movement sparked by the publication in 1930 of *I'll Take My Stand,* a volume of twelve essays written mainly by Vanderbilt professors and their former students. This reassertion of Southern tradition against the fragmentation and anomie of urban industrial society captured Weaver's interest, for like many young Southerners in the 1930s, he was exploring the meaning of Southernness. Weaver's two years in Nashville completed his disaffection with the liberalism he had imbibed at the University of Kentucky. Agrarianism provided him with a bedrock upon which to ground his subsequent thinking.

His adoption of the Agrarian creed has misled many interpreters to type him as a mere disciple of his Vanderbilt mentors, but Weaver was more than an epigone: having absorbed the Agrarians' ideas, he reshaped them, impressing upon them his own special mark. Unlike most of the original Agrarians, who were mainly poets, novelists, and literary critics, Weaver combined the sophisticated tools of the historian with the penetrating vision of an astute observer of contemporary culture. His erudition empowered him to trace the roots of the current malaise far back into the Middle Ages; his grounding in rhetoric gave him a keen sensitivity to the current corruption of language, logic, and the arts of persuasion; and his engagement with Agrarian principles, long after many of the contributors to *I'll Take My Stand* had de-

bouched in other directions, enabled him to adduce a power-
ful critique of American culture in the 1950s. In a sense,
Richard Weaver carried to completion the task begun by the
Agrarians in 1930.

While Weaver's far-ranging mind embraced many subjects
and crisscrossed several disciplines, the history of the South
remained at the center of his thinking. Although he never
wrote a full-scale history of the region, he did examine the
period from 1865 to the turn of the century in *The Southern
Tradition at Bay,* and in numerous essays he adumbrated his
view of the full sweep of the Southern past. Like the Agrarians, he admired the South's preservation of older European
modes of thinking and living, a phenomenon he spied in
everything from the Southern devotion to chivalry to the
"medieval" nature of Southern religion. Ten years before the
historian C. Vann Woodward, an opponent of the Nashville
school, published his famous essay "The Search for Southern
Identity," Weaver spotted the characteristic marks that
Woodward would later single out: the poverty, defeat, and
tragic sense which the Civil War had saddled upon the region.
More than any of the Agrarians, he perceived the overarching
significance of "the burden of Southern history" (to borrow
the title of one of Woodward's books).

Weaver derived his appreciation of liberty from Southern
history as well, for he discovered in his native land the evolution of a "social bond individualism" that he pitted against the
"anarchic individualism" that had emanated from the envi-
rons of Concord and Walden Pond. He coupled individual
liberty with duty and social responsibility to advance a concept of disciplined freedom, a stance he saw epitomized in
John Randolph of Roanoke. In the South's historic deference
toward the gentleman he seized a means of combating the rise
of the mass man that so disquieted the Spanish philosopher
Ortega y Gasset. His grasp of Southern history enabled him
to impose meaning on the unsettling international events of
the 1940s and 1950s. In the South's allegiance to a traditional

society he discerned a source of order and freedom to assert against the totalitarianism and nihilism of both fascism and communism.

While Weaver loved the South with a fierce passion, he avoided one of the besetting sins of some of the heirs of the Agrarians: a constricting sectionalism that thrives on the belief that all would have been well south of the Potomac had the Confederacy bested the Union armies. Weaver perceived that the infirmities of modern Western civilization transcended the dichotomy between North and South, for those problems were rooted in a decline of the medieval synthesis, a decline that long predated the collapse of the Confederacy. True, the South had much to teach the rest of America—lessons that the South itself came to learn only in the school of adversity after Appomattox—but the region had been no pristine Eden violated by rapacious Yankees. Weaver's appreciation of the best the North had to offer informs his respect for Abraham Lincoln, whom Weaver placed high in the ranks of American statesmanship. Witness to "the general retreat of humanism before universal materialism and technification," the conserver of Western civilization found himself as isolated in the South as in the North; the struggle to maintain humane values has no geographical boundaries. As Allen Tate wrote in the 1930s, with a similar disregard for geography: "All are born Yankees of the race of men."

Unlike some of his Agrarian mentors, Weaver sought no haven in the bitterness of despair. Although he was not much of a churchgoer, he possessed a deeply religious sensibility that allowed him to face the trials of modernity with equanimity. He was acutely aware of the frailty of humankind and of man's capacity for perverting and twisting the good, but he harbored as well a faith in man's ability to restore lost virtue and to pursue the right. He refused to surrender to the notion that Western civilization was doomed to ineluctable decay and disintegration. In 1952 he wrote: "There have been revolutions in human affairs which appear miraculous in the light of the conditions which preceded them. Ultimately it is the human psyche which determines the kind of world we live in, and history is marked with radical changes of phase which could undermine even so seemingly impregnable a thing as our modern scientific-technological order." This belief permitted Weaver to be that odd creature in the twentieth century: a resolutely hopeful traditionalist.

It is impossible to say what Richard Weaver's standing would be today had he lived beyond that truncated life of fifty-three years. There were many books he planned to write, many things he wanted to say. But we do not call his life truncated to imply that it was incomplete and unfinished; that would do Weaver a disservice. The body of work he completed speaks for itself, and one feels certain that it will be read and pondered as long as men still care deeply about civility and honor and liberty. Equally important is the personal example he bequeathed to posterity. Richard M. Weaver was a humane, decent man who confronted the modern world with courage and hope. His testimony on the merits of a life well lived remains as persuasive as ever. Those who count themselves his heirs could ask no more.

George M. Curtis, III
James J. Thompson, Jr.

George M. Curtis, III, formerly associated with the Papers of John Marshall and the Law Practice of Abraham Lincoln, is Professor of History at Hanover College, Hanover, Indiana.

James J. Thompson, Jr. is the book review editor of *The New Oxford Review* and the author of three books: *Tried as by Fire: Southern Baptists and the Religious Controversies of the 1920s, Christian Classics Revisited,* and *Fleeing the Whore of Babylon: A Modern Conversion Story.*

ACKNOWLEDGMENTS

This restoration of Richard M. Weaver's essays is a fitting celebration. Over the years, the editors, one from Weaver's South and the other from his adopted Midwest, have shared a world of historical ideas and values in which Weaver's work has assumed a greater and greater presence. As we collected Weaver's essays, a deep excitement grew as their richness became manifest. To our surprise and delight we discovered as well that the sum was greater than the parts: these essays possess a cohesiveness not often found in such collections.

In addition to Richard M. Weaver, we extend our thanks to John Stoll Sanders for his advice at the early stages of this project, to Richard T. Paustenbaugh for his bibliographic research, and to Polly Weaver Beaton for her generous encouragement.

The editors acknowledge the following journals and publishers for permission to republish these essays. "The Older Religiousness in the South," "Albert Taylor Bledsoe," "Southern Chivalry and Total War," and "Agrarianism in Exile" were first published in *The Sewanee Review*. (Copyright 1945, 1950, 1973, 1978 by the University of the South. Reprinted by permission of the editor.) "Lee the Philosopher" originally appeared in *The Georgia Review*, Vol. II, No. 3 (Fall 1948). (Copyright 1948; renewed 1975 by the University of Georgia. Reprinted by permission of *The Georgia Review* and Mrs. Polly Weaver Beaton.) "The Southern Phoenix" originally appeared in *The Georgia Review*, Vol. XVII, No. 1 (Spring

THE
SOUTHERN ESSAYS
OF
Richard M. Weaver

"Work with the Word":

Southern Literature

and Thought

1

THE TENNESSEE AGRARIANS

The often quoted saying of President Davis that if the South lost the war, its history would be written by the North, proved partly wrong and partly right. Between 1865 and 1900 the South wrote its history with vigor and in volume, and the literature of Southern apologia published in that period makes a fair-sized library. But there is some room for saying that the writers of these years wrote well rather than wisely, so that Davis's prophecy was in one point borne out. It was not so much history as special pleading which was presented; and while this may have softened, it did not materially change the national verdict.

This statement should of course not be made without due recognition of the genius and energy which were spent in defending the South's cause and in justifying its culture. The literature of the post-bellum era falls into three rather distinct phases: military and political defenses written in the shadow of defeat; romantic re-creations of ante-bellum civilization, chiefly in fiction; and continuations of the political and social argument, with some addition of perspective and objectivity. The first group contains some brilliant effort; and the South should never have been allowed to forget the herculean labors

Shenandoah, Vol. III, No. 2 (Summer 1952), 3–10.

of Albert Taylor Bledsoe, whose *Is Davis a Traitor?* is one of the great American polemics, or the militant work of Robert Lewis Dabney, whose *A Defense of Virginia and Through Her of the South* is a tough piece of reasoning. The second group was in milder vein. Represented most completely by John Esten Cooke and Thomas Nelson Page, it threw a silvery romance over all things Southern which was not entirely to the South's advantage, although the motives were unimpeachable. In the third group appeared men of such differing talents and vocations as Woodrow Wilson, Basil Gildersleeve (whose article "A Southerner in the Peloponnesian War" is worth reading today), J. L. M. Curry, and John S. Wise. To their exposition they brought the detachment of time and some feeling of re-incorporation in the Union. Yet as the period closed with the South trying to explain itself and gain recognition, there is reason to say that its history was still being framed from the outside.

The effective statement of its cause did not appear until a quarter of a century later, from men who had never worn Confederate gray, or witnessed the chaos of Reconstruction, or even cherished political ambition. These were a group of scholars and writers having a kind of center at Vanderbilt University, who found, mainly through their literary and philosophic disciplines, the means of giving the South what it had so long needed—a doctrine resting upon independent assumptions. The Fugitive-Agrarian movement took form in the early 1920's, and it presented during the next fifteen years one of the few effective challenges to a monolithic culture of unredeemed materialism. This challenge received its most comprehensive expression in a symposium entitled *I'll Take My Stand,* published in 1930. Here twelve self-confessed Southerners drew up a now classic indictment of the industrial society and its metaphysic "Progress."

Although the Agrarians were men of academic and literary profession, two things had combined to turn their attention to the question of regional difference. First, a considerable number of them had enjoyed the opportunity of European education or residence, which the older Southern spokesmen generally had not. That experience had led them to look at the South in the broad picture of Western European civilization. What they saw—what they had to see—was that the South, with its inherited institutions and its system of values, was a continuation of Western European culture and that the North was the deviation. That discovery takes on significance as soon as one reflects that by rule the deviation, and not the continuation, requires the defense. Thus there appeared a logical ground for putting the South in the position of plaintiff and the North in that of defendant, a reversal of the roles which had been played for a hundred years.

Second, an important number of Agrarians were poets. The very acceptance of poetry commits one to the realm of value, and this meant that their judgments were to be in part ethical and aesthetic. They were thus concerned immediately with the quality of the South; and this orientation put the case upon an independent footing. It was of course impossible to revive interest in the South's legal claims, and political claims alter with circumstances. But claims based upon ethical and aesthetic considerations are a different matter; they cannot be ignored at any time, and it was these which furnished the principal means of attack.

In sum, it was not until about 1925 that Southern intellectuals caught up with Lee and Jackson. The latter had known in 1862 that the one chance for the South was to carry the fight to the enemy. They fully appreciated the principle, only recently brought to public attention, though actually as old as warfare, that the best defense is a good offense. For various reasons, chiefly political, they were prevented from carrying out that policy, and the defensive struggle ended in defeat. A comparable fate overtook the Southern apologists of the next fifty or sixty years, as we have already indicated. They spent themselves in parrying, denying, and defending, and their victories were defensive victories. But with *I'll Take*

My Stand the turn came; here Southern intellectuals for the first time conducted a general offensive against the enemy positions, with some excellent results. Penetrations were made and flanks were threatened; and the enemy was alerted to a degree he had not experienced in decades. I stress this aspect despite the suggestion of the book's title and titles of some of the contributions. They sound defensive, but the tactic was actually offense. A few representative quotations will make that apparent enough.

No reader of the volume will forget, for example, John Crowe Ransom's demolishing attack upon the theory of industrial society.

> Progress never defines its ultimate objective, but thrusts its victims at once into an infinite series. Our vast industrial machine, with its laboratory centers of experimentation, and its far-flung organs of mass production, is like a Prussianized state which is organized strictly for war and can never consent to peace.
>
> There can never be stability and establishment in a community whose every lady member is sworn to see that her mate is not eclipsed in the competition for material advantages; the community will fume and ferment, and every constituent part will be in perpetual physical motion. The good life depends on leisure, but leisure depends on an establishment, and the establishment depends on a prevailing magnanimity which scorns personal advancement at the expense of the free activity of the mind.
>
> Industrialism is an insidious spirit, full of false promises and generally fatal to establishments since, when it once gets into them for a little renovation, it proposes never to leave them in peace. Industrialism is rightfully a menial, of almost miraculous cunning but no intelligence; it needs to be strongly governed or it will destroy the economy of the household. Only a community of tough conservative habit can master it.

John Gould Fletcher took the subject of education. Traditional Southern education of the classical type had as its aim the producing of good men. Now we are being asked to surrender that in favor of the type which makes "the public-school product of New York City or Chicago a behaviorist, an experimental scientist in sex and firearms, a militant atheist, a reader of detective fiction, and a good salesman." Furthermore:

> We achieve character, personality, gentlemanliness in order to make our lives an art and to bring our souls into relation with the whole scheme of things, which is the divine nature. But the present-day system of American popular education exactly reverses this process. It puts that which is superior—learning, intelligence, scholarship—at the disposal of the inferior. It says in effect that if the pupil acquires an education, he will be better able to feed and clothe his body later. It destroys the intellectual self-reliance of character, and the charm of balanced personality, in order to stuff the mind with unrelated facts. Its goal is industry rather than harmonious living and self-aggrandisement rather than peace with God.

Stark Young expressed the choice before us:

> It would be childish and dangerous for the South to be stampeded and betrayed out of its own character by the noise, force, and glittering narrowness of the industrialism and progress spreading everywhere, with varying degrees, from one region to another.
>
> We can put one thing in our pipes and smoke it—there will never again be distinction in the South until—somewhat contrary to the doctrine of popular and profitable democracy—it is generally clear that no man worth anything is possessed by the people, or sees the world under a smear of the people's wills and beliefs.
>
> This, at present, un-American idea of education may spread if in our schools and universities a less democratic, mobbed, and imitative course of things should come to be; with less booming and prating, organizing, unrest, babble about equipment, election of trustees from the Stock Exchange—all signs of an adolescent mentality and prosperous innocence of what culture may mean. I shall never forget the encouragement with which I saw for the first time that some of the dormitory doors at the University of Virginia needed paint, so sick was I at the bang-up varnishing, re-building, plumbing, endowing, in some of the large Northern institutions. If they learn little at these Virginia halls,

it is doubtless as much as they would learn at the others, and they at least escape the poison of the success idea that almost every building is sure to show, the belief that mechanical surface and outer powers of money are the prime things in living.

These were startling sentiments, but it can be said with truth, in looking back over the total response, that the nation as a whole welcomed this book. That is because the nation as a whole wishes the South to speak, and wishes it to speak *in character.* The last phrase is essential. Despite our excitement over differences, our pain over invidious comparisons, and our resentment of suspected superiorities, we desire, as long as we are in possession of our rational faculty, to hear an expression of the other point of view. That is a guarantee of our freedom and a necessity for our development. And the other point of view, to carry any conviction, must not be expressed apologetically. When you are impressed with the positive value of anything, whether it be a way of life or a creed or an art-form, you do not fall back upon defensive postures, for that is to accept defeat in advance. You go forth in the evangelical spirit and seek out the opponent. That is why *I'll Take My Stand* was read in quarters where the vapid professions of Southern liberals aroused no sign of interest.

Of course there were elements by which the book was not welcomed, and they can be pretty well tagged by the brickbats they threw. Among them were, as would be guessed, the philistines, including especially journalists of both the literary and newspaper variety. The ground of their opposition is not far to seek. Being opposed to culture as such, they no doubt realized that any genuine revival of culture would leave them exposed for what they are. The mortal enmity of philistine and poet was present in this clash. These opponents made much noise, but it is hard for them to touch people who work at the level of *I'll Take My Stand* and other Agrarian publications.

There was another type of critic who summed up his opposition in the familiar saying, "You can't turn the clock back."

The most charitable thing that can be said of him is that he is confused in a fundamental way. No one beyond the first grade in philosophy believes that time can be reversed. What the Agrarians, along with people of their philosophic conviction everywhere, were saying is that there are some things which do not have their subsistence in time, and that certain virtues should be cultivated regardless of the era in which one finds oneself born. It is the most arrant presentism to say that a philosophy cannot be practiced because that philosophy is found in the past and the past is now gone. The whole value of philosophy lies in its detachment from accidental conditions of this kind and its adherence to the essential. Any idealistic position must insist that circumstances yield to definitions and not definitions to circumstances. These opponents have not considered the saying of Spinoza: "In so far as the mind conceives a thing according to the dictate of reason, it will be equally affected whether the idea be of a thing present, past, or future."

A more formidable opposition appeared among what might be called the Southern collaborationists. They are men who have accepted completely the doctrine of progress, and who have their entire investment of substance, position, and prestige in it. They are the ones who want more factories, more of everything which would make the South a replica of Lowell and Schenectady and Youngstown with a consequent swelling of bank deposits and payrolls. Not all of them are disingenuous; some of them are simply unable to see an alternative. The collaborationists were not very vocal in the terms of this argument; but they work from richly upholstered offices, and it is they who have dealt the Agrarians their hardest blow. With the business man's grasp of reality, they have sensed the opposition to their order in a vital religious-aesthetic movement, and they have countered with a shrewd stroke. They have dispersed the Agrarians. Undoubtedly the Agrarians would exert an immensely greater influence if they held some city or some university, if they had a concentration of forces which would serve as a radiating center of impulse—if they had a Rome, as it were. This the business men have seen to it they do not have. Scattered now from Nashville to New Haven and from Princeton to Minneapolis they are comparatively impotent. The collaborationists have had the best of this phase, and the Agrarians are left with only a rhetorical victory.

It would be false to deny that in the practical realm things have become very much worse. There is no more melancholy spectacle on the American scene than the fact that South Carolina, which in former times set the best example of the ideal of chivalry, is now the site of the hydrogen bomb project, which prepares for indiscriminate slaughter on a scale not hitherto contemplated. Thus far there has been no objection from South Carolina. And indeed other Southern states are in no way behind in asking for industrialism on any terms and for any purpose.

Yet over against these discouraging facts one may set certain facts about human history and development. One of them is that the potentiality for change is always greater than we realize at any given moment. There have been revolutions in human affairs which appear miraculous in the light of the conditions which preceded them. Ultimately it is the human psyche which determines the kind of world we live in, and history is marked with radical changes of phase which could undermine even so seemingly impregnable a thing as our modern scientific-technological order. One could not do better than close with the final sentences of the "Introduction" to *I'll Take My Stand*. They are more important now than they were then, since an even greater fraction of our people seems to believe that we are being hurried along by uncontrollable forces toward a society like that depicted by Orwell in *Nineteen Eighty-four*:

If a community, or a section, or a race, or an age, is groaning under industrialism, and well aware that it is an evil dispensation, it must find the way to throw it off. To think that this cannot be done is pusillanimous. And if the whole community, section, race, or age thinks it cannot be done then it has simply lost its political genius and doomed itself to impotence.

2

THE SOUTHERN PHOENIX

Under the echoing title *I'll Take My Stand* there appeared in 1930 one of the great works of American social criticism. During the intervening thirty-odd years it has had a variegated history of praise and neglect, of criticism and attack; and those who have not been able to place it have resorted to the epithet "controversial," which is the language of journalism and reviewing for saying that a book touches upon real values. That much it is certainly safe to concede; now an issue in the *Harper Torchbook Series* will enable many more persons to understand what the controversy is about and at the same time to learn something of the pluralism of American culture.

The original time of appearance of *I'll Take My Stand* deserves comment. The military overthrow of the Confederacy was accomplished in 1865. By 1900, according to some historians, the road to reconcilement had been traveled to a final beatific reconcilement. During the next three decades an industrialism spreading everywhere and the First World War appeared to cement even closer the sections of the nation. In the whole meanwhile the funeral sermon of the Old South was preached so many times that most people thought it was

The Georgia Review, Vol. XVII, No. 1 (Spring 1963), 6–17.

really going to be interred. But in 1929 there occurred a cataclysm which shattered, perhaps permanently, the power of that group which had used the Civil War to gain political and financial hegemony over the nation and write finis to Southern influence. The year following saw a revival of the Southern idea of life, after all the obsequies, in a brilliant symposium of defenses by a group of poets and scholars centered around Vanderbilt University.

It is somewhat anomalous that a symposium should achieve the quality of a permanently great work of social criticism. Most symposia suffer grievously from unevenness, and in the poorer ones the contributors are likely to go riding off in all directions. Two things have been properly cited for giving *I'll Take My Stand* a unity and a uniformly high excellence. First, it was the product of a group in more or less constant association with one another. Great works of the mind have often if not usually been of this kind of origin; genius and talent are infectious; intellect responds to intellect; and the work, even if it should be finally authored or completed by one individual, is borne forward by a knowledge that others are thinking in the same way. Second, the authors were all the inheritors of a distinct and cohesive tradition, which meant that many things were understood by them quickly and intuitively— things that tedious explication can only make dull or irrelevant, as is well attested by the reports of our "national committees" and such organizations. And if I may add a third reason: an acute consciousness that their culture had been under attack for a hundred years must have been a great challenge to men who sensed that in dialectical and rhetorical power they were at least the equals of the attackers.

An interesting feature of *I'll Take My Stand* and a feature which made it obnoxious or incomprehensible to many was the fact that it was both anti-socialist and anti-capitalist. Before the public at a time when socialism in the guise of the New Deal was about to challenge American capitalism, it presented a third alternative in the form of a conservative agrarian social order. As a realized way of life in America, agrarianism was far older than either socialism or capitalism; and as an articulated theory it was at least as old as capitalism. Its intellectual origins trace back as far as Jefferson, and in some ways to Crèvecoeur. A passage from Jefferson's *Notes on Virginia* has often been cited as a canon.

> Those who labor in the earth are the chosen people of God, if ever He had a chosen people, whose breasts he made His peculiar deposit for substantial and genuine virtue. It is the focus in which He keeps alive that sacred fire, which otherwise might escape from the face of the earth. Corruption of morals in the mass of cultivators is a phenomenon of which no age nor nation has furnished an example. It is the mark set on those who, not looking up to heaven, to their own soil and industry, as does the husband-man, for their subsistence, depend for it on casualties and caprice of customers. Dependence begets subservience and venality, suffocates the germ of virtue, and prepares fit tools for the designs of ambition. Thus, the natural progress and consequence of the arts, has sometimes perhaps been retarded by accidental circumstances; but, generally speaking, the proportion which the aggregate of other classes of citizens bears in any State to that of its husbandmen is the proportion of its unsound to its healthy parts, and is a good enough barometer whereby to measure its degree of corruption.

The body of theory underlying *I'll Take My Stand,* however, received its greatest and most systematic exposition when John Taylor, of Caroline County, Virginia, published his massive *An Inquiry into the Principles and Policy of the Government of the United States* in 1814. (It is a commentary on the course history has taken that this American Cincinnatus has been relegated to footnotes.) The object of Taylor's sustained attack was "the system of paper and patronage," devised by Hamilton and later made into a reality by the Civil War and its consequences. Taylor stood for widely distributed property, distributed political power, and rigid abstention by the government from any allocation of wealth by political means.

This he put forward as the true defense of private property. His concept of government deserves to be called the purest ever held by any American in respect to its republican simplicity and the completeness with which it opposes nationalism and "development" by the apparatus of the state.

Socialism is by definition anti-conservative, and capitalism cannot be conservative in the true sense as long as its reliance is upon industrialism, whose very nature it is to unsettle any establishment and initiate the endless innovation of technological "progress." But with Taylor's political prescription and whatever of Jefferson can be stripped of his French-style radicalism, one has the theoretical foundation for a conservative order.

Moreover, this has historically been the South's social order. From the beginning to the most recent decades the South has been predominantly agricultural. Furthermore, from the struggle over the Missouri question, through the Civil War, through the regaining of home rule and the defeat of the Lodge "Force Bill" in 1890 down to today in its battle to keep control of its educational system the South has been the champion of local sovereignty as a paramount political consideration. It is a diverse region which has believed in the reality of diversity. In the South, it has been said, a man from another county is a stranger and one from another state is a foreigner. The jest embodies some truth and some political wisdom. Generalization is attenuation; affection always turns toward the perceptible and the concrete. During almost twenty years of residence in Illinois I have yet to hear anyone remark, "That is an Iowa accent," or "That is an Ohio accent." But in North Carolina I have often heard, "That is a South Carolina accent."

For generations Southerners have shown an unswerving loyalty to their section, with the exception of a few today who are exhibiting the disintegrative effects of modern liberalism. They have shown this loyalty toward a region in which many outsiders can see little to be patriotic over. It is poor, comparatively, which is held to be the modern disgrace; it has preserved more than a little of the social structure of feudalism, which is supposed to be effrontery to the forces of history; it has handed down faith in a sacred literature, which is indeed anachronistic; and it has shown some reservations about the scientific interpretation of the world, which is regarded as a scandal. In a word, it has been a stumbling block to modernism.

The contributors to the symposium are not unanimous, but they are remarkably in accord. They stand for an agrarian economy as respectable and salutary; for a way of life that exalts leisure and contemplation over money-making and success; for a culture of manners and distinction. Everything that materialism and philistinism appeared to have routed from the scene is here reaffirmed in a reasoned case, and without a trace of that mawkish apology which often attends the presenting of an unpopular view. Yet the book is addressed to the world, for the test is not whether a quality happened to have ante-bellum ancestry, but whether it properly belongs to a humane social order.

Among the Southern qualities forcefully exemplified by these writers is eloquence. Paraphrase could not do justice to many vivid passages, and therefore liberal direct quotation will be necessary. The symposium was opened by John Crowe Ransom, whose essay "Reconstructed but Unregenerate" denoted by its title that although a people might be politically reconstructed, its culture is a matter of birth and growing, hardly amenable to political edict.

> The Southerner must know, and in fact he does very well know that his antique conservatism does not exert a very great influence against the American progressivist doctrine. The Southern idea today is down, and the progressive or American idea is up. But the historian and the philosopher, who take views that are thought to be respectively longer and deeper than most, may very well reverse this order and find that the Southern idea rather

than the American has in its favor the authority of example and the approval of theory. And some prophet may even find it possible to expect that it will yet rise again.

This is by way of prologue; the analysis that follows is of the doctrine of progress and its genie, applied science. Societies in the past, Mr. Ransom points out, have not conceived it in their interest to war continually against nature. Once a reasonable material establishment had been achieved, man turned his attention to humane ends. " . . . [H]e concludes a truce with nature, and he and nature seem to live on terms of mutual respect and amity, and his loving arts, religions, and philosophies come spontaneously into being: these are the blessings of peace." But a modern industrialized society "is like a Prussianized state which is organized strictly for war and can never consent to peace." In this state "Industrialism is a menial of almost miraculous cunning but no intelligence." Hence it is that "progress never defines its ultimate objective, but thrusts its victims at once into an infinite series."

Industrialism had come to the South, and with it the necessity for a decision. There was still a chance that a community of "tough conservative habit" could master the aimless forces that industrialism unleashes. And more specifically there was the chance that the South could hope to preserve its regional culture as Scotland had succeeded in doing, by tenacious resistance against being absorbed into an alien way of life.

In the course of a long and much admired writing career, it is doubtful that Ransom has produced anything more brilliant than this. Its pages are alive with sentences that are texts for anyone addressing himself to the humane economy.

Donald Davidson in "A Mirror for Artists" demolished the notion that industrialism can play Maecenas to the arts. Industrialism prevents the conditions of life out of which true art emerges. It can create wealth; it can organize and distribute; but it destroys the one thing most needful for artistic creation: the *attitude* of leisure. "The arts will not easily survive a condition under which we work and play at cross purposes." For the leisure made possible by industrialism is not a source of fruitfulness. "The leisure thus offered is really no leisure at all; either it is pure sloth, under which the arts take on the character of entertainment, purchased in boredom and enjoyed in utter passivity, or it is another kind of labor, taken up out of a sense of duty, pursued as a kind of fashionable enterprise for which one's courage must be continually whipped up by reminders of one's obligation to culture." He went on to note that most of America's artists have been of provincial birth. "Our megalopolitan agglomerations, which make a great ado about art, are actually sterile on the creative side; they patronize art; they merchandise it, but they do not produce it." Mr. Davidson saw the crisis as so depressing that the artist was called upon to make use of his citizenship to help defeat, even on the practical level, the forces that were undermining art.

The distinguished historian Frank L. Owsley centered his attack upon Northern hegemony. Referring to Lincoln's "house divided" argument, he declared that the Civil War was an irrepressible conflict once one accepted the proposition that the nation had to be all this or all that. This position, unless it is taken very circumspectly, can result in the ultimate intolerance and enforced standardization (and to bring the matter down to date, let us add regimentation). Anyone could see that the North had partly succeeded in stamping its image upon the nation and in getting its history accepted as the story of the nation. Southern children learned to speak of "our Puritan fathers"; but "no child ever heard of the Southern Puritan fathers—the great horde of Scotch-Irish Presbyterians and German Lutherans and other strict and puritanical peoples who had pushed to the Mississippi River and far north of the Ohio before the New England population had got a hundred miles west of Boston."

John Gould Fletcher made an eloquent plea for placing Southern education again "on a sound, historical, conservative basis." The foundation of the ante-bellum Southern educational system had been the academy, which had given to selected students a basic training in the classical tradition. The old system might have been imperfect in detail, but its aim had been correct. In contrast, he declared, today's public school graduate of New York City or Chicago is prepared for being "a behaviorist, an experimental scientist in sex and firearms, a militant atheist, a reader of detective fiction, and a good salesman." Furthermore, "There is reason to believe that the public school system has had not a little to do with the industrial degradation" which can be symbolized by such places as Lowell, Massachusetts, and Paterson, New Jersey.

In many ways the most penetrating essay in the collection is that of Lyle H. Lanier, then Professor of Psychology at Vanderbilt. Like Ransom's, this is largely a critique of that most magic of modern talismans, the concept of progress. "Progress is both a slogan and a philosophy, a device for social control and a belief in the reality of a process of development toward some far-off divine event." It would be well, Professor Lanier said, if we could adopt an agnostic attitude toward progress, yet this is practically impossible owing to its tremendous social consequences as an idea in America. Though progress is essentially a modern concept, it can be traced to Francis Bacon, "the precursor of the spirit of modern life." From his view of knowledge as primarily useful have flowed pragmatism, instrumentalism, and positivism. But the philosophy of John Dewey inaugurated a new development in the idea of progress. By rejecting form and fixity in the world and by seeking to make democracy the supreme sanction, Dewey offered "a metaphysical rendering of communism or socialism." Given his set of values, the industrial system has a distinct educational function. But Dewey's theory of a reconstituted society, which would entail a remaking of human nature, rested on propositions not at all self-evident to the author, who treated them to a devastating psychological examination.

Space forbids a sampling of every contribution, but one more essay which should be noted in some detail is Stark Young's "Not in Memoriam, but in Defense." This is at once the most eloquent and the most polemical presentation in the book. Its uncompromising line appears on the first page, with the declaration that "It would be childish and dangerous for the South to be stampeded and betrayed out of its own character by the noise, force, and glittering narrowness of the industrialism and progress spreading everywhere, with varying degrees, from one region to another." Mr. Young was well aware that in some areas there were signs of "confusion and retreat." But if there was one thing which Southerners should view with special abhorrence, it was the habit of deferring to the masses, which is so widely encouraged by industrialism. "In my opinion the South should be told, flatly and coldly that, with other sections acting as they choose, such moral canting, confidence, and whining belong to a village of cobblers and small traders, and are based on ignorance, commonness, and a sense of what will pay." And further on the same head: "We can put one thing in our pipes and smoke it—there will never again be distinction in the South until—somewhat contrary to the doctrine of popular and profitable democracy—it is generally clear that no man worth anything is possessed by the people, or sees the world under a smear of the people's wills and beliefs."

He hoped that the South would return to the idea that university education "is suited to a small number only," while remaining indifferent to the "bang-up varnishing, re-building, and plumbing" which were construed as signs of educational progress in other sections.

Willingness to accept and defend provincialism as a positive good is practically a test of a Southerner's patriotism. I do not know of a more forthright or a finer statement of its virtues than the following:

Provincialism that is a mere ramification of some insistent egotism is only less nauseous than the same egotism in its purity, raw self without any province to harp upon. But provincialism proper is a fine trait. It is akin to a man's interest in his own center, which is the most deeply rooted consideration that he has, the source of his direction, health, and soul. . . . With or without knowing the rest of the world, you can, against all odds, defend your provincialism to yourself by simple inner necessity, as you think of your own nature, which you would not at bottom change with anyone else. . . . People who give up their own land too readily need careful weighing, exactly as do those who are so with their convictions. I am not sure that one of the deepest mysteries, one of the great, as it were, natural beauties of the heart, does not lie in one's love for his own land.

Now we must ask what there is unique in this agrarian "manifesto," so that for serious students of American intellectual history it must stand as a landmark. If we think of it simply as an "ism," we must note that it had a great deal of competition, even in the period of its publication. Among the rival theories and philosophies were Humanism, Marxism, technocracy, and very shortly later, New Dealism. The importance of agrarianism—an importance we should expect to be realized by the serious student, if not much regarded by cultists, special pleaders, and political and intellectual opportunists—is that it presents a complete regime. There is nothing of the narrowness of a cult about it or the specialism of a single-track solution. Humanism was very much a cult, not only unable to propagate itself generally but also unable to win stocktakers among the intellectuals for very long. Marxism was fatally flawed by its assumption that economics is the prime determinant of social organization. Technocracy was nothing more than an engineering approach to the problems of economic dislocation. New Dealism, though socialistic in tendency, hardly enjoyed the benefits of a theory at all; it was a hand-to-mouth dealing with problems created by the Great Depression, a set of improvisations which became more politicized as time went on.

When we compare any of these with agrarianism, we are struck by how much more comprehensive and coherent it is as a program. It began, as all philosophies should begin, by considering man in relation to the creation. Thus Ransom notes: "out of so simple a thing as respect for the physical earth and its teeming life comes a primary joy, which is an inexhaustible source of arts and religions and philosophies." Quite accordingly, it finds a place for religion. Both Ransom and Tate deal with the mystery of nature in her fullness and Tate with religion as providing the ultimate morale.

It has something to say about social structure, even though most of this had to be said indirectly, so as not to be too rude to democratic equalitarianism. It freely recognizes differences in people and insists that these differences ought to be built upon or utilized creatively—this in place of futile plans for erasing them. The essays on education and on the Negro meet this issue squarely.

It has much to say about the place of art in society and about the conditions that render true art possible. It stands for bringing art to the people, not by way of purchase and endowment, but through providing opportunity for creative impulses. It has something to say about those almost perished arts, manners, conversations, and hospitality. These things, which enter into the very texture of living, are always beneath the notice of Utopian theorists and social planners, and understandably so, since they could hardly flourish in their worlds.

Finally, there is a great deal said about the economy, which is to be primarily in the eyes of some contributors and substantially in the eyes of all, agrarian. Agriculture as "the best and the most sensitive vocation" makes its contribution to the good life. It keeps man in contact with nature, whose presence he ought to remain aware of; it imparts to his living a rhythm which is natural and not mechanical. Agrarian orders have been characterized by stability, whereas industrial societies, through the very character of their expansion and "progress," have proved notoriously unstable. As Herman Clarence Nixon summed up the role of the South's agricultural predominance: "The section's historic agrarianism offers a check and a contrast to America's rush from a continental frontierism to a world-penetrating industrialism under a maximum play of materialistic motive and a minimum of restraint of traditional background."

There are those who will say that all "back to the soil" movements are pure romanticism, and that they would never have found followers had not certain eighteenth century delusions taken root. They are expressions of nostalgia, of ignorance, of absurd values resting on empty idealizations.

Historically this is very far from being true. The belief that there is a relationship between the life of rural husbandry and political and civic virtue goes back to ancient times. A passage from Aristotle's *Politics* is very apposite on this point:

> The best common people are the agricultural population, so that it is possible to introduce democracy as well as other forms of constitution where the multitude lives by agriculture or by pasturing cattle. For owing to their not having much property they are busy, so that they cannot often meet in the assembly, while owing to their having the necessaries of life they pass their time attending to their farmwork and do not covet their neighbors' goods. . . . It is manifest therefore that this is the best of the forms of democracy, and why this is so—namely, because in it the common people are of a certain kind.

Even earlier we find in Xenophon's *The Economist* a picture of the "Greek country squire," the *aner kalos kai agathos.* Xenophon declares that "quite high and mighty people find it hard to hold aloof from agriculture, devotion to which would seem to be thrice blest, combining as it does a certain sense of luxury with the satisfaction of an improved estate, and such a training in physical energies as shall fit a man to play a freeman's part." According to *The Economist,* not only does the earth make men virile and fit, she also is a teacher of virtue: ". . . earth of her own good will gives lessons in justice and uprightness to all who can understand her meaning, since the nobler the services of devotion rendered, the ampler and richer her recompense."

Much the same tenor of thought runs through Horace, and we know that Southerners of the ante-bellum cultivated class found highly congenial Horace's delight in country living and his joy in the presence of familiar things.

To add a postlude here, Rome spent a century or two trying to get people out of the cities and back to the land. Her failure to do so is one of the most frequently cited causes of the death of the Republic.

Agrarianism is thus neither an offspring of modern romanticism nor a theory of life, and in part of politics, without previous intellectual sponsors. Coming down to much later times, we can place *I'll Take My Stand* in the tradition of Tocqueville for its probing of the weaknesses of democracy, and in that of Jacob Burckhardt for its concern with the things of the spirit.

The antecedents are there, but now what of the contemporary consequences? It is evident on all sides that the South has not taken the prescription of *I'll Take My Stand*. The babble about progress is more ignorant and brazen than ever before. The most conservative of old commonwealths are now frantically advertising for industry. Half-educated journalists talk of "seeds of Southern change" or write "epitaphs for Dixie." What survives seems to survive by inertia, with only here and there an articulate voice raised in defense.

On this general trend of things, two or three observations can be made with confidence. Some people appear to believe that technology is our fatality. It is something we are doomed to, and the doom is so inexorable that fighting against it only helps it along. Proponents of this view talk mystically about the "forces of history," and one can find them in the most dignified academic chairs.

But they are wrong, and why they are wrong can be answered out of John Taylor, from 1814: nothing that has a moral source is inevitable. A political and even an economic order is a moral creation; and men are ingenious and persistent enough to have what they want. It is in the obscure depths of the wanting that the real problem must be sought.

A more realistic explanation is that the world has been engulfed by a vast demoralization and no place has been spared; it has spread to Asia, Africa, and the islands of the sea. Its most prominent feature is perhaps materialism, but this has been greatly abetted by that compound of humbug, pretense, and vulgarity which can be labeled "Hollywood values." We could not expect the South to remain unaffected by a change of this magnitude. After all, one can get into an automobile in Detroit and roll well into the South in twenty-four hours. Modern mobility has had a great role in spreading the noxious as well as the salutary. Southern culture had roots, but far more deeply rooted cultures have not been able to withstand the general externalization and vulgarization, as any tourist to Europe can testify.

The South then has been caught up in this movement and is showing its effects. The movement is so tremendous and encompassing that anyone who tries to oppose or criticize it is likely to be called a crank, or, if he is taken more seriously, to be denounced as an enemy of progress.

It is rumored that today, after a lapse of thirty years, some of the contributors would no longer subscribe to their essays. If that be true, one can only speculate about the reasons. People are ready for different ideas at different times. It is humanly possible to become bored with an idea, or indifferent to it, or estranged from it; one can change his personal situation, and one can simply grow old. Let us at least note that these essays were written by men in their prime.

Faulkner at Stockholm, out of that perspective which must come from long dedication to pure art, said that man will prevail. As Professor Randall Stewart has pointed out, "prevail" is here used in the Biblical sense. Man will prevail against the forces of the adversary which are out to destroy him, and one of the ways to destroy him is to dehumanize him. With a good deal of geographical and historical particularity, that is what *I'll Take My Stand* is saying. It is possible to affirm a humane order in the face of the most towering odds, and by faith and work it is possible to achieve it. Any other outlook is bleak and hopeless. *I'll Take My Stand* is controversial because the argument goes on in the spirit, and it would be suicidal to assume that what is more humane and therefore eschatological must lose out.

At the very time when John Milton was publishing *A Ready and Easy Way To Establish a Free Commonwealth,* the populace of London was streaming down to Dover to welcome the restored monarch, Charles II. A shallow observer could well have thought that this meant the end of free commonwealths and also exposed the folly of arguing for them. The authors of *I'll Take My Stand,* who saw their compatriots turn away in large numbers from their recommendations, should not have felt any more absurd than Milton. Nor any less like prophets in their own country.

3

AGRARIANISM IN EXILE

About twenty-five years ago there gathered around Vanderbilt University in Middle Tennessee the most articulate group of thinkers situated in the South since the Civil War. Because they have been described to the public partly through caricature it seems necessary, in a review of their significance, to begin by distinguishing their true impulse.

These Southern writers gathered about Vanderbilt, who later became identified as the Agrarians, arose in opposition to an aggressive element of New South men. The latter had written off ante-bellum civilization as a mistake, or at best as a stage of culture outmoded by the passage of time, and had hastened to get on with the new way of life. They achieved marked success in business, and they made a considerable impression on education. Their character ranged all the way from the cynical selfishness of the Hubbard family in Lillian Hellman's *The Little Foxes* to the liberal idealism of Walter Hines Page, whose book *The Rebuilding of Old Commonwealths* expresses in its title the ambition of the political reconstructors. One might characterize so diverse an element by saying that it was ahistorical.

The Sewanee Review, Vol. LVIII (1950), 586–606.

The Agrarians were plainly distinguishable from that fairly numerous part of the Southern population which, while accepting freely all the gifts of modernism, attempted to trail clouds of glory from a culture of different provenance. These were the people to whom Southern background meant a pass to social prestige, or a ready-made means to personal distinction. From them came the obnoxious professional Southerner. These people have been quite willing to use whatever they possess of Southern inheritance to procure what is, traditionally, anti-Southern, and they have been impatient with those who remind them of the contradiction.

Finally, it is of crucial importance to realize that the Vanderbilt Agrarians cannot be grouped with the uncritical eulogists of ante-bellum culture. An early document made it plain that they proposed little traffic with the moonlight and magnolia tradition. They were, in certain of their methods, a modern breed, though most critics lacked the wit to detect their modernism. In their writing, for example, there was a stringency quite foreign to the nostalgic temper, and it could be said that on the whole they practiced an untraditional defense of their tradition. This was perfectly conscious, and in conception strategic. They knew that the kind of effusion which appears on many Southern battle monuments cannot possibly in our time be an instrumentality. If they took a poor view of the United Daughters of the Confederacy, it was not that they repudiated the Confederacy, but that they thought the Daughters failed to present its vital meaning. Like certain other movements which have baffled popular comprehension, they tended to bring together traditional ideals and modern potencies.

Because such a group departs from the main currents of Southern life, its formation is a subject of interest.

In the course of the Civil War the South suffered not only great physical destruction, but also severe traumatic shock. There can be no doubt that the latter was the greater injury by far. For thirty years the atmosphere was so suffused with the sense of tragedy and frustration that it was almost impossible for a Southern man to take a "normal" view of anything. He carried with him a self-consciousness tantamount to a sickness. It was not until the Spanish-American War (when the spectacle of Joe Wheeler in the uniform of a Federal major general drew mild astonishment) that the South felt itself back in the Union; and it was not until after the First World War that it began to feel on terms of equality with the remainder of the nation. In the long meanwhile its provincialism had been pointed to as a badge of shame.

Indeed, it was the First World War which gave the South an opportunity to break out of a vicious circle in which it had long moved. Its young men had attended the poverty-ridden institutions of their own section, or they had gone North to school, where things were not unnaturally predicated on the assumptions of Northern civilization. This great upheaval and its aftermath caused numbers of them to spend periods abroad. (The Rhodes Scholarship Trust moreover enabled a significant number of them to continue their education abroad. The influence of returned Rhodes Scholars upon Southern thinking after 1914 must not be discounted.)

Now when these provincials traveled to Europe and began to look about them, they were not a little interested to discover the same kind of environment they had left behind. Not exactly, of course, but they saw a deep-rooted organic society, held together by non-empirical bonds, and expressing in its structure a certain differentiation of calling. A suspicion began to dawn that the society they had grown up with in the South was in the main tradition of Western European civilization. It was the North and not the South which represented an aberration from a historic culture, and which therefore had to assume the burden of proof. It appeared broadly true, as one of them was later to remark, that the notorious conservatism of the South was but the European character of its institutions.

This is hardly a place to settle the issue of Europe versus

America, which is a large and intricate question, with mighty voices raised on both sides. There are those who maintain that the experiment of Europe is a proved failure, and that America constitutes the last fair hope of earth. Apart from the resolution of this question, it is easy to imagine that the discovery came to them with something of the force of a revelation. If their old-fashioned quality turned out to be their identification with a great tradition, it was obvious that much criticism of the South was superficially—or presumptuously—based. There had been enough criticism of the ignorant and spiteful sort to make the Southern-born defense minded, as every student of our national psychology knows. Following such experience, it was only natural that these voyagers should return home determined to take a fresh look at their inheritance, to strip from it those accretions which were historical and geographical accidents, and to see whether the remainder deserved a champion. In effect, they brought to the interpretation of the Southern past a new realism.

I desire not to direct special attention to the way in which they began their careers. It might appear from the foregoing that they would begin as publicists and early seek the forum; but here is where their distinction first became evident. They underwent a different kind of apprenticeship for their future labors. They served the muse of poetry.

Most students of this unusual movement have overlooked the significance of that beginning. It tells us a great deal about a man to know that he chooses as his form of expression the poetic medium. It tells us, I think, something about his system of ontology. The composition of poetry is evidence that for him values have a reality, and that he is capable of emotion upon the subject of value. The entire corpus of the world's poetry rests upon a theory of universal analogy which teaches that all phenomena in some degree resemble each other. There is a minimal truth in even the wildest metaphor simply because the world is, from one point of view, a unitary thing. And this amounts to saying that it is a creation. When in the Anglo-Saxon legend a vision appeared to Caedmon and told him to "sing creation," it was as if inspiration were pointing out to the poet his archetypal theme. Now if poetry is this system of universal analogy, and if the analogy mounts up toward that which most resembles everything else, or that which has the most universal being, it is true that all poetry is a form of worship. Poetry and religion have been too often conjoined in cultural history for the union to be fortuitous. It is with the symbol that we make the leap from what can be demonstrated rationally to what cannot, so that the poet as poet is a non-rationalist. And his post-rational demonstrations are about matters of value. Every comparison he makes has its implicative. The poet likens life now to a prosperous sea voyage; again to the sere and yellow leaf. These do not end with mere description. They place the subject somewhere on this ladder of universal analogy, so that we gain an insight into its relationship to true being. Metaphor, the distinguishing gift of the poet, as Aristotle pointed out, is the bridge between the phenomenal and the noumenal world, and it is no accident that there hangs about the poet, despite his often chequered mundane career, a certain aura of consecration. The practice of poetry amounts in effect to a confession of faith in immanent reality, which is the gravest of all commitments. Poetry on any other assumption would be anomaly.

One could scarcely desire a more felicitous example of poetry's true vocation than the title which John Crowe Ransom gave his first book of verse, *Poems About God.* The poems it contained were not religious in any conventional sense. But in introducing them the author made an explanation: "The first three or four poems that I ever wrote were done in three or four different moods and with no systematic design. I was therefore duly surprised to find that each of them made considerable use of the term God. I studied the matter a little and came to the conclusion that this was the most poetic of all terms possible. . . ." He went on to employ this term to make his verse poetic.

I cite these evidences to show that the future Agrarians owed their impetus to something far profounder than sociological excitement. This commitment to poetry had an influence upon everything that was later to emerge, even, I feel sure, from the non-poets.

All the while they faced the problem of living in a world which was in process of disvaluation. Their location was a city of the Old South which had undergone considerable industrialization, and which was a battleground of old and new. "Things reveal themselves passing away," and perhaps the evanescence of the old order made the question seem more urgent. Take one fairly coherent culture; allow it to be largely displaced by a second culture of different principles; then allow the second to suffer some degeneration, and you have many a Southern community of the Twenties. People live without a frame of reference, or they cling pathetically or absurdly to different frames, which may dictate contradictory courses. Nashville had the agrarian inheritance of Blue Grass Tennessee; but manufacturing had sprung up along the banks of the Cumberland, and there were few better places to witness the clash of Jeffersonian and Hamiltonian America. The Old South stood to the rest of the nation as the world prior to 1914 has stood to the world since; it was the last time, as Andrew Nelson Lytle has remarked, that a man could know who he was or where he was from.

The Agrarians met their practical situation in two ways. In their work as creative writers they observed an aesthetic formalism which was a rebuke to philosophies of disorder; and they published tracts for the times.

The recognition of their poetic achievement came soon and eventually spread beyond the nation. The elegance of their art, their refusal to pander or to accept shortcuts to attention, together with their alert critical intelligence, brought their verses before long to the notice of the sole people who count in this field, those who can read poetry for what it is. There is consolation in the fact that the news of quality always gets around. In the matter of a few years they passed from an obscure group supported by local patronage to a widely recognized movement subject to recurring discussion in the literary reviews, and I imagine that they were surprised themselves at the extent of their reception.

When one begins to import values into fields where practical men can discern their tendency, however, the time of peace is at end; and the reception of their contributions on social and political topics makes a different story. Here the response ranged from indifference on the one hand (in the case of the more theoretic and recondite works) to curiously mixed hostility and unbelief on the other.

A prime exhibition of the indifference attended that profoundest of books to come out of the Agrarian movement, Ransom's *God Without Thunder.* To say, as one leading critic has said, that this is one of the most original books written by an American is almost to underpraise it. Yet I would suggest that the most striking fact about this book was its authorship by a faculty member of a Southern university.

Candor compels its sons to admit that the South, despite its great contributions to the founding of the American republic, has never done much thinking of the purely speculative kind. If one excepts Calhoun, John Taylor's *An Inquiry into the Principles and Policy of the Government of the United States,* and certain parts of Jefferson, not much remains that is of philosophic cast. Its mentors have been soldiers and politicians, and its literature of discussion has been largely journalism and political exchange. When H. L. Mencken wrote his savage "Sahara of the Bozart," which pictured the South as a great cultural desert, he could have made a better case than he did by pointing to its philosophical barrenness. And the condition is not greatly changed. Though the modern South has become prolific in a literary way, so that the section may be said now to dominate the field of fiction in America, there is still hardly a trickle of analytical writing, apart from stuffy treatises of social science which emerge from university presses. Reporters of the local scene have appeared in swarms; novelists in shoals; poetry and drama have their following, but philosophy does not. It is furthermore true that despite the great expansion of Southern universities, Southern departments of philosophy have remained pitifully small. The bane of Southern writing has been an infatuation with surfaces.

God Without Thunder was a signal departure from that tradition. In a defense of religious orthodoxy, it employed all the means of modern dialectic to show two things: what happens to religion when it is deprived of its sternness and is reduced to a mild humanitarianism; and what happens to the individual man when he sacrifices a certain free aesthetic impulse to the tyrannous demands of efficiency.

Implicit in the author's doctrine of nature was a critique of technology which was to figure prominently in agrarian doctrine. Technology is a system of abstraction and simplification whereby nature is exploited. "By poets, religionists, Orientals, and sensitive people, nature is feared and loved—hardly the one without the other. But by scientists and modern Occidentals nature is only studied and possessed." This indictment was accompanied by a brilliant exposition of myth as an expression of essential truth. After his survey of the modern temper, the author could conclude that "perhaps we would greatly relish, and indeed it is possible that we are continually on the look-out to see if we will not discover somewhere, a brand-new myth, not shop-worn, not yet ridiculed, and not unrepresentative of what little taste we may have yet for the enjoyment of myths."

These propositions are enough to make plain that here was an essentially poetic doctrine of the world. The mere allusion to nature as a creation to be respected shows the intrinsic opposition between the aesthetic view and the utilitarian view of applied science, which serves as a kind of heuristic principle for modern industrialism. And too the mythmaking obviously presupposes a level of communication denied by those who aspire toward a language of pure notation.

It would be difficult to imagine a more direct challenge to the intellectual premises of modernism.* To make God again a stern judge and sword-wielder; and to insist that the myth is a form of cognition not displaced by rationalism, are heresies whose enormity is perhaps somewhat concealed by Mr. Ransom's suave language, but through them the issue has been joined. *God Without Thunder* excited little attention because few are accustomed to this level of treatment, and it may be supposed that most of those few had already come to appreciate the necessity of the position.

I have dwelled upon this work because it is the best example of the philosophical profundity of a movement which has been misunderstood in some quarters as a mere antiquarian revival. The power of the Vanderbilt writers to stimulate a great distance and over a long period stems from the fact that their thought, taken as a whole, offers not just a sociology, but an aesthetic, an ethic, and perhaps also a metaphysic.

A much more popularly conceived work, the manifesto *I'll Take My Stand,* appeared in the same year. This symposium, the production of twelve men, put before the public in plain terms the case for a return to a more stable order of society. The principal target of its attack was the theory of progress, and the embodiment of that theory was the North, victorious in war and equally victorious in trade, which Sidney Lanier in one of his most discerning phrases defined as "war grown miserly." There was nothing diffident about the invitation: the "Introduction" declared positively that "The young

---

*It is instructive to know that the Scopes "anti-evolution" trial, which the press of two continents made into an unparalleled sensation, was the decisive factor in turning the Nashville group against scientific rationalism.

Southerners, who are being converted frequently to the industrial gospel, must come back to the support of the Southern tradition."

It is a measure of the time that the book was not, in popular circles, taken quite seriously. The newspapers were filled with sallies and reproofs, and it is fair to say that the general tone was one of amusement (of course the rebel will be regarded with some indulgence when he is known to be harmless). Gerald Johnson confessed amazement that twelve men, literate and of legal age, could be found to prefer the agrarian tradition. I am chiefly concerned here to record that many of the taunting voices came from below the Potomac. The South is ever and anon congratulated for being upon the point of "waking up." What it is waking up to I defer to later consideration. Here I would say that the Southern gibes merely proved the Biblical prophecy, "a day shall come when a man's foes shall be they of his own household." One may as well admit that the Southern manifesto attracted more interest of the serious kind in the North than in the South, and this circumstance has an important bearing upon the later history of the Agrarians.

The doctrine excited more interest in the North because the North had already faced the dilemma. It was educated to a point at which it could read *I'll Take My Stand*. I refer here to an education of experience. The North, after all, had performed the experiment of industrialism. It had built the factories and had to a great extent organized its life around them. It was already looking at the results, and since the ugliness of industrialism is ubiquitous and the social benefactions are at least debatable, there arose a natural impulse to wonder whether the right road had been taken. Moreover, it must not be overlooked that there already existed in the North analogous movements. New England has a tough and time-honored agrarian tradition; and in the Middle West Henry Ford, who might be regarded as the world's chief sinner against the agrarian ethic, had begun to make atonement by encouraging folk dances and workers' garden projects. One might bring in also evidence from the literary realm. The peculiarly Middle Western American Vachel Lindsay composed one of his last poems in honor of the Virginians, "hard-riding, long-legged men," the kind who "consider a trader a hog." And Sherwood Anderson, after his Middle Western odyssey, retired to Jeffersonian America as represented by Marion, Virginia.

The North was beginning to see the limits of industrialism; and it had always been comparatively willing to listen to criticism. That is a point to take into account also.

In 1938 appeared the clearest and most courageous of the Agrarian documents, Donald Davidson's *Attack on Leviathan*. This was an extensive treatise on cultural regionalism, which, in its "Still Rebels, Still Yankees," found the Vermont farmer cousin to the Southern yeoman. For Davidson, a tireless exponent of Southern ideals, the valid contrast was between the old America of individualism and personal dignity and the new America, with its "glut of little souls."

In the decade following *Attack on Leviathan* there occurred a fairly general exodus of Southern Agrarians to the North. They went to the big cities, to the celebrated universities, and as a rule they remained. The hegira did not include all, but it included some of the most prominent, and it created an ironic circumstance. For a time it seemed that a good record as a Southern Agrarian was all that one needed for a call to some Northern institution with good salary and honorable status. It seemed indeed that the unreconstructed Southerner was preferred. The South possessed its liberals, but liberals were by then a dime a dozen in the North. There was no need to import them. But there was a use for the other point of view, provided that it was properly grounded and presented. That was one reason I think for the invitation. But why was the invitation accepted?

Their enemies, who include some of the most Philistine spirits in America, came forward with all the invidious explanations. It was said that the Agrarians had disagreed among themselves; or that agrarianism had been tried and had failed; or that it had never been seriously intended except as a means to publicity. Such charges are ignorant or malicious, and do not get at the source of this important dislocation. We are dealing now with the Agrarian exile. A significant number of those who defended the Southern way of life with rare eloquence have left their native heaths and are now found in the teeming cities of the North. Had they suffered a disenchantment, or did they desert their principles for a little more silver? To dispose of those questions we must look at a wider context of affairs.

The truth about the Agrarians is that they were becoming homeless. The South no longer had a place for them, and flight to the North but completed an alienation long in progress. Let us account for the fact.

It would be too much to claim that these poets, scholars, and teachers of doctrine were typical of the people whose spokesmen they desired to be. Or at the very most, they were typical in one way, but in another they were growing estranged. For as soon as the agrarian anywhere adds, or allows to be added, the *ism,* he is preparing the way for his own exile. We are simply confronted with different planes of human consciousness. Every *ism* is an intellectual manufacture; it has, in all sobriety, little relation to the people who till the soil for a living. These do not understand a language of such abstraction. Whatever it is they have, they arrive at by a different route. "Would I could turn and live with the animals, they are so placid and self-contained." The man who is capable of this elegant rumination, though he go and station himself among the animals, will never live as one. His very capacity for the reflective sentiment disqualifies him. After man has attained a certain stage of intellectual awareness, this power of reflection cannot be given up. The Agrarian intellectualized himself enough to make a case for agrarian living. In doing so, he was ceasing to be native. He had not many people at home to talk to. His philosophical doctrines were as far above the average Southern farmer as the empyrean; and though he could argue, he could hardly talk with the New South men of factories and counting houses, for this was the opposition.

Prudence may say that they had taken a false step, but wisdom will not. They had brought intellectual apperception to a certain quality of life, and if this meant for them some complication of personal status, such is no more than the destiny of one who grows. There is an important difference between being born to a certain kind of life, meeting its demands in a twilight world of stimulus and response; and coming to see its necessary rightness after a long voyage, in which there was, perhaps, seasickness. Some abide by the ancient simplicities because those are all they know; but there are others who return to them after finding that they subsume the sophistications which at an earlier stage of experience were felt to promise more. It is folly to say that the unenlightened state is preferable to the enlightened for the reason that the former will always be vulnerable. As Warren's character Jack Burden puts it after trying more than one philosophy and more than one way of life, "The end of man is to know." It is a fact that the Agrarians isolated themselves by becoming more intellectual, more perceptive men, but they left a legacy of thought. They left a doctrine which in some form will have to be assimilated before we stand the slightest chance of seeing the re-integration of man. But there were perhaps special reasons why they could not be prophets in their own country. Had the series of events been ideal, every neighbor would have been a John Taylor of Caroline, and then there would have been no exile. We must realize, however, that the South was already embarked on a course which made that chance increasingly remote. The proposal of the Agrarians never took into account a profound psychological fact which that course reflects.

Of all the lingering evils the South suffered as a result of military defeat, none was graver than the almost total extinction of initiative. Those who marvel that the section has lived so much in memory, that it has seemed satisfied to whirl about its "dead leaves of recollection," should recall that for a long period it was denied the right of exercising leadership. The denial was not so much legal as moral, but the effect was the same. The South slipped into the habit of following the national trend in everything except a few local customs and prerogatives. I believe that its reputation for lethargy derives from this abandonment of initiative, and not from any actual torpor. But here, in the Agrarians' proposal, was a demand that it take the boldest initiative ever urged upon it, not excepting the attempt to set up as a politically independent state. In view of its historical conditioning, there was but the slightest chance that the bid would be accepted. It had become enamored of going along. The South, as I once heard Warren vividly express it, was bent on being "the tail of a kite that is going down." Or, as Davidson had put it in *Attack on Leviathan*: ". . . modern civilization has been stricken with profound convulsions at the very moment when the South seemed on the point of making a belated choice in its favor." It had before it the lesson of the machine age, underscored with many a frustration and danger. Had its virtue been up to the mark, it might have enjoyed a sort of poetic justice in saving itself from some dismal chapters which the North, through its victory in the sectional war, had to experience. But it did not respond to the challenge. Not only the city dweller, but the rural folk too in appreciable numbers, were convinced that the business and industrial civilization whose story was being sung through every channel of publicity was the upward path.

It comes as corroboration to know that the battle of the Agrarians against the contemporary South was even then being mirrored in the novel. William Faulkner had observed the two worlds, and had made their struggle the underlying theme of his body of powerful fiction. As George Marion O'Donnell has brilliantly shown, the entire mythology of Faulkner grows out of the contest of Sartoris and Snopes in the South. The Agrarians are Sartorises, not necessarily through family or inheritance, but necessarily through sympathy with a socio-ethical pattern. One has to recognize them as traditional Southerners, publicly confessing belief in the ethically responsible will. But this traditional Southerner dwells in an increasingly Snopes-ordered world; he is faced with an opponent of terrifying vitality, pushing up from below, seizing the substance of the land even as he shatters the old forms and amenities. He represents the reign of animalism which is bound to hold sway when the old gods have gone and no new gods have arrived. Snopes is immeasurably aided by the fact that he carries no baggage of sentiment (in his world business is always business and sentiment is always "false sentiment"). The modern dissolution of values has so prepared the way for him that the contest is ridiculously unequal. By this I mean that whatever Sartoris does *qua* Sartoris will be quixotic, and whatever Snopes does similarly will be competent and *à la mode*. Or, as Warren presents the contrast of the Mastern brothers in *All the King's Men*: the pragmatic Gilbert (the one who remarked of Jefferson Davis, "What we want now that they've got us into this is not a good man but a man who can win, and I am not interested in the luxury of Mr. Davis's conscience") is more at home in the new world of the ruthless entrepreneur than he was in the old; but Cass, who studied Greek and engaged in soul-searching, is not at home in any world. The Agrarians have had many a brush with Snopeses, and some of these have been within universities, where one would not expect the type to find a harbor.

There remains, however, one very important fact to distinguish the Agrarians from Mr. Faulkner's Sartorises. Their response to the total situation has been more intelligent. There is, as Mr. O'Donnell noted, a formalized response to tradition which is mere blindness, and it is this which brings the Sartorises to their various dooms. By contrast, the Agrarians have not ended in aimless violence because they have not misconstrued the nature of the actual world. Instead, they have correctly estimated the forces arrayed against them; and a number, like the character in Ransom's "Persistent Explorer," after giving "a rueful grin," have resolved "to seek another country." That country has been the North, and if it is true that they are regional expatriates, it is equally true that they have found a home where their ideas are negotiable, and where their convictions do not clash with local immaturities.

In the battle against anti-humanist forces one does not desert by changing his locale for the plain reason that the battle is world wide. At the same time it is a battle in which one must beware of the fool's gambit. Nothing would have been more satisfying to their opponents in this phase than to see them rush out and make a failure of some practical demonstration and leave this failure as an evidence that their philosophy was wrong *ab initio.* It is a tenet of agrarian thinking that flesh and blood cannot contend against steel, and today the humanist is ringed with steel. There are millions of this generation who do not believe in war who have gone to war. There are great numbers riding in cars and busses who wish that we were riding horses again. The solution is not for the single protestant to ride a horse to his Manhattan office tomorrow. After all that has been said about for whom the bell tolls, the lesson should have been learned that no man saves himself alone. He saves himself, if at all, by bringing the community around to right reason. This the Agrarians have tried manfully to do. Their failure has not been greater than that of many true prophets and teachers who could be named.

Thus what has been represented as the flight of the Agrarians may appear on closer examination to be a strategic withdrawal to positions where the contest can be better carried on. Up to now the South has not shown much real capacity to fight modernism. A large part of it is eager to succumb; the part which would resist makes the over-formalized response and so hastens its own downfall. There are few effective allies here. And since the ideological character of the Civil War, which was perceived by only a handful of its contemporaries, has now been brought to general view, one no longer has to take part as a sectionalist. The sections fade out, and one looks for comrades wherever there are men of good will and understanding. I think the issue has broadened in this way for all who saw it first under narrower horizons.

It is not surprising therefore to find that those Agrarians who have remained at home have not been wholly spared through their tenure of place. For as modernism fills the interstices more and more, they tend, against their will, to become temporal exiles, or anachronisms. They are left little islands of protest, or eccentrics whom the regime can tolerate just because it possesses so complete a mastery. They are like men who would propose the teaching of Latin or of poetry in a vocational college, or who would distribute in Detroit leaflets attacking the motor car. The sense in which they remain "Southern" grows more ambiguous, or more traditional.

We can no longer avoid seeing that this little upheaval is not a regional affair, or an American affair, but a particular instance of a movement which is taking place all over the world. It is, to repeat, a phase of the general retreat of humanism before universal materialism and technification. And this is the real reason that geographical residence has ceased to be an important fact about the Agrarians. The struggle here related, which appeared in the guise of an American family quarrel, has its counterpart in many areas of the globe. For an instance rich in its correspondences with the Southern picture, we might turn to contemporary Ireland. There is another country which, like the American South, is "backward," religious, agrarian, mythopoeic. One needs only to look at its brilliant modern renascence to learn that its literary and philosophical sons fared little better than the disinherited of whom we speak. They were a group of men who saw a peculiar chance for Ireland in its very legacy, just as the Agrarians had seen one for the ex-Confederacy in its surviving values. And they had much to work with: a fierce spirit of nationalism, a distinct language, and an ancient literature. But their successes were hardly proportionate. We read of the coldness, incomprehension, and ill will with which their work was received. It used to be said that no Irish writer looked for an understanding review in an Irish journal; and the struggle of Yeats and Lady Gregory to keep the Abbey Theatre going against indifference and political hostility is a well-known chapter of modern literary history. Ireland was the stimulus to the imagination of these men, but their reputations were made in England, on the Continent, and in America. Stephen Dedalus's bitter phrase about Ireland, "an old sow that eats her farrow," is not inapplicable to the South. In both cases these were conspicuously filial sons who, in the main, stood up for their countries in the wholeness of their pasts. Both offered a conception of humane living, which was truculently rejected.

Warren has pointed out that a leading characteristic of our culture is a passion for abstract power, which leads to such perversions that the wielders of that power derive their greatest pleasure from regimenting and tormenting those who have a few shreds of humanity left. Under various catchwords and programs they are seeking to extirpate this humanity—calling it sentimentalism or nostalgia or cowardice, or some other name implying weakness. And after all views have been consulted, it seems most accurate to regard Agrarianism as an expression of this humanism. Though in this particular exposition it had a Southern setting, its goal was general: the humane life, celebrated in many literatures and cultivated in certain epochs of history. It is a free and unmeasured sort of life, rich in social intercourse, with its attendant manners and irrepressible conversation; it revolves around little poles of distinction (none great enough to excite those lusting after abstract power); it recognizes the fireside, the old custom, the traditional pieties; it is a life easy enough to tolerate that little tincture of absurdity without which, according to Dr. Johnson, no man can win affection. But the most important thing to say of it is that this kind of life must be appreciated in its physiognomic character or *not at all*. It is completely foreign to the statistical, bureaucratic, reformistic temperament which has come to dominate metropolitan America. The census taker can never get at this form of life, and indeed, census-taking is a potential threat to it.

In their professional work with literature too the Agrarians created a humanist trend. It is generally known that in this country the study of letters had been turned over to historians and statisticians, who worked at their tasks in the spirit of scientists. More than any other group, the Vanderbilt writers were responsible for taking literature away from this sort of custodianship and raising it again to the status of *belles lettres*. Since they have insisted that the work of art have a certain autonomy, and consequent dignity, one may say that this part of their doctrine parallels the humanist insistence that personality be respected, and not simply resolved into its historical factors. The willingness of the universities, now engaged in a critical battle to save the humanities, to adopt their method seems proof of its importance.

I have reserved for last that part of the Agrarians' philosophy which distinguished it from many other contemporary movements seeking the elevation of man. This is its admission of a theism. In this phase of their thinking they have been unafraid to step beyond the phenomenal world, and here, I believe, is the secret of their power to continue. Most readers will recall that at the time of its inception, Agrarianism was in competition with a movement styled Humanism. Yet it has proved highly fertile, and the rival has not. A group of university scholars led by Irving Babbitt and Paul Elmer More assumed that man could find his destiny through a discriminating study of his own achievements. It was sufficient for him to look back over the best that had been thought and said, and from that to learn the canons of excellence. They proposed a singing school that assuredly would have been "studying monuments of its own magnificence." They began with literature and from it deduced life; and they failed to perceive that man needs a stronger support than this really to be human. The Agrarians saw the issue more clearly. They understood from the beginning, as I have sought to show through their reverence for the office of poet, that man requires some conception of the absolute to maintain his humanity. In effect, they gathered up the implications of humanist philosophy. Accordingly we have Ransom's searching critique of humanized religion; Tate's premise that man is by nature incurably religious; and Warren's subtle studies, in verse and prose, of original sin and the problem of redemption. One feels, therefore, that they had the courage of their commitments, and that their humanism is a way into something deeper and more meaningful, where there is no evading the question of whether man has a final cause.

The great contribution of the Agrarians has been their achievement of total awareness. By compelling us to see the price that is paid for severance from nature and for the ignoring of final design, they have made us realize why we today are partial men. And if man is to be saved at all, that solution must come through self-knowledge. It is because he does not understand himself that Warren's Perse Munn is constantly being pushed around by the forces of this world until he ends in isolation and tragedy. It is for a similar reason that modern man is constantly being ridden by forces that he thinks he is riding. He cannot control them because he does not know "the carriage of his action, set and sprung."

This knowledge, when it comes, brings a degree of humility; and unquestionably their theory of human nature has made the Agrarians odious in certain quarters. In its implication the theory demands of man an atonement. Modernism is peculiarly vulnerable on this score and has to resist with all its might the thought that there is in man an essential defect. One may lay man's tragedies to nature, to institutions, to certain sets of bad men (whose badness is of course not accounted for); but one may not lay them to him. As soon as one begins to hint that the strain of wickedness in the human race recognized by Hebrew prophets and Greek philosophers long before Christian theologians is still with us, he is called an obscurantist and is disqualified from further public hearing. Now the tables are turned, and a realist who has been silenced by this Rousseauistic dogma will face his inquisitors from the social sciences, and in the manner of Galileo after his forced recantation, will say, "But he *is* wicked." That the Agrarians have done with pertinacity in their later and more imaginative writings.

{ 4 }

CONTEMPORARY SOUTHERN

LITERATURE

There is no need to detail the position held today by Southern literature. In fiction certainly, in criticism to a large extent, and in poetry and drama to a considerable extent, the South has enjoyed leadership. A people derided for its illiteracy now furnishes much of the literature of the nation. There is really no mystery in this occurrence, except perhaps for those who confuse the meaning of culture. The South did not become prolific in literature by following the advice of its outside critics. It did not do so by deciding to put on shoes, to go to school, to "embrace the national ideals," to make itself indistinguishable from the rest of the country. It prepared itself for its role by eschewing much bad counsel, by retaining its humanism, and by keeping at the heart of its faith a belief in the dual nature of man. Of the ideas it has preserved, none is more important than its humanistic concept of man. It is this image which accounts in large part for the realism and power of its literature, and for the inability of some of its critics to ignore what I am afraid they would very much like to ignore.

Texas Quarterly, Vol. II, No. 2 (Summer 1959), 126–144.

For our knowledge of man and of his behavior in this concrete world, literature has always been the great organon. And rightly so, for in insight, depth, subtlety, range, and perspicacity, it has no rival among the means to knowledge. The very freedom of literature inspires confidence in it, and hence the literary artist, whether he is working truly or falsely, is likely to produce the influential picture of man.

Of course not all literature is great literature, and we can mark instances where its rendition of man has been less than complete and convincing. If we look back over American literature, we find two major examples of systematic distortion, which included whole schools and had far-reaching pernicious influences. The first of these erred by postulating that man is by nature good, and therefore not responsible for evil. The second erred by assuming that man is merely the creature of circumstances, and again not responsible for evil.

The first of these writers were the Transcendentalist romantics of New England, with Emerson as their great teacher and avatar; the second were the naturalists, or, as some choose to call them, the realists, who followed at the end of the nineteenth century. These two groups left American literature in a condition from which recovery was possible only through the kind of reaction that we are now witnessing in contemporary Southern writing.

It is not easy to muster oneself to attack Emerson, the prophet of the "over-soul" and the teacher of self-reliance to generations of Americans. He appears serenely possessed of the truth, and his delivery of what he has to say is winsome. But the destructiveness of his influence can now be traced. Some years ago I heard a teacher say, "Emerson was the man who put the dynamite under New England." It was some time before I understood the import of that remark, but, when I did, I saw that he put the dynamite under much of the rest of the country too, owing to the widespread influence of New England education and of his branch of New England literature. Still later, when I encountered the remark of a Southern essayist, roughly contemporary with Emerson, that "the theory of the natural goodness of man will blow up any society which is founded on it," the images curiously cohered.

The denial of evil is a very great heresy. If we are interested in classifying, it is a phase of the Gnostic heresy, whose chief impulse, originating in arrogance and egocentrism, is to substitute a dream world for the structure of reality. Emerson taught that evil is essentially nonexistent; it was, in his view, only a privation of reality, and so had no ontological standing. For the frustration and suffering that everyone encounters in this life, he had no explanation other than that it was all delusion. He depicted a world in which a divine nature and a Godlike man looked upon one another with mutual satisfaction. Thus for Emerson the world was monistic. The great struggle between good and evil, taught by the religion which he gave up, and dramatized by the greatest literature, does not exist because the Great Adversary, the power of evil, does not essentially exist. To be natural is to be good, and all things work harmoniously by divine prompting.

Presumption can sometimes disarm by its blandness, and here I think it is the case. Consider what must issue from this concept. When we meet in actual life a person whose conduct seems to say, "What I am doing is the right thing because I am the one who is doing it," we set it down as arrant egotism. But what are we to say when we encounter the same idea shored up by philosophical speculation and claiming some authority from mystical intuition?

This form of Man, whom we often find apotheosized in the work of Emerson and Thoreau by being spelled with a capital letter, is a purely dialectical entity. If you place all the attributes you consider desirable for man in one category and then say, "This is man," or, "Only those who participate in this have manhood," you have a definition which may work well enough in a dialectical operation. But it is a definition contemptuous of history, and therefore useless for literature. If you write about man using a purely stipulative definition, you may come out with a conclusion that is formally valid, but it will be a conclusion having few points of contact with existence. If you start with a creature who was never on land or sea, you may expect to end up in cuckoo-land. In doing so, you soar away from all the problems that persistently tug at the human being.

It is interesting to note that the elder Henry James, father of the great novelist, saw through Emerson in this respect. Though professing an admiration for him, he stated that Emerson was "all his days an arch traitor" to the existing order. He was, James went on to say, "fundamentally treacherous to our civilization without being at all aware himself of the fact." This was so because Emerson had no conscience; that is to say, no consciousness of evil in himself. It is the nature of conscience, James pointed out, to cry, "God be merciful on *me,* a sinner," but Emerson was incapable of passing that kind of judgment on himself. "He recognized no god outside himself and his interlocutor," and what he understood as holiness was simply innocence.

These criticisms are all well aimed, and the passage of time allows us to see how close they came to the man's real weaknesses. He was a wonderful mirror of opinions, a perceiver of abstract relations; but in the final accounting he was empty of personality, of self, of what gives a man his stuff. Such was the mind which for two or more generations helped to deprive our literature of a sense of reality. (We may remember that Emerson tried to persuade his great admirer, Walt Whitman, to expurgate the later editions of *Leaves of Grass.* Whitman tells us, in a delightful account of their meeting, that he was overwhelmed by Emerson's eloquence, but that he knew in his heart he must *disobey.*)

Emerson had simply banned the problem of evil from consciousness. Having decided that there was nothing divine outside himself to issue demands or pronounce rebukes, he arrived, not at victory but at complacency. It was not accident that shallow romanticism and the genteel tradition were all that could exist in the rarefied world left by Ralph Waldo Emerson.

The reaction against this "unrealism" produced another kind of distortion. If Emersonianism was a heresy from the Gnostic dream world, naturalism was a heresy from the world of scientific materialism. The leaders of the school of naturalism wrote as if it were a new and complete revelation that man is affected by his environment. Frank Norris, Theodore Dreiser, and others embraced in varying degrees the scientistic fallacy, which one is tempted to call the "nothing but" fallacy. The scientistic fallacy is the theory that man is "nothing but" that which material circumstances can account for, or, as the literary practitioner has to apply it, that man is but one atom or collection of atoms in a vast system of interlocking causalities.

Dreiser is by far the greatest exponent of this school, and the most interesting study in its limitations. If we take him on the face value of his philosophical passages, he is indeed a prophet of despair. He tells us in *A Book About Myself* that after reading Huxley, Tyndall, and other nineteenth-century scientists, he arrived at the conclusion that "Man was a mechanism, undevised and uncreated, and a badly and carelessly driven one at that." And so he wrote in *The Financier:* "The damnable scheme of things which we call existence brings about conditions whereby whole masses suffer who have no cause to suffer, and . . . whole masses joy who have no cause for joy. . . . We suffer for our temperament, which we did not make, and for our weaknesses and lacks, which are no part of our willing." And in *The Titan* he remarks, "This is a world in which nothing is proved, all is permitted." In such a world neither intellect nor moral will has any efficacy. But there cannot be a story about a man who has no moral choice; there can be only a chronicle, and between the two lies a great gulf.

How then does one account for the undeniable power of his best novels? The answer is that Dreiser was an inconsistent mechanist. Or to put this in another way, Dreiser the novelist and Dreiser the philosopher go marching off in opposite directions. Clearly some of his characters do not share his views, nor do they behave as if those views were true. They find meaning in love and in power and in wealth. Against the forces that surround them, they manage to oppose a self. In the role of a creative artist Dreiser presented a number of convincing pictures of man as a struggler. But Dreiser as philosophic editor was always stepping in to tell the reader that things were not the way they looked; they were really much worse. An early alienation from his father's religion kept him narrow as a thinker, and narrower than he might have been as an artist. In *An American Tragedy,* his greatest effort, he does stick pretty close to his doctrine and presents his principal character as a helpless victim of "chemism." It is precisely this fact which keeps *An American Tragedy* from being a tragedy. He proved, both where he succeeded and where he failed, that a mechanistic world cannot be seeding ground for literature.

For in such a world there is nothing to write about. We cannot be interested or even diverted for long by being told that A is forever followed by B. (Our hunch is that this is not the pattern of occurrences, but that after a given event, many different things may occur, and for different reasons.) That a man walks upon the surface of the earth, that he nourishes himself and that he procreates his kind like other organisms are indeed general truths. But they do not tell us where the man will walk, or whether he will get his sustenance by industrious labor or by theft, or what kind of mating arrangement he will enter into. One does not tell the whole story by showing man pushed by one circumstance and bumped by another. If in the Emersonian view man is exalted beyond any level which wisdom will grant, in this latter view he is degraded below what observation and inner conviction tell us is true.

The naturalists did nothing more than take the old theological concept of providence and degrade it beyond recognition and meaning. They took "predestination" and stripped it to "destination." They had to believe that we were destined to go where we were going because we were parts of that vast system of interlocking causalities and had behind us the irresistible pressure of all previous forces. But they reduced such facts to unintelligibility by rejecting the concepts of Aristotle's first and final causes. It should not be overlooked that the components of the term *providence* signify "prevision" or "foresight." The word thus contains the idea of seeing, of knowing, of recognizing a conscious purpose. But the determinism of the naturalists in literature, in philosophy, and in science is a blind process. The process does not know where it is going; neither does anything outside the process. A good example of this confusion is the statement by a representative modern biologist that the evidence in nature compels us to believe that nature has a purpose. But this is not a conscious purpose, he adds, nor can we ourselves define it, since any final end or purpose is inconceivable. His determination to keep out all religious or metaphysical ideas forces him to talk about purpose which is not purpose (since nothing is aware of it) and of a goal which is not a goal (since it infinitely recedes). The theologians who used to debate "fixed fate, free will, foreknowledge absolute" never got into muddles like this. This encourages the hope that from evolutionism and other forms of naturalism some good metaphysician may yet deliver us.

In very broad outline this is the picture of American writing down to the beginning of the Southern movement. An older literature, based upon the postulates of a stern religion, gave way to heretical optimism—heretical because it denied the existence of evil and in effect set man up as a god. Then newer literature, showing at least the strength to react against falseness and insipidity, tried to find its heuristic principle in the doctrine of scientific materialism.

Into this situation modern Southern literature moved, as into a partial vacuum. What was there to resist it? The world of the romantic optimists was a dream world. The world of the naturalists was a half world, a world in which the material was elevated to sole principle—a view which mankind has always refused to accept for any length of time.

There was wanting a literature of true realism, and this the Southern writers of our time have proved especially able to create. Their literature has brought back a truer image of the world and a truer image of man, and herein lies the meaning of the Southern renascence. The world of the Brook Farmers, the world of Whitman's solitary singer in the west, the world of Zenith in the state of Winnemac, the world of Clyde Griffith, the world of a strike-torn factory town, the world of a society dominated by wealth and psychopathology are at the most parts of the world. They do not comprehend its wholeness.

In what way does the world of our best Southern writing differ from these just mentioned? I should begin by answering that it is an incarnate world, like that which Eliot evokes so subtly in *Four Quartets*. It is a world of place and time, but it is also a world which includes the mystery of the timeless. It is a place in which the transcendental is apprehended in the actual, and the actual is never without some link to the transcendental. The real and the ideal, the act and the idea, man as he is and man as he ought to be, nature and supernature are presented in their inextricable involvement. Nothing is crudely simplified into merely this or that; the meanest actions somehow remind us of highest expectations; and the noblest actors have clinging to them some of that dross of which no man is entirely clean. The characters in these creations are men in this visible world, not men in an imagined heaven. Yet they are not altogether of this world, since one senses in them a yearning for answers that no amount of bread can give them. Where man has the feeling that existence is not a one-story affair, his least actions will have implication. For life is conceived as a drama; at stake is happiness in the ultimate sense, and the powers of evil are known to set very innocent-looking snares. This world cannot be apprehended by the eye alone; the imagination is necessary, and, more than this, the moral imagination. Therefore Professor Robert Hazel could say very truly, "While the house in Ohio settles into an earth unhaunted by anything more portentous than the failure of a national administration to hold farm price supports, the house in South Carolina holds echoes that incriminate, terrify, and purge." And so we could go on to the house in Virginia and Georgia and Tennessee and the whole region where an older religious heritage and a sense of obligation to tradition have thwarted both the ethics of utility and the idea of economic determinism. The house in Ohio rests upon the ground simply and unproblematically, whereas the house in South Carolina communicates from the outset a sense of meaningful tensions. Ideas of order and questions of right and wrong surround it; it becomes at once the center of a story.

As I cross the Ohio River on my way to the South, I have a feeling that I am entering a region where things are somehow known mysteriously. They are known not through the flat, open, external means which positivistic science has told us to trust exclusively, but through other means which can carry many nuances beyond the power of the first to transmit. It is the feeling that my presence and my place are somehow duly registered, but not in a way that I could ever learn directly. There is something in it that makes me think of Kafka's castle, that mysterious and unreachable headquarters, where things are taken down and noted and arranged without one's ever being informed of the operation. This gives one an oddly reassuring sense of being counted and of belonging, though without any visible sign. The mystery is deepened by the fact that one can never discover any rational plan behind the disposition of things. If one attempts to telephone the castle and find out about one's situation, one discovers that the connection is poor and that there is no central exchange to handle the call. If one gets through to a branch exchange, he discovers that either the receiver has been left off the hook, or that the answers he gets are nonsensical or irrelevant. It is a miracle of inefficiency, yet the real miracle is that in the end things do get sorted out. No clear reason, of the kind that would satisfy the rationalists, is ever given for the arrangements that are made; they must always be justified by reference to auxiliary circumstances. Still, there is a final adjustment, so that one begins to sense the operation somewhere of supernal wisdom and supernal grace. There is a passage in the story which may illustrate the difficulty of understanding the South in simplistic and rational terms. The landlady of the village says to the chief character, "Your ignorance of the local situation is so appalling that it makes my head go round to listen to you and compare your ideas and opinions with the real state of things. It's a kind of ignorance that can't be enlightened at one attempt, and perhaps never can be, but there is a lot you could learn if you would only believe me a little and keep your own ignorance constantly in mind." Similar words could be addressed to every journalist and sociologist who crosses the line wanting to learn about the South while in a state of ignorance of what constitutes its true culture.

It may be asked whether this feeling will not be communicated by any culture that is highly developed. Every culture is a response to the need of human beings for certain psychic fulfillments, which cannot be described in the language of material exchange. They depend upon the appreciation of a set of intangibles, and it is impossible to account rationally for the way in which these sort out, dispose, arrange, and settle things. The master impulse of every culture seems to come from some kind of vision, some idealization of a value which can never be translated literally. Culture is akin to religion in that it may ask us to believe absurd things and perform useless ones; and indeed cultural fulfillment never seems complete without some kind of religious orientation. Culture has been described as a bridge between strictly religious ideas and the mundane concerns of life.

For this reason the world of every culture is a qualified world. It is not snobbery, but historical observation, to say that the South has a distinct and rooted culture. The basis of its culture, like that of all true cultures, is transcendental. In a world thus qualified, things are not just what they seem; they are suggestive and predictive of things beyond the seeming. The initial failure of some who have written about Southern life and literature is the failure to see that nearly all Southern writers write as members of this culture, and that, to the extent that they employ Southern settings, they write about characters who are members of a culture. This means that the attitudes and behavior of those characters are going to have from the beginning a certain complexity reflecting the hierarchy of values under which the characters have been nursed. The unwary outsider is prone to clutch a certain fact, say the fact that a sharecropper is poor. Then all at once this fact alters under his gaze; he discovers that the sharecropper does not consider his poverty the most important thing about himself. Or the visitor looks upon the antics of some politician and cannot decide whether they are demagoguery, buffoonery, or simple knavery. He does not know that in the South some forms of politics are a folk art, with a certain amount of daring, bravado, and even effrontery not only expected but even demanded by the electorate. I make these points in the hope of demonstrating that Southern characters in a Southern world are acting in a context. They are not baffling if one is prepared to see that in a culture reasons do not add up like two and two. The South is a qualified world, and in a qualified world, things resist quantitative analysis.

With this obstacle removed, let me turn again to the image of the South as an incarnate world. Incarnation has two halves, each necessary to the real event. It is just because the Southern author feels safe in the presence of the transcendental and the timeless that he is able to give loving attention to the physical particularities and limitations of man's existence. The physical aspect, the flesh of this life, is neither airily dismissed, as by the genteel tradition, nor viewed with bleakness and despair, as by Dreiser and his school. It is regarded rather as a provision of creation, and therefore by no means necessarily evil. This attitude toward creation prevents the writer's alienation from the physical setting of life. These are brought in with a certain grace and kindness, often with humor, and are large elements in both the charm and the truthfulness of the writing. I have long felt that among the most revealing lines ever written about the South are these appearing in one of the lesser known poems of Robert Penn Warren:

> The seasons down our country have a way
> To stir the bald and metaphysic skull
> Fuddling the stout cortex so mortally
> That it cries no more, proud heart, be still, be still.

Here is a view which declines to see man as mere "bald and metaphysic skull," and which insists on seeing beneath this a surging heart, very prone to be influenced by things like seasons and landscapes, and capable of rising up in rebellion against the head. Warren has given a faithful and poetical attention to the physical factors which enter, not decisively, but nonetheless pertinently, into the course of man's life. The Crucifixion scene in his ballad "Pondy Woods" is a rich example of this phase of his art:

> The Jew-boy died, the Syrian vulture swung
> Remotely above the cross whereon he hung
> From dinner time to supper time, and all
> The people gathered there watched him until
> The lean brown chest no longer stirred,
> Then idly watched the slow majestic bird
> That in the last sun above the twilit hill
> Gleamed for a moment at the height and slid
> Down the hot wind and in the darkness hid.

When the buzzard, who is allowed to moralize upon the situation in the poem itself, speaks, it is "with a Tennessee accent."

All of these local factual accompaniments to the expression of ideas build up a keen regard for the ineluctable presence of the particular, of the hard and often angular fact, which is the final assurance of reality.

This same intuition of the physical, expressed with more delicacy and with more awareness of irony, is to be seen in the poems of John Crowe Ransom. In "Blue Girls," the young ladies of a fashionable seminary move about under the towers of their school, listening to their teachers, who are "old and contrary" and "never believe a word." In "Piazza Piece" the lady whose "ears are soft and small" will not hear the old gentleman in a dustcoat who is trying to make her hear. In his "Prelude to an Evening," the theme of domestic discord is half presented, half adumbrated through the most felicitous choice of circumstantial detail.

> But now, by our perverse supposal
> There is a drift of fog on your mornings;
> You in your peignoir, dainty at your orange cup
> Feel poising round the sunny room
>
> Invisible evil, deprived and bold.
> All day the clock will metronome
> Your gallant fear, the needles clicking
> The heels detonating the stair's cavern,
>
> Freshening the water in the blue bowls
> For the buckberries with not all your love,
> You shall be listening for the low wind,
> The warning sibilance of pines.

This love of the particularity of the world, this acceptance of the partly conditioning fleshly half, is to be found throughout Southern fiction. I need only mention William Faulkner, Warren, Thomas Wolfe, Jesse Stuart, Eudora Welty, Katherine Anne Porter, and Andrew Nelson Lytle. One of the strangest misapprehensions in literary history was the early view of Faulkner as a systematic falsifier, for no writer has been more faithful to what can be observed. A critic in the London *Times*

Literary Supplement said a few years ago, "Faulkner is all true—
he is poetically the most accurate man alive, he has looked
straight into the heart of the matter and got it down for
good." And Thomas Wolfe had one predominating passion, a
search for the real; his air of rejecting everything is but the
converse of this. He hated sham because it got in the way of
reality, and he succeeded well enough in his search to give us
many unforgettable pictures of the American scene.

The brute empirical fact is given, but it is not allowed to
dominate, nor is its presence allowed to generate self-pity, as it
sometimes appears to do in the work of the naturalists. It is
given poetically, as the critic noted in Faulkner. The fact is
there in a capacity and with a function which helps to under-
score the precariousness and the ambiguous position of man.
A Chicago poet told me that during his service in the Army he
noted that the Southern boys rarely used bawdy and obscene
expressions without giving them a little metaphorical twist.
Even in this curious instance one sees the instinct to make art
out of circumstance, to make even obscenity significant. So
Faulkner's bawdiness, like Shakespeare's, is never simply
bawdiness; it leaps out of a situation and sheds its bit of
illumination.

A literature which thus honestly presents man in his physical setting will not proceed far without presenting man in his
passion. How true it is that many of the characters in Southern novels are people of strong passion. These characters
possess hearts which will not always listen to the bald and
metaphysic skull. They are driven by demonic and angelic
urges—the Thomas Sutpens, the Colonel Sartorises, the
Eugene Gants, the Willie Starks, the Ashby Wyndhams.
That fact helps to explain their humanity. For when we examine the history of the term we find that passion signifies
suffering.

All emotion is perhaps a kind of suffering, and here is the
key to the passionate character. It is an ancient doctrine that
man is in this world not just to make his way by dialectical skill,

but also to suffer his passion and finally to discover, if he can, the right channel for that passion. No real person may go through this life unaffected; he is born to feel. Only those who do feel deeply and poignantly realize what it is to be a human being. The rule of this life is to weigh and choose and abide the consequences, to suffer the effects of one's will. The idea that this is a world of action and liability, and that one must pay for one's choices, is nowhere more forcefully dramatized than at the end of *All the King's Men*. The survivors of that tragic action realize that they must go out "into the convulsion of the world, out of history into history and the awful responsibility of time." That is what it means to say that man is born to suffer, to endure his passion, and to find redemption, if he finds it, through effort and struggle. To be born into history is to be born with an inescapable mandate; one must act, for even inaction is a kind of action. And if one believes in a moral order in the universe, all action is liable to accounting. T. S. Eliot has observed, "It is true to say that the glory of man is his capacity for salvation; it is also true to say that his glory is his capacity for damnation." So, at the end of the story, the once cynical Jack Burden abandons his theory of the Great Twitch, which we may understand as a theory of man governed by his reflexes.

> He had seen his two friends, Willie Stark and Adam Stanton, live and die. Each had killed the other. Each had been the doom of the other. As a student of history, Jack Burden could see that Adam Stanton, whom he came to call the man of idea, and Willie Stark, whom he came to call the man of fact, were doomed to destroy each other, just as each was doomed to try to use the other and to yearn toward and try to become the other, because each was incomplete, with the terrible division of their age. But at the same time Jack Burden came to see that his friends had been doomed, he saw that though doomed, they had nothing to do with any doom under the godhead of the Great Twitch. They were doomed, but they lived in the agony of will.

There is an intimate relation between the acceptance of the role of passion in life and the vein of high rhetoric to be found in much Southern writing. The South is a culture which has never surrendered its belief in the value of sentiment. We are beholding in our time a widespread attempt to discredit all rhetoric on the ground that its appeal is to the subjective. Rhetoric plays upon the feelings; the feelings, so the argument runs, are things that man would be better off without; therefore, rhetoric is grouped with the black arts. It should be instantly apparent that this attack upon the subjective as having no reality, or as having a lower order of reality than the objective, is an attack that can be directed equally well against all humanistic expression. It is a part of the general movement to deny the validity of anything which cannot be externalized and quantitatively measured. We believe in art just because it is an expression of feeling, and we cultivate rhetoric just because it does enable us to display and to direct feeling. Anything contrary would be treason to the humane tradition.

When I say that there are in Southern writing splendid exhibitions of rhetoric, I do not mean rhetoric in the service of some external cause; that is, rhetoric bringing a precept to an audience. I mean rhetoric showing the world under some aspect of motivation, as it appears to a character in a story. As an example there is the illiterate and beautiful "Statement of Ashby Wyndham" near the opening of Warren's *At Heaven's Gate*:

> The pore human man, he ain't nuthin but a handful of dust, but the light of God's face on him and he shines like a diamint, and blinds the eye of the un-uprighteous congregation. Dust, it lays on the floor, under the goin forth and the comin in, and ain't nuthin, and gets stirred up under the trompin, but a sunbeam come in the dark room and in that light it will dance and shine for heart joy. I wasn't nuthin. I was under the trompin, which was cruel hard. But a man don't know, for he is ignorant. There ain't nuthin in him but meanness and a hog holleress and emptiness

for the world's slop. A man don't think of nuthin but sloppin, and dodgen when the kick comes. I laid on the floor and didn't know, and the trompin. But the light come in the dark room, like a finger apointin at me through the hole, and it was the hard trompin had stirred me. I shined in the light.

It was so, and truth sober. Then, that time, and for a long time, me goin or stayin, on dry land or the river. O Lord, make me to be shinin agin, and do not turn away yore face. For I have spelled how it is writ, and water come sweet from the smote stone, and light in the dark place.

One could also cite the harangues that Wolfe puts in the mouth of Old Gant or of Bascom Pentland, or any of the innumerable passages in Faulkner, where tumbling streams of image-bearing and evocative words create the speaker's world of value and inclination. Thus at the outset of *Absalom, Absalom!*:

From a little after two o'clock until almost sundown of the long still hot weary dead September afternoon they sat in what Miss Coldfield still called the office because her father had called it that—a dim hot airless room with the blinds all closed and fastened for forty-three summers because when she was a girl someone had believed that light and moving air carried heat and the dark was always cooler and which (as the sun shone fuller on that side of the house) became latticed with yellow slashes full of dust motes which Quentin thought of as being flecks of the dead old dried paint itself blown inward from the scaling blinds as wind might have blown them. There was a wistaria vine blooming for the second time on a wooded trellis before that window, into which sparrows came now and then in random gusts, making a dry, vivid dusty sound before going away: and opposite Quentin, Miss Coldfield in the eternal black she had worn for forty-three years now, whether for sister, father or not-husband none knew, sitting so bolt upright in the straight hard chair that was so tall for her that her legs hung straight and rigid as if she had iron shin bones and ankles, clear of the floor with that air of impotent and static rage like children's feet, and talking in that grim haggard amazed voice until at last listening would renege and hearing-sense self-confound and the long-dead object of her impotent yet indomitable frustrations would appear, as though by outraged recapitulation evoked, quiet, inattentive and harmless, out of the biding and dreamy and victorious dust.

We may ask whether this frank delight in the power of words does not have its root finally in a reverence for the word, which in turn may go back to a belief that "In the beginning was the word." The conviction that feelings are real and that discourse can be a devilish or a divine instrument stands at the farthest remove from the mechanistic and sterile theory of notation which the modern teachers of "communication" are trying to foist upon us.

If I imply that writers from other groups and schools seem to be comparatively hesitant in their use of rhetoric, I merely point to their comparative colorlessness, to their evident embarrassment before the bravura effects of language. They seem too desirous of having the word under complete control. Theirs might seem a valid literary posture, but what about those occasions when words seem suddenly to leap ahead and to enter into configurations which the rational mind has not fully foreseen? To accept these is to trust in the real creativity of language, to make use both of its traditional meanings and its inherent vitality. If one really loves language, one may even offer it the show of abuse. The real mistake is not to believe in its fidelity. In this respect I think that Southern writers have been more at home with their medium and that they have managed better their passages of rhetoric and of moving description. But all this would be pointless if it were not granted that man is here in his passion, and that his passion must find expression in the language of propensity and inclination.

A literature which thus shows man in his passion will not proceed far without showing him in his sin, and one of the great merits of contemporary Southern literature is that it has faced the problem of sin. Passion, in the sense in which I have used the word, is not sin; it may indeed be a means to virtue. At the same time, because of his partly depraved nature, it is often the means by which man is led into guilty action. Original sin is the parabolical statement that man is somehow originally flawed. He has the temptation, known allegorically as the curse visited upon the descendants of Adam, to do what he knows he ought not do. This flaw is no respecter of person or place or station. Its distribution is through the whole range of society, and this is precisely the treatment of it we get in the most thoughtful Southern writing. No circumstances are too reduced to allow it to appear, and no social rating is high enough to fence it out. Warren has made this the subject of one of his most interesting poems, "Original Sin: A Short Story." The theme is one of "no escape." Original sin follows the character in the poem from country to city, where modern sophistication fails to put an end to it. Later it follows him from Omaha to the Harvard Yard, where New England piety and learning might be expected to exorcise it. The character moves often and rarely leaves an address, but the result is always the same: "It thought no bed too narrow."

We sometimes encounter the complaint that Southern literature abounds unduly in monsters. I would reply that this literature's willingness to depict monsters is one of its strongest claims to validity. Monstrosity is one of the authentic modes of existence. The world regularly produces monsters, and to recognize them is part of the truth of art. The literatures of Greece and Rome certainly had no difficulty in accommodating them, and the plays of Shakespeare contain some shocking ones. It is my impression that Southern writers, instead of rationalizing away monstrous evil, as the sociologists try to do, or averting their gaze from it, as the romantics try to do, choose to give it epical proportions (as did the author of *Moby Dick*). The monsters of Southern fiction are not there for the purpose of shocking, or of presenting the South as an Africa of strange beasts; they are there because an honest artistic vision has found them.

Faulkner's work is filled with monsters, and this is one reason the critics approached him so uncertainly at first. One thinks of Flem Snopes, with his tobacco cud in his cheek and his "shifty, mud-colored eyes," a perversely vital, amoral, and destructive monster. Or Joe Christmas; or Thomas Sutpen, who can calmly put aside his wife when he realizes that she is "not adjunctive to the forwarding of the design"; or Rosa Coldfield, or Miss Emily Grierson, or any of the creations of his genius who reflect incomplete or distorted humanity.

Warren has in some ways an even greater understanding of monsters. Here one finds a veritable parade of them, from Perse Munn (in his later stages) in *Night Rider,* through Sue Murdock and her father Bogan Murdock in *At Heaven's Gate,* to Willie Stark and Sugar Boy in *All the King's Men,* to perhaps the greatest of them all, Lilburn Lewis in *Brother to Dragons.* Lewis, a nephew to Thomas Jefferson, by murdering a slave in a particularly cruel fashion, mocks his famous uncle's doctrine of the natural goodness of man. It has actually been argued that Warren should not have written this because it calls into question that tenet of Jeffersonian optimism—such being the level of fatuity to which sentimental liberalism can sink.

In Wolfe there is Old Gant, a man larger than life in his florid harangues, rages and dissipations. I can never think of Wolfe himself, in his personifications as Eugene Gant and George Webber, except as a modern Gargantua with a monstrous appetite for experience. In the stories of Jesse Stuart the Kentucky hillmen achieve huge proportions in their drinking and fighting and in their power to endure what an urbanized generation calls "hardships."

It may well be that this acceptance of monsters is closely related to a belief in heroes and heroism. If there is a centaur, there must be a Theseus; if the hydra exists, a Hercules must be found. It is one of the most certain signs of a collapse of values that the true hero is disappearing from modern imaginative life. After all, the hero is the man apart from the crowd, the man who refuses to participate in its cowardice and servile emotions. It makes a crucial difference whether you try to push all men toward a norm or average, or push them further apart by making the appropriate distinctions between good and bad, bravery and cowardice, honor and dishonor. The latter is done by those who write of heroes and monsters. A generation ago the Marxists were talking about merging the hero with the mass, of de-individualizing him, and of keeping him from being the measuring stick for the rest of us. True, the tragic hero is all too human at times; he may even be a monster in some respects, but he is still a great man greatly striving. It is my feeling that the best of our Southern writers show no disposition to give up belief in the hero. Despite the darker side of their natures, Colonel Sartoris and Thomas Sutpen and Perse Munn and Willie Stark are heroes. Eugene Gant and George Webber are heroes of a long odyssey of experience, surviving many clashes with environments and people. Allen Tate in the "Ode to the Confederate Dead" turns our eyes to that "immoderate past," where we see rising "demons out of the earth" and hear echoes of Shiloh and Antietam. In many of his poems, John Crowe Ransom presents heroes, albeit heroes crossed by a wry fate. I think particularly of his "Captain Carpenter," going forth to battle against sundry rogues and knaves until he has lost everything except the will to fight. His justly admired "Antique Harvesters" is virtually a call to heroism, with its reminder that the South is a land where heroes stood "and drenched it with their only blood."

Two centuries ago Alexander Pope said of man that he is "the glory, jest, and riddle of the world." Each of these terms deserves careful consideration. To say that man is part glory is to accept a deep-rooted belief that he has a nature which transcends nature, that he is a special creature with a contingent destiny. To say that he is part jest is to take note of the painful and ludicrous postures into which he is forced by the necessities of living in the world, of the many ways in which he can be deflected by circumstance and victimized by his own ignorance. To say that man is part riddle is to acknowledge the mystery of human personality and to affirm the impossibility of ever resolving him into anything simple.

One school of writing tried to present man as all glory. A later school tried to present him as all jest—for that is what he must be if he is considered merely the pawn of circumstances. Only the contemporary Southern school has combined the glory and the jest and remained faithful to the riddle of man which may never be answered.

In this lie its greatness and its frankness.

In asking myself why I find such spontaneous pleasure in reading Southern literature, I am always brought back to this matter of frankness—the frankness with which complexity is faced. Frankness is an attractive quality; it is the attribute of nobility, for its source is truthfulness. We are weary of plots and characters which are no sooner sprung upon us than we become aware of tendentious purpose—that is to say, non-artistic purpose. Much modern literature is rife with ill-concealed "special pleading." If the characters are marked by poverty and lack of education, we are reminded that we should feel sorry for them. If degeneracy in low life or high life is presented, we are supposed to read this as the "inside story," which the anxieties of a false society would like to keep hidden. If a struggle between rich and poor is depicted, it is subtly suggested that we should enlist under the banner of collectivism.

The writers I have been describing are free from impertinencies of this sort. They speak frankly of "crackers" and "niggers," of "lintheads" and "hillbillies," of "rednecks" and "quadroons," and they are equally ready to describe cases of murder, theft, incest, and suicide in the "best" families.

This spirit of frankness operates on a far profounder and more important level. Through it the Southern writers deal with something that the modern world seems increasingly prone to deny: the presence of tragedy in life. Here is a fact to be considered, for if you do not recognize a tragic theme in a literary work, your explanation of that work will likely be either sociological balderdash or amateur psychoanalysis.

The Southern writer is twice prepared to recognize tragedy and to come to grips with it. First, he has never given up his belief in a dualistic world and in the freedom of man to choose between the upward or the downward path. As Professor Randall Stewart has shown in his recent *American Literature and Christian Doctrine,* there is no possibility of tragedy in the Emersonian or Dreiserian scheme of things. "Tragedy requires a responsible being, who must choose between good and evil." A dominantly Christian point of view has preserved in the South the idea that man can fall. This is why Southern literature, within the context of Southern belief, has been able to recover the theme of the greatest literatures.

Second, the South has had much tragedy spread before its eyes. Compared with the Southerner, the American from other parts seems like the adolescent son of a well-to-do family, who has never done anything but eat well and drive around in the sports car that his father obligingly provides. It is natural for him to suppose that "life is like that." He has no education in life. Tragedy is probably the most deeply educative experience; it is in a sense the typical experience. Certainly the Southerner, if we examine him over the span of a century, has had this typical experience, and he has been frank to say what it is like. If our perspective is broad enough, we recognize the Southern experience not as abnormal but as more normal than that of other sections of America. The South is the region that history has happened to. People who have never experienced tragedy are the deviants. Southern writers have told much of that tragedy, and in doing so they have told us important things about the human condition.

It is not only satisfying artistically, it is of great importance socially that the image of man inculcated over a period of years by a people's literature should be a truthful one. We may freely admit that it is not the prime purpose of literature and of art in general to edify; still, no art can avoid providing materials which will be used for instruction. As a great philosopher of the aesthetic has pointed out: we cannot conceptualize unless we have data in the form of images, and it is the exercise of the aesthetic faculty which provides these images. The artist provides the basic content of our knowledge through his faithful seeing and truthful expression. It becomes important in the long run for our most practical concerns that the artist be loyal to his vision. A people can go fearfully wrong by assimilating false data. True art maintains a steady, even heroic, insistence that "this is the way things are."

Here is the chief glory and the continuing mission of Southern literature. It holds up an image of man which is derived not from some partial philosophical system, but from observation, history, traditional beliefs older than any "ism," and from the final artistic apperception. The fact that this image seems to be capturing the imagination of the country may be a sign that we are girding ourselves inwardly for the struggle against those haters of humanity and despisers of all human affections who today control a good part of the world. Those who capture the imagination of the country are, no matter how unofficially, in a position of leadership. The South, which has spent so many years as America's stepchild, is proving to have the gift which may save the household from destruction.

"The Contemplation of These Images": The South in American History

5

TWO TYPES OF AMERICAN

INDIVIDUALISM

O urs is an age in which individualism is publicly praised and privately snubbed: individual liberty is called the chief goal of all our striving, while at the same time we hear off-stage whispers to the effect that the social cost of individualism is too great a charge to be borne by a democratic world. Like all questions which give rise to one public attitude and a differing practical procedure, this one may be said to be vital, involving contradictory urges. Individualism is too deeply a part of the heritage we have been taught to prize to be yielded up easily or thoughtlessly. At the same time our modern world engenders forces which keep it on the defensive and drive it to seek refuge among the interstices of living.

Light can be shed on our problem by examining two types of American individualism, each of which has had a major prophet. One of the types is not now, and I think never was, a feasible form of individualism, though there is something about it which fascinates a part of our nature. The other is not only feasible but is today very much needed, when the forces

Modern Age, Vol. VII, No. 2 (Spring 1963), 119–134.

of regimentation and the example of totalitarianism are threatening to sweep away every principle of distinction that stands in their path.

What I am going to propose will be a transvaluation of values, in which a figure now rather obscure and deprecated will be presented for the lesson he has to teach, and another figure illustrious and much lauded will be criticized. However, before even mentioning the names I shall be dealing with, I will offer a quotation which serves well as a prologue to the general problem. Reinhold Niebuhr has written that there are two ways "of denying our responsibilities to our fellow men. There is the way of imperialism, seeking to dominate them by our power. The other is the way of isolationism, seeking to withdraw from our responsibilities to them." It is my purpose to study two characters from the American past who exemplify in their lives and their thought different responses to this exorable situation. Niebuhr was expressing a dilemma which arises perennially out of the question of the individual's degree of commitment to society. One way to meet a dilemma, as logic tells us, is to seize a horn; that is, to accept one of the alternatives offered but to cast doubt on the causal reasoning which underlies it. This was the method attempted by Henry David Thoreau, whom I am citing as one of the two major prophets, in the bulk of his social philosophy. Thoreau stood for individual isolation, but failed to see the consequences. Another way of meeting a dilemma is to slip between the horns, which means to find a third alternative without the painful consequences of the other two. The exponent of that method was John Randolph of Roanoke, now a half legendary figure, termed a "political fantastic" by one of his recent biographers and called a dangerous person by another critic, yet a figure of unique interest to one who has studied his career. Randolph stood with equal firmness against imperialism, especially in its disguised form of government welfarism, but he found an alternative to this and to simple withdrawal. I shall take up my examples in the order in which they appeared on the world's stage.

Randolph, like many of the class to which he belonged, was born on an ancestral estate, "Cawsons," near Petersburg, Virginia, on the eve of the Revolution. He grew up a member of the gentry at a time when, in the words of an early biographer, "the gentry gave law to the state, and the state gave law to the Confederacy." From his early years he was filled with a restive spirit, so that his education shows a great deal of shifting about. A brief attendance at a grammar school in Virginia, a year at Princeton, less than two years at Columbia, and a few weeks at William and Mary gave him a kind of educational odyssey. This was followed by three years of reading law under his uncle, Edmund Randolph, who was Washington's attorney-general.

The earliest vivid picture we have of Randolph comes during his first public speech, in which his opponent was none other than the aging Patrick Henry, then making his farewell appearance. Henry had in the meanwhile aligned himself with the Federalists, and Randolph attacked him in a three-hour argument defending states' rights. The great orator of the Revolution did not reply, but later he addressed this advice to his youthful opponent: "My son, I have somewhat to say unto thee . . . keep justice, keep truth, and you will live to think differently." But Henry was wrong in the prophecy. Randolph never came to think differently. "He was," says his biographer Joseph Glover Baldwin, "the most consistent of all the politicians that ever lived in the republic"—a judgment which may well stand today, a hundred years after it was made.

The defense of states' rights in this maiden speech is the key to Randolph's political career and to his political philosophy. One may say political philosophy because whereas other leaders, North as well as South, rallied behind local autonomy when some special interest of their section or region seemed menaced, Randolph upheld it in every case in which the issue ever arose, whether the threat seemed great or small, near or remote. In the course of his famous debate with Hayne, Daniel Webster was to taunt the opposition with the question: "Does consistency consist merely of casting negative votes?" In the case of Randolph it almost may be said to have done so; he was probably the greatest oppositionist that ever appeared in Congress, but his opposition was to a consistent trend which he saw as carrying the nation away from republican principles, which in his mind constituted the anchor of liberty.

Elected to Congress at the age of twenty-six, he held his seat for fourteen years, or until 1813, when he lost it as a result of opposing the War of 1812—another of his many stands of opposition. He was an ardent Jeffersonian, but he broke with Jefferson on a number of issues during the latter's second administration. He drew further and further away from Jefferson's doctrinaire democracy. Back in Congress in 1815, he spent the rest of his career in dogged fights against all nationalizing tendencies, especially the tariff and the national bank. When he learned that Madison had signed the bill incorporating the Bank of the United States, he expressed himself in a typical burst of rhetoric, the qualities of which I shall discuss later. True to his principle, he was denying that this power lay within the national government.

Sir, if I cannot give reason to the committee, they shall at least have authority. Thomas Jefferson, then in the vigor of his intellect, was one of the persons who denied the existence of such powers—James Madison was another. He, in that masterly and unrivalled report in the legislature of Virginia, which is worthy to be the textbook of every American statesman, has settled this question. For me to attempt to add anything to the arguments of that paper, would be to attempt to gild refined gold—to paint the lily—to throw a perfume on the violet—to smooth the ice—to add another hue unto the rainbow—in every aspect of it, wasteful and ridiculous excess. Neither will I hold up my farthing rush-light to the blaze of that meridian sun. But, Sir, I cannot but deplore—my heart aches when I think of it—that the hand which erected that monument of political wisdom, should have signed the act to incorporate the present Bank of the United States.

An episode near the end of his career throws special illumination upon the spirit of the whole of it. In the election of 1828, Randolph supported Jackson for the presidency and was thereafter rewarded with the post of Minister to Russia. (Just why Jackson picked Randolph to go to Russia is a matter for curious speculation. A sardonic interpreter might suggest that what Jackson really wanted was to get him out of the country.) At any rate, ill health caused him to resign that post after a short tenure, and he returned to the United States to face profound disillusionment with the new president. There had been nothing to indicate that Jackson was opposed to states' rights. He had certainly been elected by states' rights supporters, and he had campaigned against the policies of Adams and Clay, which had operated to give more power to the general government. Then came the controversy over nullification.

South Carolina, opposing the tariff laws of 1828 and 1832, passed an ordinance declaring them null and void for that state. This was the sharpest conflict between federal and state authority which had yet appeared in the forty-odd years of the republic. President Jackson, as is well known, asserted the federal power, made preparations for the use of force, and even threatened to hang the nullifiers. This development came like a thunderbolt to Randolph, who now saw the supposed champion of states' rights utilizing the most naked sort of coercion to suppress the action of a sovereign state. The centripetal tendency—the tendency toward centralization—which he had fought for three decades now, was showing itself more ominously than ever before. At this time Randolph was within a year of his death and in a very failing condition. But he had himself lifted into his carriage and went about his old district addressing the people and asking them to support resolutions against the President's proclamation. In one speech he brought in the name of Henry Clay—his old political enemy, with whom he had fought a duel many years before. "There is one man and one man only," he said, "who can save this Union. That man is Henry Clay. I know he has the power, I believe he will be found to have the patriotism and firmness equal to the occasion."

How much effect Randolph's campaign had upon the final outcome one can only conjecture. The outcome was a compromise, brought about in fact by Clay, who once more used his peculiar talent for composing differences to resolve a crisis. A compromise bill was passed, the principle of protectionism was discarded, the tariffs were reduced, and South Carolina remained uninvaded.

If I have sketched this episode at some length, it is to stress a salient feature of Randolph's political philosophy. As a defender of the dignity and autonomy of the smaller unit, he was constantly fighting the battle for local rights. But it was the essence of his position that the battle must be fought within the community, not outside the community and not through means that would in effect deny all political organization. By instinct Randolph was perhaps a secessionist—every individualist is a secessionist in regard to many things. Individualism is a rejection of presumptive control from without. But Randolph never lost sight of the truth expressed in Aristotle's dictum that man is a political animal. His individualism is, therefore, what I am going to call "social bond" individualism. It battles unremittingly for individual rights, while recognizing that these have to be secured within the social context. This last gesture of his life was symbolic: Randolph rushed to the defense of South Carolina, but called upon his old opponent and enemy Henry Clay—Clay the Westerner, the nationalist, the advocate of the "American System"—to save the situation. Not because he desired either Clay or the system, but because this seemed the *political* desperate remedy. The point I seek to make is that Randolph could not visualize men's solving political questions through simple self-isolation. Throughout the controversy he declared himself opposed to nullification, which would have been simple unilateral action.

Going back a few years in his career, we find a rare anomaly when we discover Randolph, with his pronounced localist views, lecturing New England upon the unwisdom of seceding from the Union. But less that two decades before the crisis over nullification, he had appealed to the "erring sisters" of the Northeast not to withdraw from the partnership of 1789. The New England secessionist movement had its climax in the Hartford Convention, an episode well known to students of American history as the first seriously meditated step toward the setting up of an independent confederacy. During the War of 1812 New England had suffered grievously under the Embargo Act and in general had found the war adverse to her interests. In 1814 a group of her leaders assembled at Hartford for the purpose of making a separate peace treaty with England, withdrawing from the United States, and organizing a New England nation. At least those steps were in contemplation. At that time Randolph addressed a letter to a prominent New England senator, having been advised that "his admonitions would receive their just consideration." A few quotations will convey its thought and sentiment.

> It belongs to New England to say whether she will constitute a portion, an important and highly respected portion of this nation, or whether she will dwindle into that state of insignificant nominal independence, which is the precarious curse of the minor kingdoms of Europe. A separation made in the fullness of time, the effect of amicable arrangements, may prove mutually beneficial to both parties: such would have been the effect of American independence, if the British ministry could have listened to any suggestion but that of their impotent rage; but a

settled hostility, embittered by the keenest recollections, must be the result of a disunion between you and us, under the present circumstances.

For, with every other man of common sense, I have always regarded union as a means of liberty and safety; in other words, of happiness, and not as an end to which these are to be sacrificed. When I exhort to further patience—to constitutional means of redress only, I know that there is such a thing as tyranny as well as oppression; and that there is no government, however restricted in its power, that may not, by abuse, under pretext of exercise of its constitutional authority, drive its unhappy subjects to desperation.

Randolph's theory of how such disagreements could be resolved is clearly indicated in the closing passage.

Our Constitution is an affair of compromise between the states, and this is the master-key which unlocks all its difficulties. If any of the parties to the compact are dissatisfied with their share of influence, it is an affair of amicable discussion, in the mode pointed out by the constitution itself, but no cause for dissolving the confederacy.

This provides another interesting view of Randolph's theory of the obligation of the smaller unit to the larger. In one part of his irascible nature he was a Hotspur of Hotspurs, inclined to cavil over the fraction of a hair when he discerned an issue. But in another part he was a man of prudential wisdom, which is to say, political wisdom. Nowhere in this letter does he say that New England's secession would be unconstitutional. He can even imagine a situation, involving tyranny and subjection, where it might have to be undertaken. What he is urging is that now in present circumstances it would be very unwise. And this would be his estimate in any normal situation. His theory of politics did not favor a simple withdrawal as a solution. This was a renunciation of political privilege rather than the exercise of it. With all his individualism and eccentric bearing, he had too strong a sense of the social bond to see it as a practical recourse, unless things got so out of joint that subjection was the only alternative. As we shall find later, what Randolph saw as a last and a problematical choice, Thoreau was inclined to see as a first step.

At any rate, for Randolph as a politically conscious person, the fight should be waged within the whole and not outside it in some undefinable or ambiguous position. On the other hand, he was equally unyielding in his opposition to surrendering local rights out of veneration for some super political organism called a "union" or "nation." His whole course was in a direction away from this, and now we must ask how the two positions can be reconciled. His theory of remaining within the whole while maintaining local rights, I will suggest, rested upon what military people call "defense in depth" and what political theorists call "dispersal of power"—two names for the same kind of principle in different realms. The essential feature of it is that the further one tries to encroach against local autonomy, the more difficult it is to make headway. In military language again, the depth of the resistance devitalizes the attack. It is left relatively easy to carry the outer works, but the next barrier is more difficult, and the next still more so, and so on. And the smaller and more cohesive the unit, the greater the discretionary power it has. As Randolph used the principle in practice, he fell back first upon what might be called sectional solidarity. The next line of defense was the state. How far back could the defense actually go? This is a question I think he deliberately would not have answered. In his view it would have been one of those "theoretic speculations," the sort of question which would have appealed to dialecticians, of whom he was openly scornful. It was enough to have the working principle for use against the large, abstract, and uncomprehending force from the outside. Yet I think we might in a way answer it for him. The defense could never fall back as far as the single individual. Men have to work in some kind of concert. It is well if general objectives can be broad, and we should recall his appeal to New England not to allow the United States to be overthrown or dismembered by a common enemy. Yet it is important too for local jurisdictions to be equipped with a stout defense. In our traditional practice, it could be pointed out, we do fall back as far as the jury unit, whereby a small number of local people decide whether or not a man has been in violation of the law.

Randolph was personally involved in one of the dominant issues of the time, and we can test further the consistency of his theory by considering how he stood on slavery. Like many Virginians of his class, he was the inheritor of Negro slaves, there being over three hundred on his lands. In 1819 he wrote a will, of which this was one of the opening clauses:

> I give to my slaves their freedom, to which my conscience tells me they are justly entitled. It has a long time been a matter of the deepest regret to me that the circumstances under which I inherited them and the obstacles thrown in the way by the laws of the land, have prevented my emancipating them in my lifetime, which is my full intention to do, in case I can accomplish it.

Two years later he wrote another will; again among the opening clauses were the following:

> I give and bequeath all my slaves their freedom, heartily regretting that I have ever been the owner of one.
>
> I give my ex'or a sum not exceeding eight thousand dollars, or as much thereof as may be necessary to transport and settle said slaves to and in some other State or territory of the U.S., giving to all above the age of forty not less than ten acres of land each.

Randolph wrote later wills—there were signs of mental unbalance near the close of his life—but it was this will, the will of 1821, which he affirmed on his deathbed and which the Virginia Court of Appeals eventually declared to be John Randolph's true will.

It is not the purpose of this citation to make Randolph appear a philanthropist, which he was not. The very mention of that word probably would have uncorked those sources of abusive eloquence which he possessed in such abundance.

The point of interest for this exposition is that at the very time he was writing out the emancipation of his slaves he was deeply involved in the Missouri Question, trying to bring Missouri into the Union as a slave state.

He took an extensive part in the debates, making speeches of three and four hours, but they may be boiled down to this essence: Missouri had a right to be admitted as a slave state, and Congress did not have a right to pass on the constitutionality of its constitution. Only the electoral college had this right, he maintained (and we may note again the dispersal of authority).

Now, the superficial inquirer might ask, what becomes of his much-praised consistency? He manumits slaves with one hand and with the other he seeks to extend the slave territory. But this inconsistency dissolves when we look again at his major political premise. Matters of this kind must be dealt with by those who bear the impact of the responsibility. At the bottom was his theory of the necessity of a homogeneous basis of government. "Government to be safe and to be free," he said, "must consist of representatives having a common interest and a common feeling with the represented." This is the authentic Randolph note. Common interest was the final justification of government, the source of the means of operation, the assurance that it would not become perverted or despotic. Rightly or wrongly in this case, Randolph believed that other forces were the prime movers in the attempts to make the admission of Missouri a critical question. He saw a struggle for sectional dominance carried on by men personally far removed from the institution, but sensing in the feeling against slavery a strong horse to hitch to their wagon. He even declared that he did not believe in the sincerity of the professions of most of them. Yet the crucial issue for him lay in the relation of power to those being affected. And this is always the crucial question for the anti-imperialist.

This interesting story has a sequel, which should not be omitted here. Owing to a long period of litigation, it was the mid-Forties before those charged with executing Randolph's will were in position to carry out its terms. Then Judge William Leigh, one of the executors, bought 3200 acres of land in Mercer County, Ohio, with the object of settling 400 freed Negroes upon small farms. But the Midwest was at that time very anti-Negro, and the inhabitants of the county forcibly prevented the Negroes from taking up residence. My sources do not tell what ultimately became of them.

Randolph deserves to be called a political conservative individualist for two reasons which I hope by now are apparent: his belief in the limited though real role of government, and his defense of the smaller but "natural" unit against the larger one which pretends a right to rule.

Closely related to Randolph's political conservatism was his scorn of what he called dialectic. He was not always precise or knowing in his use of this term, but what we actually find in his discourse, if our attention is not diverted by the surface brilliance of the language, is a classical instance of the rhetor, or the master of rhetoric, contending against his enemies. Now the enemy of the rhetor is the dialectician. What I am saying here is to make a point, though it is only half true. As Aristotle maintained, rhetoric and dialectic are counterparts, each one needing the other. But rhetoric and dialectic may become dangerously separated, and then the users of them become enemies ceasing to help each other as both strive to go it alone. In this event the dialectician becomes the mere abstract reasoner, and the rhetorician becomes a dealer in sensational appeals. The one ceases to recognize circumstances, which are somewhat determinative in all historical questions. The other ceases to refer his facts to controlling principles and ideals. For the first there are a good many jocular epithets, of which "egghead" is a modern instance; to the latter the term "demagogue" is most widely applied. Kant observed that concepts without percepts are empty, and percepts without concepts are blind. This will define the two opposed positions.

Randolph thought he discerned among his enemies mere

dialecticians; that is, men willing to crucify the conclusions of history and common sense upon some cross of logic. When he felt this way about the opposition, he went on with his usual impetuosity to attack the method of dialectic. Though these attacks are fragmentary and tend to be outbursts rather than careful analyses, they provide an exciting case of the rhetorician assailing the method of his counterpart. The focus of his attack was this: the direction of the state should never be given to a mere dialectician, whose habit of mind incapacitates him for dealing with affairs of public concern and urgency. In a speech replying to Senator Everett of Massachusetts, he turned to the subject thus:

> There is a class of men who possess great learning, combined with inveterate professional habits, and who are, *ipso facto,* or perhaps I should rather say *ipsis factis* (for I must speak accurately as I speak before a Professor) disqualified for any but secondary part anywhere. . . .
>
> The mind of an accomplished and acute dialectician, of an able lawyer, or, if you please, of a great physician, may, by the long continuance of one pursuit—of one train of ideas—have its habits so inveterately fixed, as effectually to disqualify the possessor for the command of the councils of a country.
>
> A man may be capable of making an able and ingenious argument on any subject within the sphere of his knowledge; but, sir, every now and then the master sophist will start, as I have seen him start, at the monstrous conclusions to which his own artificial reason had brought himself.
>
> Thus a great diplomatist, like a certain animal, oscillating between the hay on different sides of him, wants some power from without, before he can decide from which bundle to make a trial.

But rhetoric and history go hand in hand. The rhetorician always speaks out of historical consciousness because his problems are existential ones.

The fact that Randolph is here employing a rhetoric of an energetic kind must not blind us to the realization that he is addressing himself to a deep-lying problem. The problem of

whether subtle reasoners, who leave out the kind of knowledge and consciousness that I am placing under rhetoric,
should be permitted the direction of practical affairs, where
their decisions must involve many other people, returns on
various occasions to perplex us.

Randolph's style of thought and utterance was that of the
statesman—rhetorician rather than the dialectician. This is
to say, he did not pass through methodical trains of reasoning,
but dived at once to his concluding proposition and tried to
make it vivid with illustration. He did not rely upon drawn-
out logic for his persuasiveness, but rather upon "the world's
body" made real and impressive through concrete depiction.

In gathering up the significance of his style, we can profit-
ably attend to some points made by his biographer Baldwin.

> His conclusions did not wait upon long and labored inductions.
> His mind, as by an instinctive insight, darted at once upon the
> core of the subject, and sprung, with an electric leap, upon the
> conclusion. He started where most reasoners end. It is a mistake
> to suppose that he was deficient in argumentative power. He was
> as fertile in imagination as most speakers; he was only deficient in
> argumentative forms. His statements were so clear, so simplified
> and so vivid, that they saved him much of the laborious process of
> argumentation. Much that looked like declamation was only illus-
> tration, another form of argument.

"He started where most reasoners end." This may well be
the text that opens up the true view of Randolph's mind. And
now it begins to appear that whereas logic and dialectic are
the method of the scientist and the democrat, intuition is the
method of the artist and—despite the unpopularity of the
word, I must use it—of the aristocrat. A dependence upon
mere logic seems to be the habit of those who are afraid of the
act of divination; and "wisdom is a kind of divination." I
would add that divination sometimes takes the form of recognizing the universal in the single instance. The direct
approach springs from those aristocratic qualities of self-

confidence and simplicity. Anyone may possess the intuitive type of mind, but when he does, he is prone to be impatient of those redundancies which consist of spelling out a logical process. For him the process is too mechanical, and it is even likely to substitute means for ends. This is the ground for saying that the aristocratic mind is anti-scientific and anti-analytical. It is concerned more with the status of being than with the demonstrable relationship of parts.

So, with simple directness, men of this habit move to their conclusion, and their argument consists of demonstration with all the forms, colors, and pressures of the actual situation. The method is not so much a begging of the question as it is dealing with the conclusion in historical and poetical ways. Such a mind comes to wrestle at once with the true objects of rhetoric, the impulses of attraction or aversion that form men's passions.

Such, in part, was the mind of John Randolph. An ultra-individualist, he began his career by breaking a lance with Patrick Henry and ended it by tilting against Andrew Jackson. A defender of states' rights and of the original philosophy of the constitution, he adhered to its tenets "even after they had been abandoned by the fathers of the church," to quote the inimitable Baldwin again. He was a follower neither of men's opinions nor their fortunes, and he did not feel that a bold utterance needed apology. He was the kind of person who feels that he must be right because he knows that he is a great man. There is great potential danger in this, but there is also power. In some men the feeling is productive of conceit and blindness, but in others it is the very substance of proof without which the forms of logic are but dry perfections.

[II]

To some persons it will seem an impudence to link the names of John Randolph and Henry David Thoreau. The former has not gone down as a thinker, although his reputation does something less than justice to his actual power of thought. He was a political figure, who left no body of writings to serve as texts for future generations. So far has the tide of opinion receded from Randolph's position that only occasionally is he resurrected by some scholar of special interest, as by Russell Kirk in his recent *Randolph of Roanoke.*

With Thoreau it is altogether the other way around. His name is writ very large in American literature. He is the bachelor of nature, the chaste and ethereal spirit of the Concord group. His *Walden* survives as a literary classic. A steady flow of monographs about him appears in the scholarly journals. In politics he was the teacher of an extreme philosophical radicalism, the inspirer of Gandhi and other revolutionaries. But let me emphasize that this is a study of individualism, and where that is the center of interest, the two men can justly be considered together. Here in fact are two powerful individualists, living at a time when our American culture was beginning to form. Both thought a great deal about the relation of the individual to the state, and both carried on a more or less continual warfare with the government in power. Both were great "nay" sayers in the Carlylean sense; and they were fond of hard sayings, or of expressions so bold that the underlying principles were immediately revealed.

Since Thoreau is a far better known figure than Randolph, a few biographical facts may serve as reminders. He was born in 1817 in Concord, of an ancestry that included English, Scottish, and French strains. From early youth he came to know the delights of fields and woods. He entered Harvard in 1833 and there led a rather seclusive life, preferring an alcove in the library to the company and sports of his fellows. When he graduated, one biographer has noted, he was far from the head of the class, but he was probably the best read member of it. After Harvard, he taught school in several places. In 1839, when he was twenty-two, Thoreau made with his brother John a trip on the Connecticut and Merrimack rivers, which was to be the subject of one of the two books published in his lifetime. It was on the Fourth of July, 1845, that he took up his residence in the hut at Walden Pond. This experiment in living apart from civilization, continued until September, 1847, was to furnish the subject of one of the famous books not merely of American literature but of literature in English. Following the Walden experience, Thoreau moved back to his father's house on the main street of Concord and there supported himself with the family's inherited business of pencil making.

Meanwhile *Walden* was being written, though it was not published until 1854. Shortly after its publication, Thoreau developed symptoms of tuberculosis, and the remainder of his life was largely a battle against ill health. His last effort to mold the public opinion of his time was made in 1859, when he championed the cause of John Brown after the famous raid. He spent his last months confined to a sickroom, and his life came to an end in 1862, before he had attained his forty-fifth birthday.

An analysis of how Thoreau arrived at his theory of individualism may well begin with the kind of impression that he makes upon a reader today. The English critic Holbrook Jackson, in an essay meant to be appreciative, has what seems a discerning estimate of him.

> Thoreau's weakness is that he cannot trust his more concrete concepts or even his own abundant common sense. He feels a need to idealize and to intellectualize, and in doing so he is in danger of missing the life he so abundantly seeks. The curious thing is that he knows idealism leads inevitably to disappointment—but he persuades himself it is the real and not the ideal which has let him down. . . . His friends rarely live up to his illusion of them, so he tries to remember them only as ideals. . . . The finite and temporal leave him with an "unsatisfied yearning."

Now when one looks deeply or analytically into what goes on in his writing, this proves to be a remarkably accurate diagnosis. For what we find is that Thoreau belongs to that class of dialecticians which Randolph so anathematized. He is not a complete one—but he is a good enough one to get into trouble. This fact alone will explain why, with all his resources and all his charms, he is so often found out on a limb—that is, taking a position which is not merely unpopular but is actually untenable. The clearest example of this tendency appears in the celebrated essay "Civil Disobedience." Here by the operation of a dialectical movement both man and the state are refined out of existence; they are made into ideological constructs quite adapted to their author's play of fancy, but out of all relationship to history. It is simple to place man beyond the effect of such things as taxation and slavery if one de-incarnates him. Still, a criticism thus sweeping of so famous a document needs some defense.

The progression of thought in "Civil Disobedience" is reducible to a very neat scheme. Thoreau does not follow the scheme consecutively, but no one reading the essay need miss the stages. It is a dialectical progression toward the author's ideal, which is finally offered very winningly, but in complete isolation from the facts of life. In Thoreau's vision there are four levels of man, each one transcending the one below it in a movement upward toward a kind of ineffable purism. At the bottom, of course, is the slave. The slave is the most degraded form of man because he is a mere instrumentality. The slave does not even own his own will; his status is one of complete deprivation. He is the nether pole from which the ascension upward begins.

Somewhat higher but still in a deprived condition is man as subject. Subjection too is a degraded state, implying limitation of the will of the subject and of course his inequality with the ruler. It is in this class which Thoreau puts the U.S. Marines, against whom he declaims so forcefully at the beginning of the essay. The Marine is depicted as a man "made with black arts" and as "a mere shadow and reminiscence of humanity." The Marine is not owned outright, but he is in a subjection almost as servile as the slave when he carries out the bidding of the state, according to Thoreau.

Above the subject is the citizen, characteristically of a democratic or popular state. He has achieved considerable freedom and dignity, since he is a participant in government, and he may be said in a sense to rule himself. Still, he is not free with a complete freedom. He is involved with things like elections and laws, and he has the problem of what to do about the decisions of majorities when they are repugnant to him. He has the problem of his conscience.

Consequently there has to be a higher level still, and this is represented by man as an apotheosized being, who does not need the state, to whom the laws are only impedimenta, and who will discharge all of his duties out of an inner enlightenment. He may live a neighbor to the state, but he will not be embraced by it; he has matured beyond requiring anything it can do for him, and so he lives in philosophical anarchy.

This final creature is not, of course, historical man, but an idealized figment more abstract, I submit, than that produced by any other philosopher. Yet it must be obvious that Thoreau, in dealing with the problem of human existence, has left the task conspicuously uncompleted. It is no difficult work to imagine man freed of all his intractable qualities and then to say of what remains, "This is man." We are indeed thankful to those who have furnished us with ideals. But there lies ahead the task of conceiving how this or any ideal is going to be conditioned by historical existence, and then of saying something helpful about how this conditioned being can live, cooperate, and compete in a civil order. Here, I am afraid, Thoreau is not so much a philosopher as a philosopher on a holiday. He is letting his thoughts follow his wishes and turning his gaze away from recalcitrant reality. It is characteristic of a dialectic not respectful of the facts to lead away from the existential world.

The same kind of dialectical exercise is performed upon the state. Here we find a similar ascension by stages from a lowest level to something existing out of this world. At the lowermost level is absolute monarchy, or despotism, where people are essentially in the condition of slaves. Next above this is limited monarchy, which rests upon subjects. Above this is democracy, whose members are free men, taking part in self-government but still under pressure to obey and conform. Thoreau asks rhetorically at the end of the essay: "Is democracy, as we know it, the last improvement possible in government?" The expected answer prepares for his vision of the state conceived on a higher plane "which can afford to be just to all men," respecting their individuality and leaving them alone. This would indeed be a *politeia en ouranôi*, "a polity existing in heaven," in a sense more ideal than Plato's.

At the close of his narrative of the night he spent in prison (he was put in jail on one occasion for not having paid his poll tax) Thoreau gives an account of leaving the state—the political state—which is charming on the literal level and meaningful on the symbolic one. He writes:

> When I was let out next morning, I proceeded to finish my errand, and having put on my mended shoe, joined a huckleberry party, who were impatient to put themselves under my conduct, and in half an hour—for the horse was soon tackled—was in the midst of a huckleberry field, on one of our highest hills, two miles off, and then the State was nowhere to be seen.

"The state was nowhere to be seen" is the clue. It was thus simple for Thoreau to place himself physically where that physical embodiment of the state, the jail in which he had just spent a night, was no longer visible. And the force of the image implies that any man can proceed to a height where the state will no longer offend his vision.

So, it is easy to mount the dialectical ladder until one has a beatific vision, but in the meantime the earth has dropped from view. Yet it is precisely the earth, with its thickness and stubbornness, that the political thinker has to cope with.

There occur several lesser examples of abuse of the dialectical n ethod, so that one can safely say that this is the characteristic defect of Thoreau's process of argument. Near the beginning, to cite one more interesting example, we are met with this statement: "That government is best which governs not at all." This is of course the position he arrived at in the sequence of reasoning just noted at some length. Here, however, we are brought to it in a different way, and a way very revealing of a method. The starting point is a proposition that a standing army is an evil thing. Now a standing army, it is made to appear, is but a species (an "arm") of the genus "standing government" and therefore "standing government" is an evil thing. It is a relationship of implication. What can be predicated of the part can be predicated of the whole. What involves the one must necessarily involve the other. If we reject the idea of a standing army, then we must reject the idea of a standing government. So we are propelled along by the force of the dialectical implication from the acceptance of a fair-seeming proposition to the acceptance of one that is dubious. Those common-sense perceptions which tell us that, while a standing army and a standing government may have some points of resemblance, they are not identical, have been omitted.

Furthermore, Thoreau is working here from a premise still more dubious, which is that man is a kind of creature who should never be visited with coercion, either by a thing called an army or a thing called a government. History is unanimous that however enticing this may be as a thought, it is not realizable in this world. At the very lowest estimate, society always produces a few individuals who have nothing but scorn for the common morality and who will recklessly and even gleefully invade the rights of others. For them, coercion is inescapable. That is why we are again forced to conclude that Thoreau is not talking about real men in the real world.

These defects in reasoning are accompanied by what might be called a defect of temperament which has serious consequences for his over-all case. Despite his sometimes skillful use of dialectic to make a specific point, he is not consistent in his attitude toward the state, but seems to shift ground as if by whimsy. In "Civil Disobedience" particularly, he is first here and then there in his stand on the subject of government. At the very opening he professes that he is not a "no government" man; he only wants a better government. Not only is this in contradiction with the dialectical conclusion of the general argument, where government is made to vanish away, but it also conflicts with his expressed readiness to secede at once as an individual, which would of course produce "no government." His position is neither one of continued membership in the state nor definite withdrawal from it; he seems to move from one to another of these depending on the degree of vexation he is feeling at the moment. Seen from one point of view, he admits "even this state and this American government are, in many respects, very admirable and rare things, to be thankful for." And he says further, "I will cheerfully obey those who know and can do better than I, and in many things those who neither know nor can do so well." These statements, however, are nullified by other professions. "The very constitution of the state is the evil," he declares. Yet "it is not my business to be petitioning the Governor or the legislature any more than it is their business to petition me." And finally, "As for adopting the ways the state has provided for remedying the evil, I know not of such ways. They take too much time and a man's life will be gone. I came into the world not chiefly to make this a good place to live in, but to live in it, be it good or bad." There is no way of overlooking the fact that this is effectually a repudiation of the responsibility, acknowledged earlier, for improving the condition of things. It is indeed a pose of moral indifferentism, quite out of harmony with most that he has been professing right along, and of course incapable of maintenance. This attitude seems to express the feeling of one who sees that the problem is really insoluble on the grounds that he has taken.

When Thoreau decided not to pay the church levy, he

prepared this formal statement: "Know all men by these presents, that I, Henry Thoreau, do not wish to be regarded as a member of any incorporated society which I have not joined." Later he added that he would resign from all the societies he had never joined if he had been able to find a complete list of them. Would this include the political society of which he was born a citizen? Now whether an individual can be born a member of a church is perhaps an arguable question. But that a man is born a member of the state which protects and nurtures him is a practically universal concession. There is no original "social compact" which he signs for admission to citizenship. His living under the laws and customs of the state is regarded as evidence of his membership, of his participation in the social union. Thoreau's solution, however, points in the direction of a complete severance of the social bond, which would permit him to become apolitical and hermitic. There is a concealed note of arrogance in his assertion that he came into the world to live in it; this goes too far, to say the least, toward assuming that one is the author of his own being. Thoreau dwells almost not at all on one half of the story, which is how much Cambridge and Concord helped him to become what he was. They supplied education, such companionship as he chose to avail himself of, conveniences such as the shoe repair shop which he has just patronized, and other things which can exist only when men live within the "social bond." It is hardly a fair return for this to say to society, "a plague upon you, for your difficulties are many, and they get in the way of the untroubled life I would like to lead."

The long-continuing power of this essay, and I do not underrate its fascination, proceeds from the natural delight we take in haughtiness toward the state and in that spirit of independence we recognize in anyone who says he is going to make his conscience his guide, come what may. But an analysis not prejudiced by Thoreau's great reputation must regard this, I am afraid, as an example of high but irresponsible thinking. To be responsible one must take cognizance of all the facts and realities—and one must be patient. Whenever it suits Thoreau not to deal with realities, he puts them aside, or on a lower plane of existence. To cite an example from another source, in his "Life Without Principle" he says, "What is called politics is something so superficial and inhuman that, practically, I have never fairly recognized that it concerns me at all." This way of bowing out may bring comfort, but then comfort is seductive; it is with the complete picture that the political counsellor has to deal. For him there is no abdication of that responsibility through homilies upon the nature of man fictionized. That course is political fantasy, not a consideration of the *conditio humana*, and what this condition entails. When Randolph wrote out the emancipation of his slaves, he made economic provision for them. In Thoreau's anti-slavery papers one looks in vain for a single syllable about how or on what the freedmen were to live. The matter for him began and ended with taking a moral stance.

An anarchic individualism coming down through a transformed Calvinism in the shape of an otherworldliness thus meets us in the pages of the Concord sage. His prescription is defective because it does not recognize both the driving forces and the inertia which cause human beings to behave as they do. A dissenter from dissent even in New England, he diverged thus far from that conception of man as a whole which underlies Ciceronian humanism and the later development of Catholic Christianity.

Of that tradition Randolph, even the crotchety, eccentric Randolph, is plainly the heir. His attitude was one of scorn for those who evade reality. His tactic in dealing with an evil was to hold it up in all its repulsiveness and then urge that something be done to overcome it. If time permitted, I could instance this well from his speech on the great Yazoo Land Frauds Case. Thoreau's tactic was to avert his gaze from it, or ignore it. Here I speak more literally than might at first be supposed. At the time of Fort Sumter, Thoreau was writing to a friend that the best thing to do—the only thing to do—was to ignore it, that being "the most fatal . . . weapon you can direct against evil." If you know of an evil, then you are *"particeps criminis"* — a partaker in the crime. Therefore one should not read the newspapers or the President's messages; one should keep himself pure by not hearing of these things. Surely this is one of the most curious positions ever taken.

It is possible that I have given credit for more than is due to Randolph's genius or native power of thought. Possibly he was not so much a political genius as a man kept on the right path by his tradition. He was born to politics and perhaps he was saved from errancy by his tradition. I am at least willing to consider this as an alternative explanation. But this calls for looking more closely at what that tradition was.

The tradition which shaped Randolph's thinking had preserved a belief in the dualism of man's nature. He did not, of course, get it directly from Catholic Christianity, by which it has been most widely taught, but rather from his reading of the classics and from that Anglican Christianity which was widely diffused throughout his part of Virginia. He had been baptized in the Church of England. After a long period of indifference he was reconverted about 1818. In writing to his friend Dr. Brockenborough, he attributed his apostasy to a dislike of "prelatical pride and puritanical preciseness." The phrase "puritanical preciseness" could well include, I think, those extremes which can be reached by a dialectical kind of thinking which leaves out the matrix of circumstances in which issues are found.

At any rate, Randolph appears a Christian humanist to the extent that he accepted the earthly part while making profession of that spiritual part which owes a transcendental allegiance. In politics both practical and theoretic he was a conservator, distrustful, on principle, of innovations. But even conservation demands some measure of renewal; and his principle of "wise and masterly inactivity," which he urged upon all governors, and his advice never to disturb anything which is at rest must be taken as emphasizing his dislike of restless change. In this matter of reform especially he stands in contrast with the great New England individualist. Randolph's vision of reform is social, and it is anti-millennial. Though he was possibly unaware of it, he was in the mainstream of the thinking of patristic Christianity on this subject. Change by reform is Christian; change by revolution is not. The Christian philosophy of reform firmly rejects millenarianism, or the idea that perfection can be realized on this earth. Neither man nor society can be perfected in this life; progress toward perfection is the ground of renewal and the measure of reform. This Thoreau ignores in many a fine gesture, but Randolph kept it steadily in view throughout one of the most singular political careers in our history.

I mentioned at the outset that this would be a transvaluation of values. The half-mad Virginia statesman appears, at least in the light of this exposition, a safer source of political inspiration than Thoreau. There is no need to grow uneasy over detraction from Thoreau. His powers of description and that peculiar intimacy with which he entered into nature will leave him always as one of our distinguished writers. But if we are interested in rescuing individualism in this age of conformity and actual regimentation, it is the Randolphian kind which we must seek to cultivate. Social bond individualism is civil and viable and constructive except perhaps in very abnormal situations. Anarchic individualism is revolutionary and subversive from the very start; it shows a complete despite for all that civilization or the social order has painfully created, and this out of self-righteousness or egocentric attachment to an idea. Of the many radical statements to be found in Thoreau, none is more radical or more subversive in import than that one appearing near the close of his "Life Without Principle": "where there is a lull of truth, an institution springs up." This notion that there is an utter incompatibility between truth and human institutions, the one forever denying the other, is again not a proposition for this world. It is charged with a lofty disdain for the human condition, not the understanding of charity. It is not Christian to accept such a view; or, if that is too narrow, it is not politically wise; or, if that is too narrow, it is just not possible. Such a view ends in the extremism of nihilism. The other more tolerant and circumspect kind of individualism has enjoyed two thousand years of compatibility with institutions in the Western world and is our best hope for preserving human personality in a civil society.

6

TWO ORATORS

For generations young Americans, brought up on the legend of America's unvarying success, have been given the impression that Daniel Webster's "Reply to Hayne" is one of the
great forensic triumphs of history. The phrase itself has become a stereotype, carrying with it connotations of both
sound political doctrine and decisive rebuttal, so that little
temptation exists to look into the actual argument, to see

Modern Age, Vol. XIV, Nos. 3–4 (Summer–Fall 1970), 226–241. This essay, edited
originally by George Core and M. E. Bradford, is taken from copy which they
considered to be a third draft. Parts of the paper exist in two versions, and there
is no single continuous whole. Editorial emendations have been kept to a bare
minimum, and they consist mainly of determining and excising the material
(chiefly quotations) which, without doubt, Weaver would have left out of his final
draft—and in correcting obvious errors. The italics in the quoted passages have
not been supplied by either Richard Weaver or the editors. Footnote 1 is the
author's; the remaining notes have been provided by the editors.

In May of 1962 Richard Weaver wrote to Randall Stewart: "I have completed
about half of another book. I feel that this one will be, whenever I am able to
finish it, a rather original study of American literature and culture." "Two
Orators," like "Two Types of American Individualism" (*Modern Age,* Spring
1963), was intended to be a chapter in that book.

The editors wish to express their gratitude to the late Kendall F. Beaton and
to his wife, Polly Weaver Beaton, Richard Weaver's literary executors, who
kindly made the original manuscript available to them and encouraged its
publication.

exactly what issues were broached and how they were treated in an exchange which is rightly viewed as one of the critical debates over the future of the United States.[1]

It is not new to say that Webster's speeches against Hayne (there were actually three of them in the course of this engagement) are the opening gun of American nationalism. But, in what senses this is true can be particularized in ways very significant for the development of American culture. And to understand fully the shape of things, certain historical accompaniments must be noted. By 1830 the "Era of Good Feeling" had departed from American history, and the struggle over the Missouri Compromise had raised dangerous sectional animosities. The decade of the 1820's saw the beginning of a clear alignment of parties. And the spirit of Jacksonian Democracy, with its heavy support from the West and its large promises for good and evil, was spreading throughout the land. Another source of singularly bitter division was the new tariff system, increasingly supported by the new manufacturing centers of the Northeast and opposed with great determination by the distinctly agricultural areas of the South.

But no one is prepared to understand the unfolding of the drama without looking at it in far wider political background. The French Revolution was now twenty-five years in the past, and it required about that length of time for its doctrines and the force of its example to cross the Atlantic and show their influence upon basic political thinking. As Lord Acton was to point out in his searching essay "Nationality," the French Revolution had engendered a spirit of nationalism which was

---

[1]That it was critical to this extent was sensed by some at the time. Shortly after the debate took place, former president John Quincy Adams was talking with Martin Van Buren. Van Buren declared that he had not read the debate. "You will do well to read it," Adams said. "I think it is the most important one that has taken place since the existence of the Government. The two doctrines are now before the nation. The existence of the Union depends, I fully believe, upon this question." See Samuel Flagg Bemis, *John Quincy Adams and the Union* (New York: Knopf, 1956), p. 228.

something new in the world. It was a doctrinaire idea divorced from history and it was at war, militarily and ideologically, with everything different from itself. Analytically considered, the important effect of the French Revolution upon France was as the breaking point of all intermediate structures, sometimes referred to as the feudal heritage, and the forging of the French people into a single entity, "the nation." Under the impact of some of Rousseau's large ideas, the French people were "collectivized"; they were instituted as a sovereign, and that historical system of checks and balances which had grown up under feudalism was swept out of existence. Local prerogatives and loyalties were impeached, and something enthroned as the "general will" was made the supreme arbiter. In passion for liberty, equality, and fraternity, structure was sacrificed to a political unity of an extremely unrelenting kind. That this type of revolution was intended not just for France but for the world can be read in the statements of many of its leaders. Furthermore, it was ordained, by the forces that had been unloosed, that the new nationalized France would embark upon campaigns of conquest.

The same features were not missing in the later American development. Democracy and nationalism are two political forces often found going hand in hand; and when they do, only the wisest statesmanship or the most fortunate circumstances can keep the former from becoming aggressive. Nationalism, as Lord Acton demonstrated, begins as a protest against some form of wrong or oppression or denial of rights. A people who feel themselves historically to be a community become charged with a desire to throw off the injurious yoke. In this way nationalism has at first the character of a liberating movement. Clearly the American Revolution can be so described. The American people had become differentiated from the people of the mother country. Three thousand miles of distance, a large and virgin territory, and divergences in religious and political institutions to some extent were giving them a distinctive character, which made itself felt in different needs. When it became evident that these needs were not going to be satisfied, they rose in rebellion to secure what they saw as their rights. Whether the actual grievances of the moment were enough to justify such drastic action is hardly a question worth arguing; the grievances would have continued and probably would have worsened. The slogans of that rebellion were appropriately "Liberty" and "Independence" (not then "Union"). The war for secession was successful, and a new nation resulted, which may be regarded as answering to a fact of nationality. Historical development had prepared the way; the Declaration of Independence gave it some reasoned defense.

In the sequel there was of course the question of what to do next. Should the new nation continue to exist under a disposition of freedom, which is a negative kind of condition in the sense of involving self-restraint and respect for others' rights, or should it embark upon a program of positive expansion, with its numerous powerful temptations? The period of infancy kept this question in abeyance for some three decades, but by the time under study, it was beginning to appear insistently. The United States was gathering bulk and power, and the mere availability of power is capable of exciting passions and images of grandeur. By the end of the third decade of the nineteenth century the stage was set for a crisis over the question, and at a crisis one has to choose.

It is even poetically appropriate that the clash between Hayne and Webster, personifying, we may note, South Carolina and Massachusetts, arose out of a motion on the disposition of the public lands. On the 29th of December, 1829, Senator Foot of Connecticut had offered a resolution directing the Committee on Public Lands to report on the amount of land remaining unsold, and to recommend whether it would be expedient to extend the surveys of these lands and to hasten the sale of them. A measure innocent seeming as this was enough to touch off an explosive sectional controversy.

Nevertheless, the issue touched the heart of the latent political conflict. What the general government did with these lands would unavoidably carry implications regarding its constitution and powers. The mode of disposition would become a source of inference and prophecy. Two rival philosophies of the nature and purpose of the Union thus ranged themselves following a dispute over the common inheritance.

The subject had already been introduced by Senator Benton of Missouri and by Senator Hayne when Senator Webster took the floor on January 20, 1830, for his first speech. This along with the following speeches will be partly summarized.[2]

Mr. Webster declared that he originally had no intention of entering the discussion of the question, but opinions had been expressed the day before "on the general subject of the public lands, and on some other subjects, by the gentleman from South Carolina, so widely different from my own that I am not willing to let the occasion pass without some reply." He believed that the public lands should be offered in such a way as to encourage settlement and avoid land speculation. He did not believe that the national government had been illiberal in its policy regarding the western lands, but at the same time he opposed the suggestion of giving them away or making their purchase easier. The cry had been raised, he said,

[2]Foot's Resolution and Daniel Webster's three speeches upon it may be found in Webster's collected works. The editors have followed the text of the fifth edition which was published in 1853 by Little, Brown and Company in Boston; the relevant material appears on pp. 248–355 of Vol. III. For Robert Young Hayne's two speeches the editors have used the *Speech of Mr. Hayne, of South Carolina, on Mr. Foot's Resolution, Proposing an Inquiry into the Expediency of Abolishing the Office of Surveyor General of Public Lands, and for Discontinuing Further Surveys, &c.*, January 21, 1830 (Washington: Duff Green, 1830) and the *Second Speech of Mr. Hayne, of South Carolina: In Reply to Mr. Webster; The Resolution Offered by Mr. Foot, Relative to the Public Lands, Being Under Consideration*, January 27, 1830 (Washington: Gales & Seaton, 1830).

that the income derived from their sales was a factor in "consolidating" the government. But "consolidation" had become a bogey; he was in favor of this kind of consolidation. "This, sir, is General Washington's consolidation." He ridiculed the idea that the revenue derived from the sale of these lands and the existence of a public debt tended to corrupt the people. He stressed his conviction that action by the general government may be beneficent and lead to general improvement. He believed that the remarks of the gentleman from South Carolina tended "to weaken the bond of our connection."

Turning then to a related issue, he denied that the East had in any way been hostile to the West. A representative from Massachusetts had been responsible for the Northwest Ordinance, which had been immensely beneficial to the West, and which had established a model for the disposition of new territory. In a slightly digressive vein he observed that Kentucky would have been much better off had she been formed in accordance with the Northwest Ordinance—an obvious sally against slavery, which had the effect of greatly widening the area of debate. Declaring that he felt he had vindicated the character and honor of the state he represented, Mr. Webster concluded.

Senator Hayne's reply was delivered on the day following. In a somewhat roundabout opening, he wondered why Webster should have chosen him to attack, since it was Senator Benton who had preferred the charge of Eastern hostility against the West. But detecting in the speech a number of aspersions upon his own South Carolina, he was determined to reply.

The real difference between Webster and himself was over how the public lands ought to be regarded. He regarded them as a sacred trust, not as a common treasure, especially because the latter signified a monetary bond of union. Mr. Webster would look upon them as "so much money in the Treasury," to be expended for objects "constitutional and unconstitutional." The South could not be accused of showing hos-

tility toward the West if the only ground was her constitutional scruples against voting for federally financed
improvements. Moreover, it was not true that New England
had always been a supporter of Western interests. That support dated definitely from 1825 and was the result of a deal
made between Adams and Clay whereby the former accepted
what was called "the American System."

Though Webster had declared that he was in favor of pay-
ing the public debt, his actions and other of his remarks
indicated that he wished the debt to remain because it would
be a means of binding the Union together. "Sir, let me tell that
gentleman that the South repudiates the idea that a *pecuniary
dependence* on the Federal Government is one of the legitimate
means of holding the States together," Hayne said.

He would meet frankly Webster's slur upon the South as a
slaveholding community. Whoever bore responsibility for the
origin of that institution, the South had to deal with a practical problem, not an abstraction. And as for the way in which
it was solved, he had satisfied himself by actual observation
that the slaves of the South were in far better condition than
the free man of color in the North. Neither was it true that
slavery was a cause of weakness, financial or military. The
South asked only to be left alone to regulate its affairs, safe
from the inference of "false philanthropy." It was wrong to
suppose that slavery was degrading to the character of slaveholders. Hayne then pointed to Washington and to other sons
of the Old Dominion.

Next he passed to the subject of consolidation. The object
of the framers of the Constitution had been not to consolidate
the government but to consolidate the Union. Then moving
to the heart of the issue, he said,

> Sir, anyone, acquainted with the history of parties in this country,
> will recognize in the points now in dispute between the Sena-
> tor from Massachusetts and myself, the very grounds which
> have, from the beginning, divided the two great parties in this
> country....

Much of the subsequent part of the speech was given to a recapitulation. Hayne reminded Webster first of how he had shifted his position on the tariff between 1824 and 1828 and then of how New England had failed to support the Union during the War of 1812, citing especially the Hartford Convention.

In the conclusion Hayne returned to the chief issue by stating the doctrine of reserved power.

The worst enemies of the Union were the promoters of consolidation.

The "Carolina doctrine" was merely a re-affirmation of the Kentucky-Virginia resolutions of '98. It was republican doctrine:

> Sir, as to the doctrine that the Federal Government is the exclusive judge of the extent as well as the limitations of its power, it seems to me to be utterly subversive of the sovereignty and independence of the States. It makes but little difference, in my estimation, whether Congress or the Supreme Court, are invested with this power.

South Carolina had tried to preserve the Union by the only means through which it could be preserved—resistance to usurpation.

He closed with a quotation from Burke: "You must pardon something to the spirit of liberty."

By this time the conflict of interests was clear. Hayne's speech was not a great oratorical accomplishment. It was, as the above summation will reveal, somewhat wandering, and it hardly merits for its maker the title of "silver-tongued orator." But the effect was a different thing. He had managed to touch upon several of the chief topics of sectional difference and the sore spots of regional character, and he had injected into the exchange one word about which the whole argument may revolve logically—the word "liberty."

Webster began his second speech on Foot's resolution, the longest and the most central in substance of the three, with considerable flourish and circumlocution.

Mr. President,—When the mariner had been tossed for many days in thick weather, and on an unknown sea, he naturally avails himself of the first pause in the storm, the earliest glance of the sun, to take his latitude, and ascertain how far the elements have driven him from his true course.

He then opened the argument by chiding Senator Hayne for having talked about everything but the resolution. (Webster's commentary on the way the debate had been conducted covers about six pages of a printed version.)

He next restated his belief in the wisdom of the Northwest Ordinance, but denied that this was a reflection on the South. Southern touchiness on the subject of slavery, he observed, had been a powerful lever in the political machine; and Southern jealousy, he charged, had led to the exclusion of Northern men from influential positions in the government. But he was willing to accept the situation as it was. "I go for the Constitution as it is, and for the Union as it is."

He maintained that the North as a whole had no disposition to violate the constitutional compact; and he attempted to dispose of the Hartford Convention by making this series of points: 1) the Hartford Convention was without influence as a precedent; 2) it was much more studied in the South than in the North; 3) other conventions had gone further than that one; and 4) he had never read the journal of that convention.

He next denied that he had been inconsistent in his attitude toward the public lands. He favored voting funds for "local" improvements because they benefited the nation as a whole. The doctrine of localism he rejected as "narrow-minded." "In our contemplation Carolina and Ohio are parts of the same country. . . ."

A study of the Constitution had convinced him that the government had in its power the authority to make internal improvements. He declared that he was in favor of consolidation of the Union but not of enlargement of its power.

Toward the close of his speech he opened a direct attack upon the doctrine of interposition.

There could be no middle ground, he argued, between submission to laws and open defiance. It was of course necessary to distinguish between the right to revolution, which he admitted, and the doctrine of interposition. Hayne's doctrine of interposition would make the Union a creature of each of the twenty-four states, severally. He presented a view that the government was a creation of the people: "It is, Sir, the people's Constitution, the people's government, made for the people, made by the people, and answerable to the people."

The states were not sovereign in the sense of being empowered to levy war, coin money, etc.

Suppose South Carolina should annul the tariff law but Pennsylvania and Kentucky should accept and uphold it?

He denied that New England had ever supported the interpositionist doctrine, and he used the Embargo Act as a test. It was held in New England to be both unconstitutional and harmful, but there was no talk of nullifying it.

He avowed clearly his belief that the national government is the judge of the extent of its powers:

> ... For I maintain, that between submission to the decision of the constituted tribunals, and revolution, or disunion, there is no middle ground; there is no ambiguous condition, half allegiance and half rebellion.
>
> I hold it [the United States] to be a popular government. ...
>
> This government, Sir, is the independent offspring of the popular will.

He named the Supreme Court as the body established to decide questions involving scope of authority.

Here he employed a *reductio ad absurdum*: a Union with power, subject to twenty-four diverse interpretations!

"Talk about it as we will, these doctrines go the length of revolution. They are incompatible with any peaceable administration of the government."

He developed an illustration of what would happen if South Carolina tried to interfere with the collection of duties.

The Constitution is not unalterable. It can be amended. If the "Carolina doctrine" were accepted, the Constitution "will exist in every State but as a poor dependent on State permission."

His peroration was to "Liberty and Union."

The closing speeches by Hayne and Webster merely developed the matter and manner of their earlier arguments.

With these summations, it is easy to see the opposing bases of the arguments. Hayne was resting his case upon the rhetoric of history, which involved reasoning from historical fact and literal interpretation. Webster, on the contrary, was basing his upon a dialectic about power.

We have noted that this issue came up in a way that is seemingly indirect, though it is certainly implied in the question of what to do about a common property, the public domain. Hayne, to repeat, stressed the fact that he regarded the public lands as a sacred trust, not as a common treasure. A sacred trust is something to be handled with scrupulous regard for the nature and purpose of the Union, and not a source of means by which this body can be transformed. He objected pointedly to the idea of a monetary bond of union. Already the subject of money is beginning to appear, and attitudes toward this subject will distinguish significantly the two mentalities which are here locked in debate. By its very nature money is on the side of the dialectician. In speaking of the public lands, Hayne had to defend the South against the charge of indifference to the West. The apparent indifference, he contended, was not a sign of lack of interest, but of meticulous respect for the terms of the Constitution. Here we are of course observing in Hayne's speech a literal interpretation of that document. Contrary to what his opponent had been saying, the interest of New England in the West had been neither consistent nor disinterested. It dated from the

politically controversial agreement of 1825 and was destined
by that to serve the sectional ambitions of New England.

Linked with the subject of the public lands was that of the
national debt. Despite some equivocal assertions on the subject, Webster was obviously in favor of continuing the public
debt because this would serve as another bond of union.
Again the reference by Hayne to money appears in a strong
and perhaps tactless way:

> Sir, let me tell the gentleman that the South repudiates the idea
> that a *pecuniary dependence* on the Federal Government is one of
> the legitimate means of holding the union together. . . . A mon-
> eyed interest in the Government is essentially a *base interest . . .*
> opposed to all the principles of free government, and at war with
> virtue and patriotism.

In this there were of course echoes of the feudal age, but
the sentiment was authentic with Hayne, who was speaking
out of tradition.

In his references to the Northwest Ordinance Webster had
animadverted upon slavery. Nowhere is Hayne more clearly
in the rhetorical mode than in the passage where he replies to
this. He begins by pointing out that for the South the problem
of slavery is not one for mere dialectical exercise. It was not an
abstraction to be played with, but a practical material exercise.
It was a fact of being which could not be simply reasoned away.
Referring again to the historical record, he reminded the
Senate that New England had had a large share in the creation of that problem. The South had the task of working out
some manageable solution, and he did not think that it had
succeeded badly. The history of the case thus gave Hayne
ground from which he secured rhetorical leverage. We have
found him talking continuously about what had been and is.
Examples and antecedents and consequences are the formal
sources of his argument.

Hayne's appeal was to history also in answering the charge
that slavery was a source of weakness. He cited the Southern

contribution to the nation's military record and the economic value of what it produced. To deny the charge of harmful effect upon character, he mentioned Washington and other illustrious sons of Virginia.

But the most serious attack in the political sense which he had to meet concerned South Carolina's loyalty to the Union. Insinuated throughout Webster's speech were remarks tending to make it appear that South Carolinians were a disloyal faction, planning to weaken the Union if not indeed to dissolve it. The main force of Hayne's counterargument would depend upon his showing that the course of his state had been dictated by pure patriotism to the Union as originally conceived. In doing this he found it necessary to offer a definition, and then to refer to the historical record. It must be granted that he was successful in detecting if not in answering the dialectical reasoning that Webster set in train. He pointed out that this conflict of philosophies had been present at the founding of the Union, and that it had been settled in favor of the limited confederacy. This too was a historical fact. Again:

> Sir, anyone, acquainted with the history of parties in this country, will recognize in the points now in dispute between the Senator from Massachusetts and myself, the very grounds which have, from the beginning, divided the two great parties in this country. . . .

He then directly described the motives of the two parties: "Sir, there have existed in every age and every country two distinct orders of men—the *lovers of freedom* and the devoted *advocates of power.*" Webster's dialectical conception of the nature of the Union was inspired by a love of growing power, not of settled right and liberty.

After all, how does one best prove loyalty to a country? A convincing way certainly is through willingness to sacrifice for it even when one's immediate interests are not at stake. Such had been the action of South Carolina both in the Revolution and in the War of 1812. In neither of these struggles did South Carolina have as much depending as did New England, but no state had shown greater effort, sacrifice, or suffering. If there had been a state which had shown "zealous, ardent, and uncalculating devotion to the Union," it was South Carolina. He went on to stress New England's comparative treachery in the War of 1812.

Naturally in his role Hayne was acting as a defender of the tradition and the *status quo*. He did not wish to see the public lands used as a source of increased revenue for the central government. He likewise opposed a continuing public debt, because this would perpetuate an objectionable pecuniary dependence upon the government. As for slavery, he fell back upon two current defenses of the system: the argument which called attention to its massive presence, regardless of who might be to blame for its origin, and the contention that free men of color had not been found to improve their condition under emancipation. The Union as it had been founded was a free covenant, designed to provide for certain general needs and at the same time to protect local rights where general measures were inapplicable or objectionable. The "Carolina doctrine" only restated the Kentucky-Virginia resolutions of 1798, which were in turn a reaffirmation of the original principle of the Union. The real enemies of the Union were not those who were striving to preserve its original purity of purpose, but those who were trying to consolidate it in the interest of a power hostile to liberty.

A rhetoric of history presents images which have been actualized, and in these Hayne's speech is far richer than his opponent's. He takes the Union as it was designed; he regards the public lands as a "sacred trust" and not as something to be utilized. He defends the spirit of liberty, which was the true genesis of the American republic. He acknowledges the inheritance of slavery as a legacy from the past. These things are to be enjoyed or endured, as the case may be; all that he asks is protection against the growth of a centralizing power and against "false philanthropy." It is a defense of the past and the present against charges which he saw only as threats to freedom and happiness. So the rhetor of history asked that what was good or tolerable from the past be preserved against enthusiastic visions which would prove delusive to those who followed them and hurtful to those whose conservative realism trusted the actual more than the envisioned and preferred liberty to power. It is essentially a libertarian case, opposed to the promise of welfare through governmental interference and finding contentment in a present state of things where the individual is left to make his own accommodation to the circumstances in which he finds himself. It breathes much of Randolph's "wise and masterly inactivity" as a prime factor in social stability and happiness.

In one passage of his speech, as we have seen, Hayne approached the subject of national consolidation and the tariff through a historical review of American parties. The principles in dispute between Mr. Webster and himself, he averred, were the same principles which had divided the country politically since its beginning. One party, which he went on to name, was in favor of a centralized national union; the other, prizing liberty above all, was in favor of limitation of power and a federal union. A similar conflict between the lovers of power and the lovers of liberty could be found throughout history:

> The same great leading principles, modified only by peculiarities of manners, habits, and institutions, divided parties in the ancient republics; animated the *Whigs* and *Tories* of Great Britain, distinguished in our own time the *Liberals* and *Ultras* of France, and may be traced even in the bloody struggles of unhappy Spain.

He considered history eloquent enough upon this subject to justify his viewing "*the consolidation of the Government,* AS THE WORST OF EVILS."

In the exchange over the intended nature of the Union, the tariff was a subject which made itself insistently felt. Each antagonist accused the other of inconsistency in regard to the tariff, but Webster's personal shift of position seems to have been the most striking instance of an altered stand. In 1820 and again in 1824 he had appeared as a leader of the free trade sentiment of New England, but in 1828 he voted for the "Tariff of Abominations," which John Randolph was to characterize as the most selfish piece of legislation ever passed by a government. Webster defended himself in this speech by declaring that he had voted for the tariff only after it had become a settled policy, when the one thing to be done was to adjust it to the other national exigencies. In other words, he had swung to the side of protection only after it appeared that this was going to be the fixed and permanent policy of the country.

It could be asked whether Webster is not here arguing from history, whether, seeing that a change of feeling toward the tariff had taken place between 1824 and 1828, he did not accommodate the situation with as good a right as Hayne had to accept and defend slavery. To this objection it must be answered that the change was too abrupt, and anyhow this was not consistently Webster's way of defending a policy. An argument from history is not simply a pragmatic argument with whatever fact comes last tipping the balance. History has extent and depth, revealing lines of growth over a period of time, so that the historical-minded person can ordinarily reconcile tradition and principle. Webster's almost sudden about-face hardly admits of this perspective. His own sense of discomfiture is revealed by the disingenuous question: "Does political consistency consist in always giving negative votes?" To this a writer in the *Southern Review* of August 1830 replied: "Yes, upon identical propositions involving the same policy."[3]

It should now be sufficiently apparent that Hayne's argument is largely an argument from the record. It contains little

---

[3]"Debate on Mr. Foot's Resolution," an unsigned editorial, appears in Vol. VI, No. XI of *The Southern Review* for August 1830 on pp. 140–198. Weaver recurs to it later in the present essay; and the writer's view complements Weaver's at certain points.

in the way of theoretical speculation. His method was to bring forward certain broad historical truths, here and there supported by factual detail to show that the cause of South Carolina and of as much of the South as agreed with her was in the mainstream of the American political tradition.

We are now in position to examine the forensic character of Webster's reply. He spoke of the irrelevance of much of the debate to the original resolution; he corrected Hayne's misapplication of a quotation from Shakespeare, and he chided him for his ignorance of Nathan Dane, the mover of the Northwest Ordinance. All this is fair warning that Webster was not going to be confined to the facts of the record; he was making himself free, as it were, for an adventure among ideas. And much of the remainder of the speech consists of drawing out the implications of a position asserted as desirable. The actual reply does not in fact begin until he moves to the subject of the Northwest Ordinance, and his statements with reference to that must be regarded as curiously incompatible. They were that the provisions against slavery were wise and beneficial for the states formed out of this territory and would have been so for other states, and that there was nothing in this view which would be regarded as prejudicial against the South. Evidently Webster was walking a fence, endeavoring on the one hand to accept certain facts, and on the other to put forward propositions which could but doubtfully be reconciled with them. Here appears the root of the inconsistencies against which he had to defend himself.

After a passage of some length in which he denies that he has been inconsistent on the subject of the public lands, he moved to the real issue of the argument, the nature of government with whose interests the senators were charged. Here it appears most convincingly that the true basis of Webster's argument was not historical but dialectical. His speech is not indeed without excursions into history, but these had been made for the purposes of correction and refutation of some minor points. When he reached the real source of leverage for his argument, this turned out to be a concept—a concept of the Union which is without historical support. By this route he had arrived at a concept of the "common good" which must separate him from the upholders of the "Carolina doctrine."

> "What interest," asks he [the gentleman from South Carolina], "has South Carolina in a canal in Ohio?" Sir, this very question is full of significance. It develops the gentleman's whole political system; and its answer expounds mine. . . . Sir, we narrow-minded people of New England do not reason thus. Our *notion* of things is entirely different.

Attention must be given to his usage of the word "notion." This is something formed in the mind, which by the very semantic history and connotation of the word may have little to do with existing circumstances.

This was obviously a way of stating his conviction that the policy should be one of tighter union. Whether the part or the whole should have precedence in cases where their desires conflicted was the question, stated in the most abstract terms, which underlay the long-developing controversy and which was not decided until the settlement of force was invoked in the 1860's. But lying even behind this question is another for the student of cultural and political institutions—the question of which of these priorities is more friendly to liberty. We have noted that Hayne's speech was conspicuous for its apostrophes to liberty. His historical argument was devoted to the proposition that the United States had been founded primarily to secure the blessings of liberty. For Hayne the implication was clear that liberty required the independence and dignity of the parts, with local attention to and disposition of local affairs. In what may seem to many an excess of particularism, he opposed local improvements financed by funds of the general government. Yet from a strict point of view Hayne was but facing and accepting the price of liberty. Freedom is something that gathers around the hearth, inheres in local associations, and endears to a man his place of habitation. It was a protection to enable him to enjoy things, not a force or power to enable him to do things.

Now a new notion was beginning to be broached. It was that happiness lies in magnitude and potentiality. New lands had to be disposed of and new conveniences had to be provided for commerce, and protection had to be given to a burgeoning industry, or so thought the now emerging advocates of consolidation. Webster by 1830 had become a bold spokesman for these. But the reasons he gave for his stand were "notional" rather than historical. He does indeed try to give it the cloak of testimony and authority. Thus at one point in his speech he offers an accounting for his new orientation:

> Under this view of things, I thought it necessary to settle, at least for myself, some definite notions with respect to the powers of the government in regard to internal affairs. It may not savor too much of self-commendation to remark that, with this object, I considered the Constitution, its judicial construction, its contemporaneous exposition, and the whole history of the legislation of Congress under it; and I arrived at the conclusion, that government had power to accomplish sundry objects, or aid in their accomplishment, which are now commonly spoken of as *internal improvements.*

But this remained generality. He immediately confessed that he was not prepared to argue at large the grounds for this position. His tactic was instead the dialectical one of involving South Carolina as having blazed the way for internal improvements and the tariff.

Webster's treatment of the Hartford Convention is another good illustration of his method. He repudiated the convention not because of historical circumstances but because of a principle. With him the primary consideration was not that it had adversely affected the strength and morale of the nation in the time of war, but simply that it had disunion as its object.

The material question is the *object*. Is dissolution the *object*? If it be, external circumstances may make it more or less an aggravated case, but cannot affect the principle. I do not hold, therefore, Sir, that the Hartford Convention was pardonable, even to the extent of the gentleman's admission, if its objects were really such as have been imputed to it.

Once more the reader may be invited to note that the clash between Hayne and Webster is a clash between history and asserted principle. Hayne takes the view that historical situations may condition the right to claim a privilege. Webster takes the view that certain rights or obligations must be regarded as above or independent of historical situations. With this he is of course ready to put forward his concept of union as a self-justifying ideal which can in the present and the future be maintained even to the detriment of local interests.

Now, in the last part of the speech, which glows with increasing zeal and takes on more of the embellishments of rhetoric, Webster made his case for the indivisibility and indestructibility of the Union. It is plainly in accord with his use of the dialectical method, which I have insisted on from the beginning, that he attempts to catch Hayne in a dialectical trap. What he does, in brief, is offer Hayne a disjunctive choice between allegiance or submission and revolution. The right to revolution he does not dispute; he leaves this clear alternative. It is to be recognized as a right inherent to all people. But to the question of whether there is a middle ground between the right to revolution and the duty of obedience, his answer is not without qualification. There is no means by which the people can legally resist the actions of the general government to which they belong. In this passage of his argument, Webster is not simply unhistorical, for it would be more accurate to say that he deserts history and falsifies it. Asserting that the Constitution must be understood in the light of its origin, he declared, "It is, Sir, the people's Constitution, the people's government, made for the people, made by the people, and answerable to the people." And he stated furthermore: "The general government and the State governments derive their authority from the same source."

Such was the construction of the Union put forward by Webster and echoed later by other nationalists. In 1850 Theodore Parker was to refer to "A government of all the people, by all the people, for all the people." Lincoln's phrasing of the same idea in the Gettysburg address is too familiar to need citing. But this concept was not historical. There was nothing in the Constitution except the phrase "the people," itself of doubtful implication, to suggest that the people were acting *en masse*. But somewhere along the path of events the French revolutionary theory of the people as a unitary whole, governing in the interest of the whole without restrictions on its power, had seeped into the political thinking of some Americans. Its effect, like the effect of Puritanism in religious doctrine, was to diminish and even to sweep away intermediate structures and centers of authority. The same impatience with an ordered and tempered relation between parts and whole now began to show itself in a philosophy of government. And even though the trend did not go as far in the United States as it had gone in France, there is no mistaking the common source of the "notion" (to repeat Webster's word). The "spurious democracy" of the French Revolution, as Lord Acton was to term it, which placed power and rule above local rights and autochthonous institutions continued its sway during the nineteenth century and profoundly altered the character of the American Union.

Against this trend South Carolina was invoking, in Webster's own phrase, the "conservative power of the state." He took cognizance of the fact that this was being done in the name of liberty. To that his retort was as follows:

In one sense, indeed, Sir, this is assuming an attitude of open resistance in favor of liberty. But what sort of liberty? The liberty of establishing their own opinions, in defiance of the opinions of all others; the liberty of judging and of deciding exclusively themselves, in a matter in which others have as much right to judge and decide as they; the liberty of placing their own opinions above the judgment of all others, above the laws, and above the Constitution.

It is clear as Webster warms to his theme that he sees the particular part as so integrated with the whole that it has no absolute right which could be asserted against the whole. South Carolina had no right to make a judgment, even of its own welfare, contrary to the Union. In the extreme application of this doctrine, she is caught in a political trap from which there is no escape, even if her extinction were being meditated. Webster was not, of course, contemplating such an extreme. His eyes were dazzled with the image of a union growing in size and power and diffusing light and blessings throughout the world. The student who is interested to see how much of the nationalist case rested upon fanciful representation must attend to the peroration of this speech:

> When my eyes shall be turned from the last time to behold the sun in heaven, may I not see him shining upon the broken and dishonored fragments of a once glorious Union; or States dissevered, discordant, belligerent; on a land rent with civil feuds, or drenched, it may be, in fraternal blood! Let their last feeble and lingering glance rather behold the gorgeous ensign of the republic, now known and honored throughout the earth, still full high advanced, its arms and trophies streaming in their original lustre, not a stripe erased or polluted nor a single star obscured, bearing for its motto no such miserable interrogatory as "What is all this worth?" nor those other words of delusion and folly, "Liberty first and Union afterwards," but everywhere, spread all over in characters of living light, blazing on all its ample folds, as they float over the sea and over the land, and in every wind under the whole heaven, that other sentiment, dear to every true American heart,—Liberty *and* Union, now and forever, one and inseparable.

This is grandiloquence, but it does not contain the philosophy of a free society. To see the applications of this truth, one must take a more comprehensive view of American history and an independent look at the "Carolina doctrine," which Webster was assailing as fatal to liberty.

Movements for reform and revolution have a natural tendency to go to extremes. The test of statesmanship is the ability to tell the critical line which they must not pass if they are to prove salutary. At the bottom of such ability lies the sense of measure; and measure, it hardly needs pointing out, requires the concept of limits. Once again we have in view the root idea of stasis.

The prudential virtues are always concerned with how far a thing will go. Theological virtues exist in an absolute form, but the political and moral virtues of this life are found, as Aristotle pointed out, between extremes. Since man is not an angel, the consideration of too little and too much must always be a guide to his thinking. It is the Faustian obsession to decry limits and to reach out for an infinitude of experience and power. If this is an illustration of what it means to become man by supposing oneself to be of a godlike capacity, the concept of measure and restraint because of the human condition is the secret of humanism. These two spirits of course have their manifestation in politics.

The historical clash which we are now studying furnishes an unusually vivid example of this principle. The American revolutionary movement, with its object of independence and its ideal of a sovereign republic in a new world, certainly can be viewed as a reform movement. There are those who have maintained that America would have done better had she continued as a part of the British Empire, and while their arguments are not comtemptible, the juster opinion seems to be on the other side. A new type of society was evolving on the western side of the Atlantic, with its own legitimate rights and aspirations, and political autonomy appears to have been needed for an adequate realization of this.

But once this object was attained, a more difficult subject arose; for success often brings problems that the pressure of a struggle has kept submerged. It now had to be decided whether the victory would be used for freedom or for power. The relation between the two is one of metaphysical subtlety, but here it can be said that on the political level freedom inheres in the local and the particular. Freedom emanates from individual desires, not large corporate enterprises. The latter are sometimes mistaken for the former, but the freedom which results from them is distant and illusory. The political question then becomes, what is the right unit of government which will insure safety and at the same time allow the expression of individual bents and preferences? Washington and many of the Federalists took this attitude because of their experience in a seven year military struggle. In time of war, no other kind of government is practical; dispersion of power means weakness, whereas in union there is strength. As a military means, there is everything to be said for the consolidated union. But the fact itself is instinct with grave prophecy.

When the military exigency disappears and the people begin to contemplate the order of their civil existence, another alternative becomes possible. The ideal of a free society with the maximum dispersion of authority and the minimum of state coercion may become the goal of those whom Hayne described as the lovers of freedom. By the very nature of things, freedom depends upon an establishment of law and custom. To be free a man has to know where things are to be found and in what form, for these are the very instrumentalities of his choice. An order which derives its impetus from a dynamism and which moves along on a collective urge cannot present the alternative choices which a conservative order holds out. The responses which are to be made are willed in advance, and progression keeps things in a perpetual unsettlement. This state of affairs is most inimical to freedom where the compelling force is a political one.

Forty years after the close of our revolutionary struggle the nation was at a crossroads where one of these courses had to be chosen over the other. The Federalist party, with its bias in favor of centralization born of the struggle itself, had been overthrown; but there appeared in its midst the advocates of a new political sentiment in favor of a more consolidated union. The Union had been created through a constitution, and now the debate polarized naturally around two points of view which may be phrased as questions: was the Constitution to be viewed primarily as a guarantor of liberty or as an instrument of power? The South, generally speaking, took the former position; and the North with the West took the latter, with the West acting as a sort of catalyst in the division.

The most widely received interpretation of the division is that the South was on the defensive, seeking to protect its "peculiar institution" against the anti-slavery and even anti-agrarian tendencies from the outside. It is manifest that the issue of slavery was drawn into the controversy, where it became the most exciting and inflammatory of the symptoms of difference. Lying beneath it and behind it in time were cultural differences which had long been tending to make the two sections different nations. In the 1790's while cotton was still an insignificant crop it had flared up in the Kentucky-Virginia Resolutions, in which the opinions of the founders of the Union had been brought forward in support of a union established primarily to secure liberty. Later the repeated demands of the South that it be left alone to manage its own affairs in its own way were turned to its political disadvantage by those who represented them as a plea for the preservation of Negro slavery. In part, and as a circumstance, they were just this; but they were also a parcel of a much wider demand for local autonomy which has produced sectional differences down to the present moment. A respect for establishment against a dynamic progressivism was the wider and deeper source of Southern resistance.

The strength of this feeling led the South to the point of defending an absolute veto, in the form of state interposition, upon certain acts of the Union. That Webster considered this the weakest point in his opponent's case may be inferred from the space he gives to it and the élan with which he presses his attack. But concede a state the right to veto an act of the general government, he argued, and the Union would become only a "rope of sand," a poor thing dependent for its force upon the permission of the several states. It is impossible to think in these terms of a union with power. Let us note again that Webster was arguing neither from history nor from text, but from implied consequences. A government which has to defer to the authority of one of its component members must be a weak government and *therefore* not the kind of government which the founders of the nation had desired to institute. The very tone of his speech in this part suggests that he formed the advocates of the "Carolina doctrine" into defending a government which would be incapable of operating.

The case was not, however, as conclusive as it might seem. All depends upon what one has in view. Webster assumed that no man of good sense and patriotism would espouse a government which is without power to expand and to adapt its operation to the demands of the "common welfare." But suppose one starts with the conviction that the highest aim of the art of politics is not an institution of magnitude and power, but "civil freedom"? That is an uncoerced state of affairs, in which the individuals are protected but are not used in the interest of grandiose projects. Then the perspective changes, and Webster's mockery loses its power to sway. This was essentially where the South stood, and it was not without means of rebuttal.

Let us now look narrowly at two points which the Southern spokesman had to meet. (1) Had Webster presented a true dilemma in his alternative of submission or revolution? and (2) if the right of interposition were recognized, would it be used so irresponsibly that the Union would become a union in name only?

In the *Southern Review* article to which reference has been made, the first of these two points is met squarely. It was the very purpose of the founders of the American Union to devise a means whereby liberties would be protected against encroachment *without* the appeal to revolution. The right to revolution was an antecedent right, existing everywhere and at all times, where situations are dire enough to warrant its use. But revolutions are costly and unsettling, and cannot be preferred modes of redress. It was the genius of the American Constitution that it provided a way to redress wrongs without the expense and agony of revolutionary upheaval. This way found its formulation in the doctrine of interposition, which permitted a local unit to oppose what it considered oppression without severing its connection with the general government. If it was in any sense revolutionary, it was revolution made to prevent revolution; but it could more appropriately be called "anti-revolutionary." The view was expressed in these words:

> The power to protect herself, in the confederacy, from an infraction of the conditions of the compact, is not a revolutionary right, but a right that belongs to her as a member of the confederacy; and we maintain, that in regard to all such powers as she has not delegated, she remains just as competent as she was before she joined the confederacy. . . .

The reserved rights of the states were therefore guarantors against revolution rather than means to inaugurate one. This was the solution which the Confederation of American States had devised to strike the balance between power and freedom. But with the advocates for civil freedom, resistance to oppression was the uppermost thought; and here was the structure designed to forestall further revolutions of the kind the American states had just passed through. It was unhistorical and wrong to say that the Supreme Court had been set up to adjudicate differences between the states and the general government. "The framers of the Constitution never intended to confer upon the Supreme Court, the political powers of an Aulic Assembly."

The objection that such veto power would leave responsible government out of the question remained to be answered. Here, in the manner of Hayne, the writer relied upon an argument which may be most clearly recognized as rhetorical-historical. He simply appealed to the weight of the situation to make it appear that the right of interposition would never be used except for grave cause. The sense of historical fact gave assurance that "nothing but the *truth* and a *deep sense of oppression* on the part of the people of the State, will ever authorize the exercise of the power." As long as the several states were attached to the idea of union by a sense of loyalty proceeding from mutual trust and benefit, there was no prospect that reckless leaders would seek to nullify the operation of the general government on slight pretext. The author asked his public to consider the results that must follow a clear recognition of the right to interpose.

> But, in order to understand more fully what its operation would be, we must take into the estimate the effect which a recognition of the power would have on the administration, both of the General and State Governments. On the former it would necessarily produce, in the exercise of a doubtful power, the most marked moderation. On the latter, a feeling of conscious security would effectually prevent jealousy, animosity, and hatred, and thus give scope to the natural attachment to our institutions.

The feeling of liberty he went on to describe as something very intimate—an appreciation by the individual of the surroundings he had always known. It grew from the affections and provided an enduring bond between himself and the habitation which had been his. Liberty was invested "with all the associations which belong to home—to the spot endeared to us by the affections of infancy, and the more sober attachments of mature life. These political associations contain in themselves the self-resisting principle to revolution."

Such liberty was not an urge to power, but a feeling of contentment and enjoyment of an order having status in the memory and nourished by all the things that enter into sentiment.

With a final reference to Webster's "slavish doctrines" and a rebuke to those who "regard our government as a consolidated empire" the review closed.

This was an attitude into which the aesthetic, as distinguished from the practical, entered heavily and in fact determined the position in regard to the purpose of the Union.

It should be by now clear that in this celebrated exchange, two theories of nationality appeared in direct opposition. For Webster a nation was something that filled the political horizon; it was a creation which tended to carry its own vindication, and for which the sacrifice of local rights was appropriate. When the author of the review mentioned that "National glory . . . combatted by his side," he was of course referring to the theme of national greatness which pulses through Webster's conception of a nationalized union with its subservient parts. The parts derive their greatness not through themselves but from the participation in the whole. It is a vision emanating from a dream by way of "construction," and it prepared the United States for that trend toward national unification which had already seized Europe and was to cause the wars of the mid-century period.

For Hayne and his fellow expositors, on the other hand, South Carolina was the nation or the nationality. That is to say, South Carolina represented legitimate aspirations toward unity insofar as these were reconcilable with liberty. Beyond that it had no right to go. A nation was a means toward a higher end, not a self-glorifying structure which improved as it gained size and authority for coercion. True nationality was always connected with historical facts which consolidated a people as far as that was compatible with their happiness in a state of civil liberty. These facts were geographical, ethnic, cultural, linguistic, and political; and they furnished the substance for any claim to independence. Political union which transcended these should be for purposes limited in proportion to the transcendence. Those unions which tended to crush these facts out savored of empire, and the readers will recall how the words "empire" and "imperial" appear as terms of condemnation in the speech of Hayne.

It was the prospect of the West which encouraged dreams of empire and began one of the most fundamental conflicts over political organizations which can occur.

{ 7 }

THE OLDER RELIGIOUSNESS

IN THE SOUTH

Of the many factors which have conspired to make the Southern people a distinct cultural group, so that it remains possible today to speak of "the mind of the South," none has received so little informative discussion as their peculiar religious temper. The liberal journals satirize the Bible Belt and attack "fundamentalism," which they identify with ignorance and general wrong-headedness, and the sociological writers, always chary of anything implying a metaphysic, handle it gingerly if at all. Yet this religious temper is definitely a survival, whose history can be traced as successfully as that of the feudal system or the tradition of chivalry. The conservative section of the country has clung to "the old time religion." It is the purpose of this paper to indicate some of the antecedents of that religion in our common heritage.

It is plain that just as there was much in the economic and social structure of the Old South to suggest Europe before the Great Plague and the peasant rebellions, so there was much in its religious attitude to recall the period before the Reformation. For although the South was heavily Protestant, its

The Sewanee Review, Vol. LI (1943), 237–249.

attitude toward religion was essentially the attitude of orthodoxy: it was a simple acceptance of a body of belief, an innocence of protest and schism by which religion was left one of the unquestioned and unquestionable supports of the general settlement under which men live. One might press the matter further and say that it was a doctrinal innocence, for the average Southerner knew little and probably cared less about casuistical theology: what he recognized was the acknowledgement, the submissiveness of the will, and that general respect for order, natural and institutional, which is piety. In short, there was a religious as well as a political Solid South, as Bishop Poteat has pointed out. Such disputes as occurred among churchmen were ecclesiastical rather than theological—saving a few striking exceptions—and the laymen themselves preferred not to regard religion as a matter for discussion. Religion was a matter for profession, and after one had professed, he became a member of a religious brotherhood, but this did not obligate him to examine the foundations of belief or to assail the professions of others. The Southerner did not want a reasoned belief, but a satisfying dogma, and the innumerable divisions which occurred on the Southern and Western frontiers must be ascribed to a religious intensity together with an absence of discipline rather than to a desire to effect a philosophic synthesis, as was elsewhere the case. In 1817 *The Western Gazetteer and Emigrants' Directory* reported of the condition of religion in Kentucky: "Baptists, Methodists, Presbyterians, and Seceders are the prevailing sects; they manifest a spirit of harmony and liberality toward each other, and whatever may have been said to the contrary, it is a solemn truth, that religion is nowhere more respected than in Kentucky." Throughout the South and West there occurred the anomalous condition of an incredible flowering of sects together with the more primitive type of emotional response to religion. Travelers expressed a double amazement at the multiplicity of sects and at the lack of friction or ill will between them.

This curious circumstance is susceptible of explanation. The religious Solid South expressed itself in a determination to preserve for religion the character of divine revelation. Superficially, the difference between a backwoods convert, with his extraordinary camp-meeting exhibitionism, and the restrained and mannered Episcopalian of a seaboard congregation, seems very great. Yet it must be borne in mind that despite the different ways they chose to assert religious feeling, both were inimical to the spirit of rationalism. And if the spirit of rationalism is looked upon as the foe of religion, then it must be admitted that orthodox Christianity was as safe in the hands of one as the other.

New England, on the contrary, was settled in the early years largely by people who had been embroiled in religious feuds, which they found occasion for renewing after they had set themselves up in the New World. The doctrinal differences which resulted in the exiling of Anne Hutchinson and Roger Williams, in the withdrawal of Thomas Hooker from the Bay Colony, and which later cost Jonathan Edwards and Ralph Waldo Emerson their pulpits are instructive cases in point. Such troubles arise only when egotistical and self-willed people make assent a matter of intellectual conviction. In New England the forces of dissent finally won the day. The right to criticize and even to reject the dogmas of Christianity came at length to overshadow the will to believe them, so greatly did the tide run against the conformists, and in the nineteenth century Emerson, Channing, and Transcendentalism killed insistence upon uniformity in this once most orthodox of sections. A conclusion to be drawn from these events is that New England, acting out of that intellectual pride which has always characterized her people, allowed religion to become primarily a matter for analysis and debate, if we take here the point of view of the conservative religionist. Instead of insisting upon a simple grammar of assent, which a proper regard for the mysteries would dictate, they conceived it their duty to explore principles, and when they had completed the exploration, they came out, not with a secured faith, but with an ethical philosophy, which illuminated much, but which had none of the binding power of the older creed. There followed as characteristic results Unitarianism and Christian Science, two intellectual substitutes for a more rigorous religious faith. While this was going on, Southern churchmen were fiercely assailing the "Arian heresy in New England" and were declaring that when man uses reason to test Scripture "the inevitable logical result is Atheism."

The results of the divergence did not appear at the beginning, for originally both Virginia and the New England colonies conceived religion as a part of the general program of government. The instructions drawn up in 1606 for the Virginia Company required that "the true word and service of God be preached, planted and used," and further provision for conformity was made by the Divine and Martial Laws of 1611, which required that everyone who then resided in Virginia, or who should thereafter arrive, should make profession of religious belief, and if found deficient, should repair to a minister for instruction. The first General Assembly, moreover, passed a law ordaining universal church attendance. This, together with various laws against profanation and the sins of the flesh, was enforced with regularity and some severity. Virginia Episcopalians and New England Dissenters thus began *pari passu* the suppression of what they considered alien and subversive views. As time went on, however, their paths separated; the religiousness which in Virginia had originally been supported by laws, remained as a crystallized popular sentiment; in New England, always more responsive to impulses from abroad, it weakened and virtually disappeared. New Englanders cultivated metaphysics and sharp speculation; Southerners generally, having saved their faith, as they thought, from the whole group of pryers, reformers, and troublesome messiahs, settled back and regarded it as a part of their inheritance which they did not propose to have disturbed.

Such religious persecution as occurred in Virginia found its victims not among heretics in theology, but among actual or potential disturbers of the peace. The Quakers, who were considered the foremost of these, were treated with extreme hostility throughout the seventeenth century. The charge leveled against these zealots was not that of doctrinal heresy; it was that their principles tended to undermine the whole institutional character of religion, and the state as well. They would not contribute to the support of the established church; they did not hold public assemblies; and they would not bear arms in defense of the commonwealth. It is little wonder that to colonial administrators these evidences savored of disaffection to the point of disloyalty, and that Quakers were commonly described as a "pestilential sect" and "an unruly and turbulent sort of people." The General Assembly of Virginia of the winter of 1659–1660 declared that their beliefs tended to "destroy religion, laws, communities, and all bonds of civil society," and passed laws forbidding the immigration of Quakers and banishing those already in the colony. They were being punished not for the sin of theological schism, but for the sin of political non-cooperation, and although these are not necessarily unrelated, the happier fate of other sects within the state suggests that the authorities were indifferent to doctrine which had only theological implications.

The history of Unitarianism in the South provides a further commentary on the Southern conception of the role of religion. While the Puritan was attempting to make his religion conform to the canons of logic, conscience, or ethical propriety, the Southerner clung stubbornly to the belief that a certain portion of life must remain inscrutable, that religion offers our only means of meeting it, and that reason cannot here be a standard of interpretation. Unitarianism, as a conspicuously speculative kind of divinity, was agreeable to those who test belief by reason, but unattractive to those who long for a sustaining creed and a means of emotional fulfillment. Captain Basil Hall in his *Travels in North America in the Years 1827 and 1828* gives an amusing account of a Unitarian preacher whom he heard in Boston: "He then embarked on the great ocean of religious controversy, but with such consummate skill, that we scarcely knew we were at sea till we discovered that no land was in sight." It must be confessed that in the South there were few congregations of a sufficiently intellectual disposition to enjoy this kind of voyaging. Bishop Francis J. Grund wrote: "The inhabitants of the South are principally Episcopalians, and as much attached to authority in religion as they are opposed to it in politics. They consider Unitarianism as a religious democracy; because it relies less on the authority of the Scriptures, than on the manner in which the authority of the clergy expounds them, and retains too little mysticism in its form of worship to strike the multitude with awe." And James Freeman Clarke found that in Kentucky the "nature of the people" demanded a more emotional discourse than the typical Unitarian sermon provided.

A fairly intensive missionary effort succeeded in establishing Unitarian societies in Baltimore, Augusta, Savannah, Mobile, New Orleans, Nashville, Louisville, and a few other cities, but most of these dwindled after a brief period of flourishing. As it became plain that religious radicalism in New England was tending toward anarchy, and more especially as radical clergymen became prominently identified with Abolitionism, Southern religious orthodoxy hardened, and the Unitarian societies became powerless to propagate themselves.

General evidence that the South afforded poor soil for religious radicalism may be further seen in the following distribution of churches: in 1860 this section had one of the 51 Swedenborgian churches in the United States, 20 of the 664 Universalist, and none of the 17 Spiritualist. In his *Autobiography* Peter Cartwright rejoiced that during the Great Revival "Universalism was almost driven from the land."

Among all classes in the South an opinion obtained that religion should be a sentiment. Where the people were refined, the sentiment was refined; where they were demonstrative and disorderly, it was likely to be such. Among the aristocratic congregations of seaboard communities, overt expression was at a minimum. The apathy with which such a cultivated congregation regarded its faith and the labors of its ministry may be illustrated through a story reported by Harriet Martineau: "A southern clergyman mentioned to me, obviously with difficulty and pain, that though he was as happily placed as a minister could be, treated with friendliness and generosity by his people, and so cherished as to show that they were satisfied, he had one trouble. During all the years of his ministry no token had reached him that he had religiously impressed their minds, more or less. They met regularly and decorously on Sundays, and departed quietly, and there was an end. He did not know that any one discourse had affected them more than another; and no opportunity was offered him of witnessing any religious emotion among them whatever." A tradition of gentility, and a belief that the content of religion was settled combined to produce this condition. All agitation was frowned upon. Restless and skeptical minds, who would dispute the grounds of the canon, were looked upon as persons inimical to a comfortable and orderly design for living. Refuting a point of doctrine brought one a reputation not so much for intellectual distinction as for perverseness and ill will. Because of her zeal for inquiry New England was contemptuously referred to as the land of "notions." A writer in *The Southern Literary Messenger,* drawing a contrast between Southern and Northern people, found the latter lacking in a sense of measure: " . . . having liberty which they do not appreciate, they run into anarchy,—being devotional, they push their piety to the extremes of fanaticism,—being contentious withal, they are led to attack the interests of others merely because those interests do not comport with their ideas of right."

What the Southerner desired above all else in religion was a fine set of images to contemplate, as Allen Tate has shown in his *Religion and the Old South*. The contemplation of these images was in itself a discipline in virtue, which had the effect of building up in him an inner restraint. And thus a sense of restraint, and a willingness to abide by the tradition were universally viewed as marks of the gentleman; on the other hand, the spirit of discontent, of aggressiveness, and of inquisitiveness was associated with those who had something to gain by overturning the established order.

In consequence it is not difficult to see why the Southern gentleman looked upon religion as a great conservative agent and a bulwark of those institutions which served him. Spokesmen of the South were constantly criticizing Northerners for making religion a handmaid of social and political reform. A critic of Dr. Channing, writing in the *Southern Quarterly Review,* declared: "It is not very usual for the clergy of our country to enter with zeal upon the arena of politics. The department of a religious teacher is supposed to lie in a different sphere, and to embrace different duties; and the people generally listen to him with aversion and reluctance when he meddles with secular subjects." Some years later a writer in *The Southern Literary Messenger* thus described the North's mixing of religious and secular causes: "Her priesthood prostitutes itself to the level with a blackguard, and enters the secular field of politics, in the spirit of a beerhouse bully: and the politician as carelessly invades the sanctuary of the priest." Although Southern clergymen occasionally invoked the word of God to defend Southern institutions, especially when these were being assailed, as a general rule they were overwhelmingly opposed to the use of the church as a tool for secular reform. The evangelical sects aimed at a conversion of the inner man; the conservative ones at the exposition of a revealed ethic; but both regarded themselves as custodians of the mysteries, little concerned with social agitation, and out of the reach of winds of political doctrine.

Reverence for the "word of God" has been a highly important aspect of Southern religious orthodoxy. Modern discussions of fundamentalism have overlooked the fact that belief in revealed knowledge is the essence of religion in its older sense, so that this point perhaps needs special emphasis. The necessity of having some form of knowledge which will stand above the welter of earthly change and bear witness that God is superior to accident led Thomas Aquinas to establish his famous dichotomy, which says, briefly, that whereas some things may be learned through investigation and the exercise of the reasoning powers, others must be given or "revealed" by God. Man cannot live under a settled dispensation if the postulates of his existence must be continually revised in accordance with knowledge furnished by a nature filled with contingencies. Nature is a vast unknown; in the science of nature there are constantly appearing emergents which, if allowed to affect spiritual and moral verities, would destroy them by rendering them dubious, tentative, and conflicting. It is therefore imperative in the eyes of the older religionists that man have for guidance in this life a body of knowledge to which the "facts" of natural discovery are either subordinate or irrelevant. This body is the "rock of ages," firm in the vast sea of human passion and error. Moral truth is not something which can be altered every time science widens its field of induction. If moral philosophy must wait upon natural philosophy, all moral judgments become temporary, relative, and lacking in those sanctions which alone make them effective. And though probably no people were more ignorant of the *Summa Theologica* than the inarticulate and little-read rural Southern population, this Thomist dualism lies implicit in their opposition to scientific monism, the most persistent of the South's medieval heritages. Then, as now, it explains their dogged adherence to what is taught "in the Book" and their indifference to empirical disproofs.

Emerson and his colleagues founded their revolt against New England orthodoxy on the principle of the continuity of knowledge and the prerogative of the individual mind to judge and determine. They were successful, and the country concluded that the victory was won everywhere; but in the South the battle has not yet been fought. In the present century, when publicity attending the theory of evolution forced the issue, there was widespread amazement that legislatures representing sovereign states were prepared to vote revealed knowledge precedence over natural, for such, in a broad way of viewing the matter, is the significance of the anti-evolution laws. This could not have surprised anyone who knew the tradition, for in the South there had never been any impeachment of "the Word," and science had not usurped the seats of the prophets. It may therefore be proper to describe the South as "backward" if one employs the word not in a vaguely prejudicial sense, but with some reference to the continuum of history. The South was striving to preserve a centuries-old distinction, which the North was condemning as error. Indeed, it has been a settled practice with Southern spokesmen to describe the differences between North and South in religious language. When the period of sectional separation came, more than one Southern churchman could be found placing the blame for the sins of New England, the most notable of which was Abolitionism, upon "the great Socinian heresy." This was an open attack upon the whole movement of deism and rationalism, which by the middle of the eighteenth century had captured the cultivated orders of Europe, and by the middle of the next, much of New England and the North. In the midst of the Gilded Age the Reverend R. L. Dabney, a celebrated Presbyterian divine, pronounced pragmatism the equivalent of atheism, and fundamentalist leaders today regard the purely scientific view of man as only the modern pose of godlessness.

It cannot be denied that during the period of the French Revolution there was much religious skepticism in certain Southern educational centers and among elements of the Southern upper class. It was, however, a transient phase, confined while it lasted to small cultivated groups, and it disappeared so completely in the antebellum years that it can be properly ignored in any account of the molding of the Confederate South. Skepticism is always an achievement of an intellectual aristocracy, who by education and through access to libraries become accustomed to the critical handling of ideas. At the close of the eighteenth century and for perhaps two decades afterwards some Southern aristocrats considered it fashionable to embrace Deism and to flaunt a disrespect for the Bible. Jefferson, who in this period translated twenty chapters of Volney's *Ruins,* is, of course, the best known Southern exponent of free-thinking. The irreligion of the day turned Williamsburg, home of venerable William and Mary College, into a veritable seat of infidelity; it flourished surprisingly at the University of North Carolina; it crept across the mountains and infected illustrious Transylvania in the Blue Grass Region of Kentucky, shocking Amos Kendall by the extent of its prevalence; and it penetrated the University of Georgia, then in its early years. It remained, however, distinctly an upper-class attitude, sharply localized and without power to affect the essential religiousness of the Southern populace. After 1830, when the South as if by prescience turned to a defense of all conservative ideals, it declined almost to the point of extinction.

One might suppose that the powerful example of Jefferson would have started a school of rationalism below the Potomac, but in this matter, as in others, Jefferson failed to take root in his section. His doctrine of states' rights and his agrarianism were cherished, but his religious liberalism, like most else that he learned from the French radicals, was ignored. His influence waned so rapidly that within a few years after his death the Presbyterians were able to force the resignation of an atheist professor from the University of Virginia, which he had aspired to make the very citadel of unfettered thought. In the same period South Carolina fundamentalists compelled the removal of President Cooper of the state university because he had questioned the authority of the Pentateuch.

Some notice must be taken of the influence of nineteenth century science upon the religious temper of the Old South. It has been a common assumption that Southerners devoted their minds to politics, the classics, and the novels of Sir Walter Scott, remaining blandly innocent of the discoveries in which this century was so fruitful. Like other generalized conceptions, this one is broadly true, but omits much which would qualify the picture. Thomas Cary Johnson in a survey of scientific interests in the antebellum South has corrected many overstatements of Southern indifference to the spirit of the age. He found natural science taught not only in colleges, where it sometimes led the list of elective subjects, but even in female seminaries; and he names a number of Southerners who proved themselves fertile in theory and invention. His study, however, affords little if any evidence that this scientific interest, more widespread than is popularly supposed, issued in a skeptical habit of mind. The truth seems clear that the Southern scientist did not carry his scientific speculation to the point at which it becomes an interpretation of the whole of life. Mr. Johnson ascribes the failure of the South to become eminent in scientific thought to the individualism of its people and their unwillingness to cooperate in common enterprises. But it appears nearer the truth to say that the traditional mind of the South, although it recognized in science a fascinating technology, refused to become absorbed in it to the extent of making it either a philosophy of life or a religion. It thus clung to its inherited religious humanism. Unlike the technician, the average Southerner did not feel that he must do a thing because he found that he could do it. It is highly significant that neither the jacobinism of the French Revolution nor the scientific materialism of the century which followed was able to draw him from the view that man holds a central position in the universe under divine guidance.

So the Southern people reached the eve of the Civil War one of the few religious peoples left in the Western World. Into the strange personnel of the Confederate Army, out of "regions that sat in darkness," poured fighting bishops and prayer-holding generals, and through it swept waves of intense religious enthusiasm long lost to history. It is on record that there were more than fifteen thousand conversions in the Army of Northern Virginia alone. And when that army went down in defeat, the last barrier to the secular spirit of science, materialism, and pragmatism was swept away.

It seems an inescapable inference that in the sphere of religion the Southerner has always been hostile to the spirit of inquiry. He felt that a religion which is intellectual only is no religion. His was a natural piety, expressing itself in uncritical belief and in the experience of conversion, not in an ambition to perfect a system, or to tidy up a world doomed to remain forever deceptive, changeful, and evil. For him a moral science made up of postulates and deductions and taking no cognizance of the inscrutable designs of Providence and the ineluctable tragedies of private lives was no substitute. Whether he was a Virginia Episcopalian, dozing in comfortable dogmatic slumber, or a Celt, transplanted to the Appalachian wilderness and responding to the intense emotionalism of the religious rally, he wanted the older religion of dreams and drunkenness—something akin to the rituals of the Medieval Church, and to the Eleusinian mysteries of the ancients.

8

ALBERT TAYLOR BLEDSOE

A hopeful interest in the New South has succeeded for the past seventy-five years in focussing attention upon aspects of change in Southern life. This has left in oblivion a number of brilliant spokesmen of the old regime, who if only for the sake of historical completeness, deserve a picture in some gallery. The opinion is widespread that the Confederacy's right to existence was defended by nothing other than political declamations and bullets. On the contrary, a good deal of cerebration took place below the Potomac after the South felt itself seriously threatened, and buried in dusty magazine files today is a respectable body of acute reasoning on the subjects of slavery and secession. Chief among the intellectual defenders of the South was Albert Taylor Bledsoe, one of the most curious intransigents in American history.

Bledsoe was born in Frankfort, Kentucky, in 1809, his family having come into this region while it was yet a part of Virginia. His father, Moses Bledsoe, founded a newspaper in Frankfort, and an uncle, Jesse T. Bledsoe, taught law and music, one of the odd combinations not uncommon in those days, at Transylvania University when this flourishing institu-

The Sewanee Review, Vol. LII (1944), 34–45.

tion of the West was a rival of Harvard for academic distinction. Like many another young man of promise in this period he was sent to West Point, and here he became acquainted with Jefferson Davis and R. E. Lee. After a brief experience in the Indian wars he abandoned military life to take up the study of theology at Kenyon College in Ohio. A period as minister in the Protestant Episcopal Church terminated when his naturally uncompromising mind found the doctrine repellent, and he changed next to the field of law.

Bledsoe spent the years from 1838 to 1848 practicing before the Supreme Court of Illinois, where Abraham Lincoln and Stephen A. Douglas were fellow members of the bar. That he was highly successful as a pleader before this tribunal is attested by the fact that he more than once received the basket of champagne which was by custom awarded to the lawyer winning the largest number of suits in a year. It is a matter of curious interest that when Lincoln was challenged to a duel by General James Shields, Bledsoe, drawing upon his West Point training, endeavored to teach his colleague the use of the broadsword. But the two men differed on the issues which split the American Union, and in the postwar era when the Lincoln legend began to take shape, Bledsoe was among the first to set down a candid estimate of the martyred president.

In 1848 he changed occupations again, this time to become a professor of mathematics, first at the University of Mississippi and later at the University of Virginia. Meanwhile his religious interest had remained strong, and in the midst of secular employment he found time to publish *An Examination of President Edwards' Inquiry into the Freedom of the Will* (1845), and *A Theodicy, or Vindication of the Divine Glory* (1853). The former work, which he described as "a complete triumph over the scheme of moral necessity," was the first evidence of his great talent as a controversialist, but his career as a champion of the South began in 1856 with the publication of a book-length tract entitled *An Essay on Liberty and Slavery.*

Most of the literature called forth by the slavery controversy is topical and superficial, but Bledsoe was profound enough to see that the real crux lay in the issues raised by the French Revolution. From this time until his death more than twenty years later he continually attacked the romantic postulates underlying this movement. A believer in the necessity of divine sanctions for government, he denied the existence of natural rights. The theory that man is naturally good he regarded as the grand heresy of the modern world, and the source of all social disorder. His basic position was that libertarianism rests upon a false metaphysic, for it is incorrect to suppose that liberty and order are antagonistic principles. This misconception, seemingly one of the permanent confusions of political thought, assumes that liberty and order limit one another, and that to increase one we must somehow diminish the other. Bledsoe sought to show that they are mutually sustaining and that increase in one promotes increase in the other: thus, when a state has gained in order, the foundation for more liberty is laid. Just as every orderly arrangement of our lives is made to free us for purposeful activity, so the regulations of a state have no meaning in themselves, but are instrumental toward its general aims. The abolitionists were absurd, he thought, when they talked of freedom as something that could be extracted and exhibited apart from the objects of the social whole. This phase of his case is substantially the Miltonic doctrine of the inseparability of freedom and right reason. Even the great Puritan rebel declared that "orders and degrees jar not with liberty, but well consist."

With this principle established, Bledsoe proceeded with its application to the institution of slavery. Like all conservatives, he believed in a structural society, and his thesis can be reduced to the proposition that a whole cannot be harmonious unless its parts are in their proper places. The abolitionists insisted on denying those differences in men which everyone knows to exist, and this out of zeal to conform to the abstractions of French political theory. It was plain that the negro in America constituted a strongly differentiated minority, and no prescription was valid for him unless it took into account his nature and the nature of the polity into which he had been thrust. Since the right to freedom is predicated upon the ability to use it, and since the negro was without experience in the conduct of a civilized state, the law could abridge his freedom as it does that of children and defectives. If liberty were an equal blessing to all, then all would have equal right to liberty. But if one accepts the fact of this difference between the races, the corollary follows that complete equality would result in "terrific inequality."

A feature of the *Essay* which will surprise readers unacquainted with the controversial literature of the time is a long section of arguments drawn from the Bible. A deficient knowledge of history has led some modern writers to express amazement that Christian ministers could make use of Scripture to defend slavery. They were overlooking the fact that this was the South and not New England, and in the South of this period the Bible was revealed truth. Slavery was an institution virtually universal throughout the ancient world; it is well recognized in the Old Testament, and it is not without endorsement in the New; indeed, a strict constructionist interpretation almost requires its defense. Nothing was more congenial to Bledsoe's mind than contention over Biblical passages, and his thorough but tiresome exposition is in the meticulous style of the seventeenth century.

The Fugitive Slave Act gave him an opportunity to point out the real nature of the sectional battle, which in Gerald Johnson's felicitous expression was essentially a contest between the Law and the Prophets. It may be doubted whether history affords a more instructive instance of the struggle between organic society and the written guarantees which were supposed to limit its choice of action. The more radical of the abolitionists were, of course, revolutionaries, appealing with Transcendentalist blessing to the law of conscience against the law of the land. But behind the Constitution, behind the Fugitive Slave Act, and behind decisions of the courts the South stood as behind barricades in the face of revolution. Such patterns repeat themselves, and today we see a strikingly analogous case as the great corporations battle behind Constitutional safeguards and judicial interpretations to protect their prerogatives and advantages.

Repressible or not, the conflict arrived in 1861, and Bledsoe, who had joined the Confederate army with the rank of colonel, was soon made assistant secretary of war. This appointment was entirely unfortunate, because the work of the office was routine, and for routine employment of any kind he had no capacity. His temperament was that of the philosophic recluse; given to long periods of immersion, he would arouse himself for a burst of activity and then lapse again into reflection. J. B. Jones in *A Rebel War Clerk's Diary* has left an unflattering picture of him engaged in the toil of this office. Under the burden of regular application he complained incessantly. Almost every day brought announcement of his resignation. On one occasion, reports Jones, he was assigned the duty of revising a manual of military tactics for use by the Confederate army. All he had to do was cross out the U in USA and write C, "and yet the colonel groans over it." His irascibility and his arrogance with superiors led to constant friction, and in 1864 President Davis found him a new field of service. He was sent abroad to gather in European libraries materials for an adequate statement of the constitutional right of the Southern states. What manner of publication was intended is not known, but before he could complete his work the war had ended, and he returned home with his notes.

Some time after the surrender General Lee remarked to Bledsoe: "Take care of yourself, Doctor; you have a great task: we look to you for our vindication." Yet in their careers the two men took precisely opposite roads from Appomattox. Lee, always a nationalist, confessing himself before the outbreak of war "one of those dull souls who cannot see the good in secession," accepted the verdict of the sword with a soldier's realism and advised Southerners to make themselves good Americans. It was impossible for one of Bledsoe's temperament to submit to forces he believed wrong on principle, and prospect that the civil leader of the Confederacy might be tried for treason led him to sit down and write "in white heat," it is said, the masterpiece of the Southern apologias. This was *Is Davis a Traitor; or, was Secession a Constitutional Right Previous to the War of 1861?* In the extensive body of Southern political writing there is no more brilliant specimen of the polemic. For the drudgery of a clerk's office he might have been unfit, but he was a born controversialist, able to reduce shapeless masses of argument to simple propositions, and zealous to drive the shot home, to make the opponent conscious of his sins and errors. Beside the prolixity of Davis's *Rise and Fall of the Confederate Government* and the tediousness of Stephens's *A Constitutional View of the Late War between the States,* his *Is Davis a Traitor?* stands as a model of conciseness and cogent argument.

The greater part of this little volume is taken up with recapitulation of the interminable metaphysical debate over constitution and compact. Bledsoe was interested in establishing three points: first, that the states had been originally sovereign and independent; second, that they had entered into a voluntary compact which carried limited commitments; and third, that certain Northern leaders had designedly and for selfish reasons spread the notion that the Constitution had been entered into by the people without the mediation of the states. Though belatedly asserted in war and lost, this case was still formidable in law and equity.

As may well be imagined, Bledsoe's chief target was Webster, and the chapter "Mr. Webster vs. Mr. Webster" is a scornful review of the record of the great expounder. Declaring that the Webster of 1833 was to the Webster of 1850 as "Philip drunk to Philip sober," he showed how the trend of events had driven the New Englander to accept the Southern view of the Constitution. "Mr. Webster's real opinion, however, seems to have been that the Constitution was a compact between the states. His great speech of 1833 may have convinced others; it certainly did not convince himself; for during the remainder of his life he habitually spoke of the Constitution as the compact formed by the states. Especially after his race was nearly run, and instead of the dazzling prize of the presidency, he saw before him the darkness of the grave, and the still greater darkness that threatened his land with ruin, he raised the last solemn utterances of his mighty voice in behalf of 'the compact of the Constitution,' declaring that as it had been 'deliberately entered into by the states,' so the states should religiously observe 'all its stipulations.' "

Bledsoe was never more happy than when dilating upon New England's poor regard for consistency. The theme of "New England hypocrisy," a favorite with all Southern publicists of the period, moved him to sardonic humor, and the perfect topic for this was, of course, the Hartford Convention. As early as the winter of 1803–4 the New England states, feeling that they were a minority suffering injustice, entertained plans for dissolving the Union. The War of 1812 with its injury to maritime commerce deepened their resolve to such an extent that a convention was called at Hartford to decide on practical steps. Meeting in 1815, the group chose commissioners to go to Washington, and according to John Quincy Adams, went to the point of selecting a military leader to serve in case its demands were not met. The signing of peace put an end to this secession movement, but a single quotation from the journal of this convention will show the trend of sentiment: "Whenever it shall appear that these causes are radical and permanent, a separation by equitable arrangement, will be preferable to an alliance by constraint, among nominal friends, but real enemies, inflamed by mutual hatred and jealousy, and inviting by intestine division, contempt and aggression from abroad."

The substance of *Is Davis a Traitor?* was that the Civil War had shifted the basis of the United States government from compact to conquest, and that however effective the victorious section had made its will, it did not have legal grounds for punishing Confederates. Bledsoe witnessed some practical result of his labor when Robert Oulds and Charles O'Conor, attorneys for Jefferson Davis, made use of the book in preparing their defense; but the Federal government, apparently feeling the weakness of its legal position, allowed the case to be dismissed.

In the year following the publication of *Is Davis a Traitor?* Bledsoe set himself a larger task of the same nature. Together with William Hand Browne, who later became a distinguished teacher at Johns Hopkins University, he founded *The Southern Review* in Baltimore for the purpose of further vindicating the South and of waging continuous war against the "disorganizing heresies" unloosed by Northern triumph. Despite great discouragements he kept it going for the remaining ten years of his life, and it is today unquestionably the best repository of unreconstructed Southern thought.

Looking as always at the more fundamental causes of social disorder, Bledsoe renewed his attacks upon the sentimental optimism of the French Revolution, against which he defended a religious, authoritarian theory of government. "With the absolute supremacy of the French School, whose doctrines are so flattering to the pride and ignorance of man, there arose the self-idolatry of the men of 1789, and also 'the dominant idea of the last century,' that governments and institutions make the people." He mocked the prevalent notion that men can be regenerated by "an idea." Because the government of the United States had not been "adjusted to the great facts and laws of the moral world," it became "a gigantic and degrading tyranny." Because the founders of the American Union had not taken into account the natural depravity of man, the system which they devised, however unexceptional from the secular point of view, was unable to stand the test of history. "The causes of the late war," he wrote, "had their roots in the passions of the human heart. Under the influence of those causes almost everything in the new system worked differently from what was anticipated." At the founding of the Union the North and the South had struggled together like Jacob and Esau in the womb "with almost fatal desperation." After the government had been established, this struggle was continued through a series of crises, and following each the majority section grew bolder and more tyrannical as it grew stronger. The fundamental error of the designers of the Constitution proved to have been the clothing of man instead of law with supreme power. " 'Man is free by nature,' says Locke, but according to the infinitely more profound aphorism of Aristotle, 'man is a tyrant by nature.' " Hence when the majority found it could have its way, it trampled the law into the dust, and so it will always be when man either singly or collectively is made the arbiter. "The legislators of 1787 did not know that man is a fallen being; or, if they did, they failed to comprehend the deep significance of this awful fact."

With this example of human failure before him, Bledsoe could return to the errors of the French radicals. The great mistake of those theorists, he argued, was the constructing of an imaginary man who was not to be found when the actual task of making institutions work commenced. "The more shallow the theory on which our politics are based, the sooner will they be ground to powder and scattered before the angry winds." The theme of man's natural depravity challenged his resources as a theologian, and he would at times rise to the earnestness and intensity of an Old Testament prophet. "The new Republic of '87, being founded on a presumptuous confidence in man, was doomed to fall, or to undergo sad changes and transformations." And, he repeated, "As often as the experiment may be made, it will be demonstrated in the grand theater of history, that the purity, the equality, and the freedom of all men, is one of the most fatal delusions that ever issued from the brain of theorist, or convulsed the world with horrible disorder." His view was summed up in the Apocalyptic cry: "Woe betide all the proud polities of self-idolizing man."

In addition to combating the secular theory of government—whose classic expression is, of course, "government of the people, by the people, for the people"—Bledsoe assigned himself the task of reviewing Northern histories of the war as they came from the press. They were appearing in increasing number, and many of them, partly because of patriotic zeal and partly because of inattention to strict facts, carried inaccurate stories and questionable interpretations. Upon these he fell with determined savagery. One can almost detect the note of glee as he warms up for such exercise. He thus approaches John William Draper's *History of the American Civil War*: "The author of course gives himself credit for perfect fairness and impartiality. . . . The promise is fair, but what of the performance? We shall judge the tree not by its blossoms but by its fruits. If these happen to be misrepresentations, calumnies, and lies, what do we care for the author's good intentions? Or for any other hollow, hypocritical thing that bears such deadly fruit?" George Bancroft was saluted in similar fashion. "There have been bad men and bad teachers always," Bledsoe wrote, "but society was safe as long as it shut them up in its moral lazarhouses. When it makes them its high priests, and spreads its garments and palm branches for them to tread on, those who love it may begin to despair." School histories of the United States of Northern authorship moved him to the highest pitch of indignation, for they were spreading the very doctrines he had established the *Review* to counteract. Characterizing them as "crude compilations of malice and mendacity," he said that he could not afford to follow their "innumerable lies, great and small," but he warned Southern parents to keep their children out of schools where such books were used.

Bledsoe could remark with approval that a collection of Southern war poetry reflected "an intense, unquenchable, personal hatred of Northerners both as a race and as individuals." When Ward Lamon's *Life of Lincoln* appeared, he seized the opportunity to set down his own recollection of the man, with whom, he declared, he had held almost daily intercourse at the bar of Springfield. "It is believed by the world at large that hatred of oppression, coupled with a love of freedom, was Mr. Lincoln's ruling passion. Nothing is farther from the truth." Instead, thirst for distinction was the "one, intense, all-absorbing passion of his life." Bledsoe grew more shrill as the years passed, and in a bitter and violent passage he described his former associate as the ideal man to lead the "Northern Demos" in its war to subjugate the South. "For if, as we believe, that was the cause of brute force, blind passion, fanatical hate, lust of power and greed of gain, against the cause of constitutional and human rights, then who was better fitted to represent it than the talented but the low, ignorant and vulgar, railsplitter from Illinois?" Lincoln was the "low-bred infidel of Pigeon Creek," in whose eyes "the Holy Mother" was "as base as his own."

The unbookish Southern people whom the *Review* championed would neither read it nor support it, and by 1870 its founder, whose unflagging energy sometimes supplied half the content of an issue of 250 pages, was beginning to feel the effects of frustration. Declaring himself "deeply impressed with the vanity of all earthly things," he resolved to dedicate his magazine thenceforward to the glory of God. Without ceasing to be a Southern organ, the *Review* became more religious in tone, and in the final issues Bledsoe found occasion to renew a theological dispute of extraordinary bitterness with Robert Lewis Dabney, another Southern spokesman as doughty as himself.

Walter Hines Page was to say that slavery, politics, and religion were the three chief curses of Southern life. When Bledsoe died in 1877, there passed away a man who had spent the better part of his career as an exponent of each, not on the level of superficial journalism, but with reference to first principles. Everything for which he battled was destined to be beaten. Slavery (waiving certain modern forms as debatable) is extinct throughout the civilized world; the question of

Southern secession has been answered as far as force can answer it; and the theology whose points he sought to sustain has been softened down into a milk-and-water humanism. Where would one look to find another such sponsor of lost causes and impossible loyalties? Can anything be salvaged from the thought of a mind which ran so perfectly counter to the path of history? The easy modern verdict will be that Bledsoe was another gifted Southerner condemned by the tumult of his age and the defeat of his people "to keep with phantoms an unprofitable strife."

It would seem on the contrary that history is again trying to teach the lesson which he vainly endeavored to make heard amid the din of the Gilded Age. This is the need of an abstract, metaphysical law which will hold when all else fails. It is the controlling belief which former ages have found in religion and in myths. His reiteration that sanctions which are merely human must fail, and that man needs protection against his own wicked impulses places him before the French Revolution and aligns him with the political realists. Modern man begins to grow weary of self-canonization and is on the threshold of recovering the old truth that dignity comes through identification with something greater than self.

The pragmatic liberalism which he fought has done its worst, and today the world, groping for some kind of absolute, totters uneasily between fascism and communism. It may well be that before it can again achieve stability, before it can again find some harmonious expression of liberty and law, it will have to accept some measure of his distrust of the natural benevolence of man.

In any case, one can say of him as a defender of the Southern faith what Enobarbus said of the followers of Anthony:

> yet he that can endure
> To follow with allegiance a fall'n lord
> Does conquer him that did his master conquer
> And earns a place i' the story.

9

SOUTHERN CHIVALRY

AND TOTAL WAR

[I]

The expression "Southern chivalry" has been occurring in discussions of the South for a century and a half, and few writers have scrupled to use it in making a point, jokingly or seriously. It has even enjoyed some currency among the masses, and during the Civil War those Northern soldiers who described the struggle as a contest between "chivalry and shovelry" apparently believed that there existed in Southerners some kind of self-idealization, or moral ambition to conform to an aristocratic type, sufficient to create a difference between the two peoples. Yet few have stopped to ask whether it stands for a solid reality in the Southern past, or whether it has had some part in defining the mind of the South. Examination will show that however tenuous its European connections may have been, there survived in the South enough of the genuine chivalric tradition to decide prevailing views on critical questions. One of these was the question of "total war," which is causing some controversies today.

The Sewanee Review, Vol. LIII (1945), 267–278.

So many accidental associations have gathered about the term that one cannot risk its employment without an attempt to learn what it meant historically. Chivalry as it was understood in Europe from the middle of the eleventh to the middle of the sixteenth century was a body of forms and sentiments of paramount influence in determining the civilization of the Middle Ages. Its origin occurred in the dark days following the dissolution of Charlemagne's empire, when cruelty, rapine, and savage anarchy so distressed humanity that there came a passionate reaction, which enlisted men in the service of an ideal good and looked to the Christian religion as a sanction. People recognized the class of knights as representatives of right and defenders of order, crowned them with all virtues, both real and imaginary, and for more than four hundred years respected them as the ruling caste. Although in its later periods chivalry associated itself with other things, including the worship of woman, it commenced as an order of men of good will, pledged to make might serve right; and although it developed forms, shows, and ceremonials, it was first and foremost a spirit. Of this spirit the Knights of the Table Round were the perfect, if legendary, exemplars, engaged in asserting a rule of justice and humanity against naked strength. Candidates for the order of knighthood were put through an initiation which made these duties explicit. An early specimen of their vow required them "to speak the truth, to succour the helpless, and never to turn back from an enemy." The ethical importance of chivalry lay in the fact that wherever this spirit made itself felt, there it alleviated, even though it could not entirely overcome, the natural brutishness of man. It furnished a code whereby iniquity could be condemned, however dazzling the success of its perpetrators, and in the darkest times it stood as an aspiration and a promise that justice would return and lawful relations obtain again among men. Chivalry was the form taken by the code of self-discipline which produced Western civilization.

One finds it difficult to say in precisely what company it crossed the Atlantic. That a certain portion of Virginia's first settlers were gentlemen, "it being so nominated in the bond," may be granted. Captain John Smith's struggles with his indolent colonists, who were "ten times more fit to spoyle a Commonwealth, than either to begin one, or but help to maintaine one," make a striking chapter of early American history, and there can be little doubt that these misplaced men-about-town and many who came after them would have been happier deciding points of honor than digging up stumps. In view of such facts one may observe that chivalry, like certain other European institutions, came over a seedling, but having struck root in the lush American soil, achieved an indigenous growth, modified, sometimes grotesquely, by the rudeness of the new environment.

In the American South the order of chivalry took the form of a gentleman caste. As soon as this class had established itself on property ownership and slave labor, it invoked the chivalric concept to set itself apart from the commonalty. The gentleman, because he lived up to a self-imposed ideal, was a character enjoying certain prerogatives. His motives could not be impugned; and above all, his word could not be questioned. The highly touchy sense of honor built up on these premises often called for the ritual of the duel, which tells us more about Southern chivalry than does anything else.

Dueling was widely prevalent in the antebellum South, where it was generally regarded as a token of social superiority. Governor John Lyde Wilson of South Carolina in his famous manual, *The Code of Honor; or Rules for the Government of Principals and Seconds in Duelling*, observed that "Tennessee, Kentucky, Georgia, and South Carolina would bear away the palm for gentility among the states of the Union" if the popularity of the duel should be admitted as a criterion. He took pride in asserting that the kind of personal abuse printed in Northern newspapers would in the South bring challenges to mortal combat. Various other writers attributed opposition to dueling to "the materialistic puritan skeptics of this country," and anti-dueling laws were generally described as "transplanted from the pernicious hotbed of puritan skepticism." The Englishman Thomas Hamilton after a journey covering much of the United States formed the impression that "to fight a duel in the New England States would, under almost any circumstances, be disgraceful. To refuse a challenge, to tolerate even an insinuation derogatory to personal honor, would be considered equally so in the South." Southern communities were accustomed to boast of the number of men "called out" by those demanding "satisfaction."

The connection of dueling with the tradition of chivalry appears plainest in the emphasis placed upon the social rank of the combatants, for the duel was reserved for gentlemen as the tournament had once been reserved for knights. A gentleman might chastise a low fellow with whip or cane for offering him an insult, but he could not meet him on the field of honor. Governor Wilson noted in his *Code* that if a man received a challenge from a person with whom he was unacquainted, he might demand a reasonable time "to ascertain his standing in society, unless he is fully vouched for by his friend." It was a general rule that a gentleman could not fight one whom he could not invite to his house. Correspondingly in the days of European chivalry knights jousted only with knights, and sometimes this privilege was insisted upon in actual battle. Thus it is recorded that at Bouvier a body of Flemish knights refused to charge a force of infantry because they were not gentlemen, and so lost the engagement.

Elizabethan literature is filled with expressions indicating that the chivalrous orders considered it ignominious to engage in fight with the base-born, or to indulge in mere killing as distinguished from lawful combat. In Massinger's *Duke of Milan* Francisco says:

> . . . And but that
> I scorn a slave's best blood should rust that sword
> That from a prince expects a scarlet dye
> Thou now wert dead.

In Shakespeare's *Henry VI* the Duke of Suffolk declares:

> Obscure and lowly swain, King Henry's blood,
> The honourable blood of Lancaster,
> Must not be shed by such a jaded groom.

Even Cleopatra is conscience-stricken enough to cry:

> These hands do lack nobility, that they strike
> A meaner than myself.

And the villainous Iago has been brought up in a martial tradition which draws a distinction between war and murder:

> Though in my trade of war I have slain men,
> Yet do I hold it very stuff o' the conscience
> To do no contrived murder.

In the *Mirror for Magistrates* Roger Mortimer is made to complain that the barbarous Irish by whom he has been slain do not observe the conventions:

> They know no lawe of armes, nor none will lerne
> They make not warre (as others do) a playe.
>
> Theyre end of warre to see there enmye deade.

Such has been chivalry's view of those whose lack of a code permits them to wage total war.

Behind these attitudes lies the deep division between mere bestial fighting, whose end is simple destruction of the enemy, and "honorable combat," which has both the form and purpose of a ritual. That the participant in "honorable combat" is defending his honor rather than his life becomes apparent when one considers the full nature of the duel. If a gentleman's word was questioned, he demanded an explanation, and if the matter could not be adjusted, he proved that honorable status was dearer to him than life by going through the ceremony of the duel. Only if he met this test was he adjudged worthy of the companionship of gentlemen, or, in the language of old, was he deserving of a place in the chivalric order. Another dueling "Code," published in New Orleans, made this very point in noting that "among the refined, virtue with women and honor with men are more valuable than life—are more worthy of the last defense."

Since civilization is in essence a struggle for self-control, the nobility in every civilized community, by whatever name they may go, and all who contribute to the cultural life, are somehow identified with the restraining forms. Those who are ignorant of the forms are not, properly speaking, members of civilization, and hence the remark that when one enters a peasant's doorway, he passes out of Europe. The significance of chivalric combat lies in the fact that because it is "formal" in the sense indicated it enables men to fight without passing beyond the pale. Warfare is assumed to be inevitable, but civilized people will conduct it as they conduct all else, with self-control—in other words, they will make it a game. Only those people who have never emerged from barbarism—or those who have lapsed back into it—fight without regard to certain binding rules, which go deeper than the war itself and make it part of the pattern of civilization. It is not too much to say that only thus can civilization survive war, for here the pragmatic standard would be fatal. If it stakes its all on the outcome of any particular struggle, civilization abandons its force as an ideal and so sinks to the realm of contingency.

[II]

In antebellum days there was much loose discussion of chivalry, but it was left to the events of the war itself to provide an interesting demonstration of the extent to which this surviving spirit lingered on in the South. From the very beginning, sharply contrasted views of the ordeal appeared. The majority of the Southern people looked upon it as an elaborate ceremonial, to be conducted strictly according to rules, and with maximum display of color and individual daring—in short, as a gigantic tournament, with the Lord of Hosts as umpire and judge. After First Manassas some Southerners were actually heard to express the opinion that the war must promptly cease because the question of manhood between the two sections had been decided and there was nothing else at issue. The South went into the first modern war thinking that it was a duel, an "affair of honor."

The celebrated Richmond journalist Edward A. Pollard declared that the people of the South prided themselves so much upon their reputation for chivalry that they were willing to sacrifice everything else in preference to it, including the hope of victory. It is true that Confederate observance of punctilio was sometimes carried to an extent which, in the light of modern practice, appears quixotic. There was a constant emphasis upon correct form to the disregard of consequence. The partisan raider John S. Mosby, who used to grow impatient over the respect for rule and regulation manifested by the Davis government, affirmed in his *Reminiscences* that "the martinets who controlled it were a good deal like the hero in Molière's comedy, who complained that his antagonist had wounded him by thrusting in *carte*, when according to the rule, it should have been by *tierce*." It is related that during the middle part of the war a Southern inventor carried before Jefferson Davis an object fashioned to resemble exactly a large lump of coal. His plan was to fill such devices with a high explosive and to distribute them in the fuel yards of Federal naval stations. The Confederate President declined the scheme with considerable show of indignation as "an unjustifiable mode of warfare." Although this may have been an instance of what Gamaliel Bradford calls Davis's "dogmatic idealism," it none the less shows a significant concept of war.

Whenever Confederate commanders were in a position to flaunt their superior chivalry, they made the most of the opportunity. After General John B. Gordon had captured York, Pennsylvania, in the Gettysburg campaign, he reassured a group of frightened ladies by promising them "the head of any soldier under my command who destroyed private property, disturbed the repose of a single home, or insulted a woman." Later, General Gordon struck the keynote of the unpragmatic Southern attitude when he wrote that the Confederate troops in the Battle of the Wilderness, though aware of Grant's overwhelming odds, "rejected as utterly unworthy of a Christian soldiery the doctrine that Providence was on the side of the heaviest guns and the most numerous battalions."

Realization that the North as a whole did not propose to regard the war as a game came as a shock to the Southern people, who had always counted the Yankees out of chivalry, but who seemingly had never reckoned what this would mean in practice. For the North had already become industrial, middle-class, and bourgeois, and if it began the war with old-fashioned conceptions, they vanished after the removal of the dramatic and colorful McClellan. Thereafter the task of conquering the South became a business, an "official transaction," which cost a great deal more in dollars and lives than had been anticipated, but which was at length accomplished by the systematic marshalling of equipment and numbers. When John Pope's Virginia campaign gave the South its first intimation that the North was committed to total war, the reaction was indignation and dismay. Perhaps it is not too fanciful to read in Lee's brief sentence, "Pope must be suppressed," a feeling that he was fighting not so much against an individual enemy as an outlawed mode of warfare. And when Sherman, Sheridan, and Hunter began their systematic ravaging and punishing of civilians, it seemed to the old-fashioned South that one of the fundamental supports of civilization had been knocked out, and that warfare was being thrown back to the barbarism from which religion and chivalry had painfully raised it in the Middle Ages. The courtly conduct of Lee and his officers to the Dutch farm wives of Pennsylvania has been perhaps too much sentimentalized, but the fact remains that these men felt they were observing a code, which is never more needful than in war, when fear and anger blind men and threaten their self-control. Sherman's dictum that war is hell was answered by E. Porter Alexander's remark that it depends somewhat on the warrior.

It was not solely the loss in dwellings and livestock which embittered the South against Sherman, for Southern prodigality has a way of making small issue of material misfortune. But he offered a mortal affront to the tradition to which it was bred, and the insult has outlived the injury. McClellan was something of a Southern hero, as was Grant; indeed, Southern admiration of Grant sometimes went to the point of effusiveness, and Robert Stiles could commend him for his "rough chivalry." These men, it was generally thought, had fought honorably according to the rules of the game, eschewing vandalism and terrorism; and the code of chivalry allows, or even enjoins admiration for a foe who had conducted himself in the proper manner. Naturally the thought of being beaten came hard to a people priding themselves on their martial traditions, but the memory that has rankled in the South for generations and has done more than anything else to support the unreconstructed attitude is the thought that an enemy, while masking himself under pious pretensions and posing as the representative of "grand moral ideas," dropped the code of civilization in warfare and won in a dishonorable manner. When Cindy Lou Bethany in *Kiss the Boys Good-bye* tells her Northern host, who had brought up the topic of the war, "Yes, but you cheated," she is expressing the serious conviction of her grandparents' generation. Clare Boothe probably intended the remark to sound merely absurd, but it mirrors the mind of an older day, as one can discover by reading the literature of Reconstruction.

This explains why the animus felt against Federal commanders was not in proportion to their success in the field. Against Meade, who fatally dashed Southern hopes at Gettysburg; against Grant, who won decisive victories at Vicksburg and Chattanooga; against Thomas, who at Nashville gave the Confederacy its most humiliating defeat of the war, there was little or no complaint. But against Sheridan, who devastated the Shenandoah so that "a crow flying across it would have to carry his provisions," and against Sherman, who was quoted as saying that he "would make Georgia howl," and that he would "bring every Southern woman to the wash-tub," words could not contain the measure of indignation.

At this point one must mention, both in pursuance of the thesis and in the interest of sectional fairness, that there were on the Southern side commanders who advocated the other style of warfare, and who, if they had got into the North with independent commands, very likely would have followed pol-icies similar to those of Sherman and Sheridan. But it is significant to note that they were not members of the gentle-man caste. They were the hard, self-made men, who believed that "war means fighting and fighting means killing." Such were Stonewall Jackson and Nathan Bedford Forrest, both men of the people and both men in whom there ran a streak of ruthlessness. Jackson was a fierce middle-class puritan, and Forrest was a frontiersman; and although both were on the road to becoming members of that caste, they were not so conditioned as to feel instinctively its restraints. It has become a widely accepted opinion that Lee was too much of a gentle-man to be the perfect commander. But when one thinks of the hatred and the anguish saved by his idealism and self-control, of his splendid exhibition of what it means in terms of chiv-alry to be a victor in defeat, would one wish him anything other than the knight *sans peur et sans reproche*?

[III]

In this war the side which more completely abjured the rules of chivalric combat won, and the way was cleared for mod-ernism, with its stringency, its abstractionism, and its im-patience with sentiment. Here, as elsewhere, Americans proved pioneers in a field whose value to civilization is dubi-ous. It is well-known that German generals have been careful students of the American Civil War, and a revealing story is told by Dr. Moritz Busch in his *Bismarck: Some Secret Pages of His History*. At a banquet given by the Chancellor in 1870 General Sheridan, who had been with the Prussian staff in the capacity of unofficial observer, remarked that he favored treating noncombatants with the utmost rigor. He expressed the opinion that "the people must be left nothing but their eyes to weep with over the war." The auditor of this statement confessed himself struck by its brutality but added that he thought it might bear consideration, as indeed it must have sometime between the first and second World Wars. It scarcely needs pointing out that from the military policies of Sherman and Sheridan there lies but an easy step to the total war of the Nazis, the greatest affront to Western civilization since its founding.

The Nazi movement has been sponsored by the lower middle class, and all of its so-called innovations are but projections of the middle-class mentality. After the economic, political, social, and psychological explanations have been sifted, the plain fact emerging is that the National Socialism of postwar Germany is an answer to the "what now?" of the "little man." And total war is a typical middle-class concept because this class, with its materialistic bias, is unable to see that there is involved in war anything other than complete destruction of the enemy, so that, as the popular thought has it, we won't be at the expense of having to do this again. It cannot see that after one has defeated the enemy, one has the responsibility of saving his soul. The code of chivalry has its formula of appeasement, but the appeasement is to come after the victory is won and not before the contest is joined, as some of our recent businessmen statesmen have thought more proper. The unpardonable thing about the war of un-limited aggression is that it precludes this kind of settlement.

The difference in character between the first and second World Wars can largely be explained in terms of this shift of power from one class to another. It is no accident that Hit-lerian diabolism had its origin in the underworlds of Munich and Vienna. And a complementary fact, so obvious it has gone unnoticed, is that the leaders of the two nations fighting to preserve what may with real propriety be called Christian civilization are both members of a hereditary upper class. In all of the countries which have undergone revolution, the heirs of the old chivalric order have passed out of power, and their place has been taken by men without belief in any standards, or men with a frank contempt for all restraints that stand in the way of immediate results. This is a large part of the price we have paid for our rage against traditionalism and "mediaeval backwardness."

Sherman was indeed a fighting prophet, and today we are seeing the fulfillment of his prophecy. Those who throw aside the traditions of civilized self-restraint are travelling a road at the end of which lies nihilism. The process is a part of that "sinking in upon the moral being" which W. B. Yeats describes as the first sign of the decay of civilization. For the consequence of putting war upon a total basis, or of accepting it upon that basis in retaliation, is the divorce of war from ethical significance. To announce that civilization is merely being suspended until the unconditional surrender of the foe is not enough. It is true, as Emerson remarked, that the ends preexist in the means. The American Civil War was the first modern war in which the end was absorbed by the means, so that it became a technician's war, with the technician's habitual indifference to ultimate ends and values. With it the pragmatic sanction began to complete its conquest of the world, which is now trying desperately to save itself by incantations to freedom and democracy.

10

LEE THE PHILOSOPHER

As the Civil War assumes increasingly the role of an American Iliad, a tendency sets in for its heroes to take on fixed characterizations. Epithets of praise and blame begin to recur, and a single virtue usurps the right to personify the individual. In the course of these formations, Robert E. Lee has emerged perhaps too exclusively as soldier and pater-familias. These careers were central in his life, but they do not exhaust the man. Lee transcended some extremely difficult situations, which must have mastered him had he not been, in addition to warrior and patrician, an intellect.

One understands readily why he has invited the customary approach. It is natural to see him first as the military genius, or as the Christian soldier, or as the personally attractive leader of a lost cause. Under the influence of these images, however, it has proved tempting to picture him as a somewhat passive embodiment of the culture of his region. He can be made to appear a natural expression of the Virginia patriarchy, and, because natural, neither creative nor thoughtful. Yet if Lee had remained merely the product of the kind of training he received, he would have been unequipped to penetrate the surfaces about him.

The Georgia Review, Vol. II, No. 3 (Fall 1948), 297–303.

It is to be strongly suspected that the unflattering portrait of Lee's son at Harvard given by Henry Adams in the *Education* has been allowed to reflect upon the father and to deepen this impression. Adams pictured young "Roony" Lee as little more than a healthy animal. "He was simple beyond analysis," the critical New Englander reported, and "no one knew enough to know how ignorant he was." The description went on to conclude that "Strictly, the Southerner had no mind; he had temperament." Adams was shrewd, and his prejudices were not of the parochial kind. I would give him credit for some true insights in certain parts of this sketch. Yet I would maintain that whatever the case of the son, the father had enough intellectual endowment to attain a wisdom. Dr. Freeman, in his massive biography, insists that the keynote of Lee's character was simplicity, but this is not at all incompatible with greatness of mind. On the contrary the two united to produce the *symmetria prisca,* the proud symmetry of personality, which made him illustrious. Lee seems in fact to have been capable of profound thought upon those subjects which engaged his attention, though a reticence, partly professional and partly temperamental, leaves us but little to analyze. He comes to us, as the early Ionians come to the modern historian of philosophy, in "fragments."

If we examine Lee first upon the art at which he surpassed, we find a curiously dispassionate understanding not just of the technique, but of the place of war in the life of civilized man. Napoleon too was a philosopher of battle, but his utterances are marred by cynicism. Those of Lee have always the saving grace of affirmation. Let us mount with the general the heights above Fredericksburg and hear from him one of the most searching observations ever made. It is contained in a brief remark, so innocent-seeming, yet so disturbing, expressed as he gazed upon the field of slain on that December day. "It is well this is terrible; otherwise we should grow fond of it."

What is the meaning? It is richer than a Delphic saying.

Here is a poignant confession of mankind's historic ambivalence toward the institution of war, its moral revulsion against the immense destructiveness, accompanied by a fascination with the "greatest of all games." As long as people relish the idea of domination, there will be those who love this game. It is fatuous to say, as is being said now, that all men want peace. Men want peace part of the time, and part of the time they want war. Or, if we may shift to the single individual, part of him wants peace and another part wants war, and it is upon the resolution of this inner struggle that our prospect of general peace depends, as MacArthur so wisely observed upon the decks of the *Missouri*. The clichés of modern thought have virtually obscured this commonplace of human psychology, and world peace programs take into account everything but this tragic flaw in the natural man—the temptation to appeal to physical superiority. There is no political structure which knaves cannot defeat, and subtle analyses of the psyche may prove of more avail than schemes for world parliament. In contrast with the empty formulations of propagandists, Lee's saying suggests the concrete wisdom of a parable.

Sandburg has remarked that Lee, despite his Christian piety, loved a good fight. In this I believe he is correct, but whether Lee loved it more than any other man loves an exciting contest at which he knows he can excel may be doubted. To Lee, as to Washington before him, the whistle of bullets made a music, and the natural man responded. But this observation rebukes the natural man and tells him that further considerations are involved. Thus Lee, at the height of his military fortunes, recognizes the attraction of the dread arbitrament, but at the same time sees the moral implications. Coming from one who delivered mighty strokes of war, the observation is itself a feat of detachment.

Most important of all, Lee seems to have felt that it is possible for civilization to *contain* war, or to go on existing in the presence of war if self-control is not entirely lost. To many persons "civilized warfare" is anomalous, but it is not truly so except for the war of unlimited objectives. The deeper the foundations of a civilization, the more war seems to be formalized or even ritualized, and the failure to hold it within bounds is a sign of some antecedent weakening on the part of that civilization. This explains why Lee always operated with a certain restraint which, some have affirmed, cause him to fall short of maximum success in the field. There is great ethical encouragement in this knowledge. To him as to a number of grave thinkers the touchstone of conduct is how one wields power over others. Whether modern invention has made all restraints of this kind a quaint delusion is something that fearfully remains to be seen.

If it is one kind of blindness to assume that man is made for war, it may be another kind to assume that he can remain indifferent to the drama of conflict. And so, if our world of peace is ever to behold the light of day, it will probably be after we have found something like William James's moral equivalent of war. Those in quest of the substitute could well begin their reflections with Lee's text, which seems to have the right proportions of realism and moralism.

As one studies Lee's opinions of the events of the angry sixties, it becomes evident that he understood the tendency of the mass mentality of war as only the most expert manipulators of modern propaganda have come to understand it, though his knowledge prompted a different kind of action. He knew that the mind of a people at war is psychopathic, that it is subject to hysteria and hallucination, that often it cannot tell right from wrong or even friend from foe, that it is likely to prefer revenge to survival. Recurring time and again in his correspondence of the years 1865–70 is the counsel of patience and silence. The two sides had not waited for the cessation of firing to inaugurate the polemic struggle. Generals published their vindications; politicians hastened into print to prove that their courses had been constitutional; publicists of every kind discussed the Northern and Southern ways of life. Amid this din Lee, although constantly importuned, said nothing. He expressed a desire to write a history of the campaigns in Virginia, but the writing was never done, and Gamaliel Bradford is probably right in saying that he shrank from the task. Attempts to engage him in conversation about his battles were met with the remark, "I do not like to think about those years."

Apparently Lee realized that the sole hope of reconciliation lay in a returning sense of justice, and that this restoration would only be impeded by protest and controversy. "At present, the public mind is not prepared to receive the truth," he wrote in 1866 to Jubal Early. This statement represented a settled conviction, which he reiterated on numerous occasions. Like the observation dropped at Fredericksburg, it becomes more troubling the longer one reflects on it. Certainly it denies the principle that the voice of the people is at all times the voice of God. It declares rather that the mind of a people, like that of an individual, may become so deranged with anger that it is simply not receptive to the realities. Because this psychopathic mentality cannot interpret objectively, it does not want to hear reason and may be offended by a proposal in proportion as it is reasonable. People must be in a state of grace to listen to the truth, more especially when it comes as a remonstrance. It is perhaps the finest triumph of Lee and the best evidence of that splendid integration of personality which was his that he could thus stand outside the popular passion and predict its end. The tide of feeling had a course to run, and syllogisms offered by victor or vanquished served only to increase the prevailing rancor. "You cannot argue with unreason; you can only describe it," Santayana has said, and this thought must have lain at the source of Lee's policy to say nothing until reason had a chance to resume its sway on both sides.

One can scarcely avoid curiosity about Lee's opinion of war as an instrument of national policy. Since he was a man of reflection, he must have pondered at times its general efficacy. On this question the world of today seems divided into two schools, one maintaining that a war settles everything, and the other that it settles nothing. Lee appears to have been less dogmatic than either. Certainly he was not a Hotspur, rushing to turn the *ultima ratio* into the *prima ratio*. In proof of this, we have the letter written to his sister in April, 1861: "Now we are in a state of war which will yield to nothing. . . . I recognize no necessity for this state of things and would have forborne and pleaded to the end for redress of grievances. . . . " Toward the close of his life, moreover, he began to face frankly the limitations of soldiering as a profession. Since the days of his cadetship, war had been his study; he had no competing interests; nor had his reading carried him far afield. Yet he had not developed the insulated mind of the professional. During his presidency of Washington College he remarked to Professor Humphreys that the great mistake of his life had been to take a military education. On another occasion he declared that military training does not prepare men for the pursuits of civilian life, an opinion which should be weighed by proponents of its educational value. "It was not by chance," Dr. Freeman writes of Lee's days in Lexington, "that he failed to keep step with the superintendent of V.M.I. when the two walked together at the head of the column of cadets." One may well inquire how many men laureled as he was have challenged the instrumentality of their fame and sought to turn the young toward other courses.

The tendency to see a thing in its moral relationships, to discipline egoistic impulse, and to subordinate self to a communal ideal of conduct appears in Lee's often quoted saying that duty is the most sublime word in the language. It is fairly certain that he did not intend here the narrow military sense in which a mission is accepted and executed. His conception seems much nearer the celebrated categorical imperative, that sense of obligation to act as one would have others act, out of a love of order and accomplishment. At any rate, duty is what Lee, on the basis of a rather wide experience of men and things, found to be the redeeming virtue. Today we can point out how much would have been saved to the world had the world made this its precept.

I would not represent Lee as a prophet, but as a man who stood close enough to the eternal verities to utter prophecy sometimes when he spoke. He was brought up in the old school, which places responsibility upon the individual, and not upon some abstract social agency. Sentimental humanitarianism manifestly does not speak to language of duty, but of indulgence. The notion that obligations are tyrannies, and that wants, not deserts, should be the measure of what one gets has by now shown its destructive power. We have tended to ignore the inexorable truth that rights must be earned. Fully interpreted, Lee's "duty" is the means whereby freedom preserves itself by acknowledging responsibility. Man, then, perfects himself by discipline, and at the heart of discipline lies self-denial. When the young mother brought an infant for Lee to bless, and was told, "Teach him he must deny himself," she was receiving perhaps the deepest insight of his life.

The ideal of duty is related to the quality which above all else gives Lee an antique greatness, his humility. He believed that there is an order of things. That order is providential in the sense that mortal wisdom is not to be compared to infinite wisdom. This truth, however, conveys nothing of fatalism or determinism; the individual is not exempt from exerting his will in the world and seeking to influence the course of things according to his light. Man cannot withdraw; he must weigh and wager, and abide the consequences. To assume that his light is always sufficient is pride. Education is discipline and education is lifelong; indeed, we have Lee's own statement that no man's education is completed until his death. If one has respect for the order of things, it is then possible for him to accept failure as instruction rather than as total repudiation. I do not see how Lee's serenity in the face of crisis and his self-possession in the days of distress can be explained save through this conviction, which is in essence the answer of Christianity to the paradoxes of existence.

As we approach that time at which his education was complete, we are eager to know whether, on the broad issues of this life, he stood with the pessimists or the optimists. This is putting the matter in simple terms, of course; but humanity has a clear mind on this issue; it will not have for its great teachers those who despair of the condition of man. It will read them for excitement; it will utilize them as a corrective, but it will not cherish them as its final oracles. It prefers Aristotle to Diogenes and Augustine to Schopenhauer. It does not wish to hear said, however brilliantly, that life is a tale told by an idiot; it wants an unmistakable, if chastened, recommendation of life.

From this point of view too we may say Lee is philosophically sound. Despite failure in the great effort of his career, and despite a twilight of five years during which, it seemed to Stephen Vincent Benet, "He must have lived with bitterness itself," he gave no sign of despondency. His expression, we are told, took on a look of settled sadness, but he never allowed feeling to assume control. Whatever of doctrine Lee knew was derived from Christianity, and there we read that God sometimes appoints to men the task of contending and falling in a righteous cause. A few days before Appomattox Lee remarked to General Pendleton that he had never had much hope for Southern independence without some measure of foreign assistance. "But such considerations really made no difference with me. We had, I was satisfied, sacred principles to maintain and rights to defend, for which we were in duty bound to do our best, even if we perished in the endeavor." All idealism can be represented as quixotic. But Lee has survived in the national mind as a hero in defeat; and it is inconceivable that he could have done so had not his own philosophy accommodated the idea of temporal failure.

Looking upon the fearful wreck of his country and the bewilderment of his compatriots who could see no future, he could say, in words which seem to plumb the depths of man's destiny: "Human virtue must be equal to human calamity." Lift up your hearts! A recent historian has declared that Lincoln alone among Americans of the nineteenth century rose to the tragic view of life. Those familiar with the Second Inaugural Address, that strangely troubled document, now remote, again near and intense, now resolute, again hesitantly confronting the problem of evil, will know the grounds. "The prayers of both could not be answered—that of neither has been answered fully." God in his own mysterious way "gives to both North and South this terrible war. . . ." Lincoln too abjured the right of final judgment. For him the practical human solution was to invoke the healing spirit of charity. In the Second Inaugural, as in the Gettysburg Address, the underlying thought is redemption. The splendid affirmation by Lee should cause us to ask whether he did not share the vision. In both men partisanship seems accident rather than essence. And here perhaps is an explanation why these two, so little resembling in background and walk of life, have been accepted as the worthiest representatives of the contending sections.

When we come to Lee's final testament, we discover a profession of faith which for courage and spiritual hope deserves to rank with the noblest utterances. For what he composed it we do not know; it was found among his papers and made public first in 1887 by Colonel Charles Marshall at a ceremony of dedication:

> My experience of men has neither disposed me to think worse of them, nor indisposed me to serve them; nor, in spite of failures, which I lament, of errors, which I now see and acknowledge, or of the present state of affairs, do I despair of the future. The march of Providence is so slow, and our desires so impatient, the work of progress is so immense, and our means of aiding it so feeble, the

life of humanity is so long, and that of the individual so brief, that we often see only the ebb of the advancing wave, and are thus discouraged. It is history that teaches us to hope.

It is a rare distillation. If Lee had been a member of that archetypal republic which a great philosopher imagined, with its orders of valor and wisdom, is it not likely that he would have been promoted a grade? I think that he would have risen from warrior to philosopher king.

"Discipline in Tragedy":

The Southern Tradition

for an American Future

11

THE SOUTH AND THE

REVOLUTION OF NIHILISM

That the South was the first section of the United States to sense an enemy in fascism was indicated not only by polls of opinion, but also by its ardor in preparing for the fight. On the surface it is an anomaly of the first order that this most conservative of sections should have discerned a foe in the regimes gathering strength in Europe, for in open debate the South would have been hard put to it to distinguish between some of the slogans of the New Order and the tenets of its own faith, sealed with Confederate blood and affirmed in many a post-bellum oration. That the Southern whites considered themselves *Herrenvolk* in relation to the Negro is one of the obvious features of our sociological landscape, and belief in the influence of blood and soil is powerful with them, as with any agrarian people. The glorification of the martial spirit, the distrust of urban liberalism, the hatred of money economy are pages that might be found in the book of any unreconstructed Southerner. The restoration of medieval concepts in Europe might almost have seemed the Confed-

The South Atlantic Quarterly, Vol. XLIII, No. 2 (April 1944), 194–198.

erate's dream of reversing history and regaining the way of life which he lost in 1865. Why then the deep, instinctive hostility of the South to Hitler and his allies?

To answer this question one must look at the continuum of history and distinguish some cultural stages. In the ideological conflict between the South and Fascist Europe the world before the French Revolution looks at the world after the French Revolution and finds it hateful.

The Fascist regimes of Europe lie not in the period of the French Revolution, but beyond it; they mark, in fact, an end to that great epoch of society. From 1789 to 1914 the ideas released by this great transformation made irresistible headway until they had destroyed in every center of influence the ancient system of feudalism. Society was changed from a hierarchy, from a state with a corporative form, held together by traditions, bonds of sentiment, and a vision of the whole, into the undifferentiated democratic mass, with free competition regarded as the sole means of measuring position and power. This meant change from a more or less articulated order into an unlimited number of groups and individuals engaged in self-promotion. It was supposed by liberal thinkers that this change represented a permanent rectification of society, in which all injustices, both those inherited from the past and those proceeding from ignorance or malice, would be removed.

The first World War and the Great Depression which followed proved that this condition, far from being a permanent stabilization, carried the seeds of its own destruction. Unregulated competition, unplanned industrial expansion, and private control of surplus and scarcity meant chaos, which rendered unattainable the bourgeois ideal of prosperity and security. When the truth of this became apparent, it was plain that the French Revolution, with its emphasis upon individual liberty and its belief in self-operating laws, had finished its role in Western society. The great experiment, which the

South with incredible stubbornness refused to try, ended in failure.

The first World War began all over Europe the liquidation of the class which that revolution had placed in power, and it was not unnatural that this liquidation should have proceeded farthest in those countries which got the worst of the settlement. With economic anarchy, with the bourgeois pushed toward the proletarian level, with professional men forced to seek employment as common laborers, it was apparent that nothing less than a complete rationalization of economic life would permit the state to endure at all. Signs are not wanting that the whole Western world is being pushed toward a reorganization dictated by these facts.

When it becomes necessary in the interests of saving the whole to abandon laissez faire, individualism, and belief in inalienable personal rights, then some new order is on the way toward establishment. In the forcing house of war, revolution, and economic breakdown the countries of Central Europe arrived at this crisis, while the more prosperous nations to the west were surviving on the strength of their accumulations.

As a general thing American social developments lag a good many years behind those across the water. Slavery made its last stand in America in the middle of the nineteenth century—a late stand. Capitalism reached its apogee in the United States after virtually all of the European nations had been driven to adopt various measures of socialism. The relationship comes down to this: the South, which has never entered the French Revolution, cannot understand the forces which are driving these nations to leave it. And more conservative than America as a whole, it shows an almost unanimous opposition to those tendencies which would destroy the poetic-religious myths and create the mass state.

The South retains enough of the medieval world-picture, enough of the impulses which gave Western civilization its forms and its coherence, to be shocked by this new and outrageous radicalism. If the French Revolution represented one stage of dissolution—and we need only remind ourselves how destructive it was of ancient forms—then this represents another and a greater. That the South was acting in accordance with deep-rooted traditions is proved by the fact that it never took the businessman's attitude toward this threat. It realized that as soon as the first encroachment is made, the battle is on, and there can be no cessation until a victor has been decided. The suggestion that a movement striking at the heart of all beliefs and able to grow with what it fed on could be bought off—unhappy delusion of our statesmen blinded by bourgeois liberalism—found no acceptance in this section, which has never made money, but which has never ceased to study human nature, and its projection, politics.

In strong contrast to the Middle West, the South has a metaphysical instinct which tells it where it stands in any contingency. It cannot analyze, it cannot explain to the world, but the secret voice is a true one, and it valiantly if hopelessly battles for its position. The Middle West has no such anchorage. It is of diverse heritage, prosperous, inexperienced in tragedy—really convinced that tragedy should leave it alone. When the challenge came, therefore, it displayed only vexation, and behaved as if it did not live in a world in which trials are part of an inevitable lot. To the Middle West history is a kind of tableau, such as one might inspect half incredulously at a World's Fair. The South has learned history the hard way; it does not have to ask of the crimes and follies of mankind, "Did they *really* do those things?"

The South perceived intuitively that the new radicalisms of Europe represent a final assault upon society as that term has been understood in Western civilization. Society implies a structure; it consists of centers of authority, degrees of power and prestige, and an inevitable system of ranking even where representative government is in effect. But the tendency of the nihilist revolutions in Europe is toward the destruction of this and the substitution of the formless mass manipulated by a group of Machiavellians. Distinctions in society, however invidious they can be made to appear by doctrinaires, are what gives richness, variety, and freedom to the life of a people, and the exchange of them for some extreme equalitarianism results in regimentation with authority lodged ultimately in a dictator. Centralism always points to an alliance between the mass as such and a single leader purporting to be their champion; and, conversely, decentralization leaves the way open for local authority and provides opportunity for individuals to express themselves as such. Actually this was the trend against which the South fought in 1861–65, although other issues were allowed to obscure that feature of the conflict. Now, as it sees society threatened by the new and extreme proletarian nihilism, it expresses once more the conservative reaction and girds for battle. It understands correctly that the promise of fascism to restore the ancient virtues is counteracted by this process, and that the denial of an ethical basis for the state means the loss of freedom and humanity.

In accordance with this pattern, the coup of the Fascists constitutes the kind of usurpation toward which radical democracy always tends. It is an old story, made spectacular by some modern techniques. Against this alliance of mass and self-appointed leader every traditional society has protested, because it realizes that in its formlessness and in its insistent pressure against the usages which have the sanction of time and experience—the "rubbish of past centuries" of the Jacobins—it moves toward a kind of extinction, often not suspected until the time is too late for reparation.

The South, moreover, is the part of the Western world which has suffered least from what Hermann Rauschning has called "the fading out of a spiritual tradition among the 'historic' ruling classes." Because the Southern aristocracy was an aristocracy of achievement far more than is generally supposed, it has some vitality left. It has never abdicated; and it commands some solid respect at home, a different thing entirely from silly adulation by elements at the North, which it would be better off without. Wherever it has been strongest, there the white-trash demagogues have made least headway; indeed, there is a close correlation between the decay of this class and poor white ascendancy in Southern States. One cannot visualize a Huey Long in Virginia for precisely this reason. The collapse of traditional society in the Southern States and in Europe has shown the same consequences.

The South, by its firm grasp of the traditions of our civilization, has had a great part in giving us one more chance for the conservative solution. While the old sources of power and self-confidence were being weakened by debunking and scientific investigation, it clung to the belief that man is not saved by science alone, that myths and sentiments are part of the constitution of a nation, and that poetry ultimately decides more issues than economics. In the choice that had to be made its voice was perhaps decisive; and the choice was between a world illuminated by religious and poetical concepts and made human by respect for personality, and a world of materialism and technology, of an ever greater feeding of the physical man, which is nihilism.

In this, and not in natural belligerency, or poverty, or loyalty to the Roosevelt administration is to be read the explanation of its role in World War II.

12

ASPECTS OF THE SOUTHERN

PHILOSOPHY

One of the significant aspects of Southern literature is that it does not contain a corpus of purely philosophical writing. It contains some of the best political commentary written in America; and Southern theologians were debating points of doctrine with a seventeenth-century seriousness some while after their contemporaries in other sections had turned to applied religion. But generally over the years, the phrase "camp and senate" fixed the poles of Southern creative activity, and the senate did not produce philosophy of the kind which deals with ultimate questions. With the exception of the recent Fugitive-Agrarian movement, there has been no systematic attempt in the South to articulate a theory of the world or a philosophy of life. Consequently one who writes of the Southern philosophy has little opportunity to speak from texts. What he says must be inferred, partly from the unexpressed postulates of a way of life, and partly from the tendencies of a non-philosophical literature.

We may find a clue to this literary fact by looking at the Southerner as we find him today and examining the points of

The Hopkins Review, Vol. V, No. 4 (Summer 1952), 5–21.

belief in which he most strongly contrasts with the dominant American type, which may still with reasonable accuracy be called the Yankee. A comparison of the two minds leaves one first impressed with the high resistance which the Southerner shows to the idea and practice of analysis. Probably there are few types of minds in the world today so little given to the analytical approach. This characteristic can be seen in the policies of Southern statesmen, in the intellectual processes of Southern college students, and in the household and financial management of the average small citizen. So opposed is the Southerner to the method of analysis that he seems to regard it as a treasonable activity, and I raise the question of whether this may not give us a better insight into his essential mentality than the explanations which are commonly put forward. Sometimes it is said that he does not analyze because he will not make the exertion; sometimes it is said that his education has not brought him up to the level of analysis, and both of these have a degree of plausibility. Yet I feel that both miss the true factor, which is that the Southerner rebels against the idea of analysis because his philosophy or his intellectual tradition, however transmitted down the years, tells him that this is not the way to arrive at the kind of truth he is interested in. It is his habit to see things as forms or large configurations, and he senses that the process of breaking these down (which is nearly always carried on for some practical purpose) somehow proves fatal to the truth of the whole. In fine, analysis is destructive of the kind of reality which he most wishes to preserve.

It is a general rule that analytical procedures issue in one kind of activity and synthetic procedures in another; and it so happens that the analytical successes are the ones upon which the modern world sets a premium. The Southerner is consequently reproached for this incapacity, which has indeed left him a laggard in many of the modern world's competitions. Yet it is possible to take a different view of his condition, for it must be borne in mind that if an extreme development of the analytical faculty suits a man for one type of work—or for one kind of life—it unsuits him for another. We have only to recall that in the achievements of the world's cultures, the work of analysis is fairly late and is somehow specialized. The form in which the messages of the great religions come, for example, is seldom if ever analytical. Such creations are synthetic; they appear to us in large groupings or visualizations which are vitiated by the operation of analysis. That is to say, if one tries to take them apart piece by piece the genius of the message vanishes. They are wholes, like stories, and we have to grasp them with a single act of the mind, as it were. The evidence seems overwhelming that synthesis is the way of religion and art and that analysis is the way of science and business, and this distinction underlies a wide range of Southern attitudes and choices. The typical Southerner is an authentically religious being if one means by religion not a neat set of moralities but a deep and even frightening intuition of man's radical dependence in this world. That awareness is something which has to be achieved immediately rather than mediately, and I suggest that the Southerner's practice of viewing the world in this way is the postulate of all his thinking, and that it causes him to demur at the analysis of life, or love, or war, or any other large subject. What he wants is a picture of it, in which the whole is somehow greater than the analyzable parts.

Naturally this distrust of analysis has kept the traditional Southerner at loggerheads with progressive elements, both those from within his own borders and those from other sections. Again and again the North, or groups representing its prevailing opinion, have presented the South with statistics showing its miserable condition. The South looks at the statistics and doesn't believe them. How can it ignore them? Well, statistics are, after all, the most abstract form of analysis, and what do they tell about an organic whole? The Southerner prefers to take in this whole through a kind of vision, in which the dominant features are a land and sky of high color, a lush climate, a spiritual community, a people inclined to be good humored even in the face of their eternal "problems" and to adapt themselves to the broad rhythms of nature. A Kentuckian of my acquaintance once described the feeling: "Statistics show that Kentucky is next to the bottom in educational facilities. But just take a ride from Lexington to Winchester. Isn't it beautiful!" It is a unitary pattern, and the attempt to segment any part of it with the aim of some practical application violates his notion of the due regard for things. There is likely some obscure connection between this feeling and those religious taboos which forbid the counting of things and especially the taking of census.

For even a threshold understanding of the Southern mind, one must recognize that the South's intractability in the face of statistics proceeds from a positive and not a negative factor, as has been more commonly supposed.

There appears to exist, furthermore, an essential linkage between this virtual defiance of analysis and the South's cultivation of legend and anecdote. No other section compares with it in fecundity of stories of all kinds; and it is almost the rule for an untutored Southerner to be adept at the telling of tales. But always for him the point of the story is in the story, and he is stopped and confused when a single statement is extracted from it for sociological or political analysis. Thus a story about mountaineers or sharecroppers will not be about the sociological status of mountaineers or sharecroppers, but about the dramatic point of the story. In such resistance to the sociological construing of the drama of his life he shows most frankly his antiscientific bias. And so in regard to his humanism, for man is something that can be perceived as a whole too; and it is a prevailing antipathy toward the specialist of the man of unshapely development which has kept the South humanistic in comparison with those sections which have followed the route of analysis and science. We may understand by the same principle why the South insists on putting forward as political leaders highly symbolic personalities rather than the colorless successes with efficient habits and the mentality of bookkeepers which moneyed urban areas prefer. With these examples in mind I wish to turn to a more widely diffused expression of the same tendency.

When we look over the roster of Southerners who have won distinction in the history of the nation we discover that virtually all of them, with the single exception of the soldiers, have been workers in the realm of words. The South has produced no scientists of front rank, few if any creative geniuses in business, no men of any real importance who have been manipulators of things rather than of words. But its manipulators of words have been in the front rank from the beginning, not omitting the most depressed periods of Southern history. As I perceive this characteristic of the Southern mind, it is no accident that the two greatest rhetoricians to occupy the White House, Abraham Lincoln and Woodrow Wilson, were men of Southern nurture. Lincoln early nourished his mind upon that exquisite rhetor "Parson" Weems and upon the frontier anecdote; later he sought to model himself upon Henry Clay. Wilson grew up in close contact with Southern theological rhetoric, of which his father was a professor. If we regard Jefferson as of equal rank, we can raise the number to three. And it seems to be Patrick Henry rather than Daniel Webster who survives in the popular mind as the nation's orator. In the department of utterance, then, the South has made its deepest mark, and we can see that with some changes in form of expression and subject matter, the tradition continues strong today.

An impressive evidence appears in the contemporary school of Southern literary criticism. It is a lamentable fact but a true one that Southern institutions of higher learning have produced nothing of sufficient merit to be followed by the nation as a whole except this literary movement. About 1920 a group of brilliant individuals, drawn together more or less by a conscious Southern heritage, began a new approach to the interpretation of literature. Within less than two decades, they succeeded in putting literary criticism in this country upon a new basis, and so completely that almost any literary critic beginning today has to take up where they are. This they were able to do without the aid of institutional prestige; indeed, one might say that they did it despite the handicap of poor institutional rating. A peculiar qualification for using the word, and for criticizing the use of the word, thus enabled them to make the single contribution of the South to contemporary American intellectual history. Then there comes as culminating evidence the fact that the only Southerner to win a Nobel prize is a literary figure and one, furthermore, whose writing has notable rhetorical qualities. In the background of these exceptional performances is the conspicuous role that Southern drama and fiction have enjoyed on the literary scene at every level of sophistication. But always, work with the word.

The explanation of so consistent a success, contrasting with the barest poverty in other fields of activity, must somehow concern the word itself. The most probable answer is that the word is a synthesizing instrumentality. It can, of course, be used for analysis, as in dialectic; but in rhetoric words make use of things already dialectically determined in a further and final expression which has to do with matters of policy and value. In this further operation the typical Southerner feels as much at home as he feels lost in the activity of rational or piecemeal inquiry, for he is made a rhetorician by the nature of the society in which he grows up. The very stability of its institutions makes possible a vocabulary which does not exist, or exists with much less authority, where things are characterized by distracting change. There are decisive advantages to the rhetorician, and along with him to the man of letters, in a vocabulary whose acceptance does not have to be called into question. Its very settledness gives him a range of opportunities—including that of meaningful deviation—which a vocabulary challenged or in flux cannot give. He enjoys something comparable to what the lawyers call "the right of assumption"; and working from these advanced positions he can accomplish things which would be far harder or impossible if he had to go back and shore up the assumptions underlying every predication.

When a culture and a vocabulary thus settle down together as correlates, there develops a natural tendency to assume that a mastery of the word is equivalent to a mastery of the institutions, and this development can reach an unhealthy extreme. On the whole, the Southerner has perhaps been too credulous about language. His responsiveness sometimes leads him to the belief that if a man can make a good speech, all other things should be credited to him. By this we may account for the great prestige which the orator has traditionally enjoyed in the South, and not merely by those who have encountered Cicero and Quintilian in their education, but also by the masses. The kind of political folk hero who has proved incomprehensible to the remainder of the nation finds the greatest source of his power in a widespread admiration of confidence and even *bravura* in the use of language. When the pistol-toting henchman of Willie Stark in Warren's *All the King's Men* tries to explain why he so admired Stark, he comes out with an answer which would satisfy an average Southern audience: "Couldn't nobody talk like him."

Yet on the other hand, if this reverence for the word can run into liability, it can also constitute an asset of a singularly important kind. For the same set of facts will explain why the South remains the stronghold of religious and perhaps also of ethical fundamentalism. Verbal skepticism is the beginning of moral nihilism; and it is just this belief that words are among the fixed things which has kept the South conservative in regard to those forces which are liquidating values. Just as soon as men begin to point out that the word is one entity and the object it represents is another, there sets in a temptation to do one thing with the word and another or different thing with the object it is supposed to represent; and here begins that relativism which by now is visibly affecting those institutions which depend for their very existence upon our ability to use language as a permanent binder. With all due recognition of semantic analysis, this distinction is one of the most perilous morally that can be made. It seems to open a hitherto excluded middle between the word and the thing signified, where every sort of relativistic dodge becomes possible. I have come to abominate the expression "Southern gentleman" because it is used presumptuously, yet there must be some connection between the old concept of "the word of a gentleman" and this view of language as having fixed pertinence.

The South is often described as differing from the rest of the nation through a disproportionate amount of piety, but it is easy to fall into an erroneous impression here. For a long while I labored under the illusion that the South is peculiarly the pious section and that the North, as its democratic professions would lead one to imagine, is opposed on principle to the idea of reverence. But years of residence in the North have convinced me that such is not true. Northerners have their piety too, as probably every people does; but Northern and Southern piety differ in a way to produce even more mischievous disagreements than the condition I had supposed to exist. I would define piety as an attitude of reverence or acceptance toward some overruling order or some deeply founded institution which the mere individual is not to tamper with. Ultimately perhaps it is religious, but immediate religious associations are not essential to it; it may manifest itself toward various objects as what Matthew Arnold called "the discipline of respect." There would in fact be some advantage in changing the term to "pieties," for the attitude sometimes shows itself in seemingly unrelated responses. In any case, the Northerner is as reverential towards his sanctioned order or objects as the Southerner is towards his, but the two orders are not the same.

Southern piety is basically an acceptance of the inscrutability of nature. Under its impulse the individual Southerner feels that nature is not something which he is to make over or change; it is rather something for him to come to terms with. The world is God-given; its mysteries are not supposed to be fully revealed; and the only possible course in the long run is to accommodate oneself to its vast pulsations. Thus nature is seen as providential, and even its harsher aspects must be regarded as having ends that we do not fully comprehend. In a word, the Southerner reveres original creation. His willingness to accept some conditions that his more energetic Northern cousin will not put up with is not purely temperamental or climatic; it is religious or philosophical insofar as it stems from this world view. Often the Yankee's effort to become complete master of his environment appears to the Southerner an effrontery against an order which is divinely provided and which, in the total outcome, is not going to be improved by busy human schemes. It never occurs to the typical Northerner, for example, to ask whether it is right to move a mountain or alter the course of a river; but it may occur to this fundamentalist Southerner, and some degree of this feeling will be encountered in every level of the population.

Northern piety, on the other hand, finds its objects in things of human creation. It shows itself primarily through attitudes toward education and learning and the kinds of conventions erected upon these. Perhaps it could be most generally described as a respect for ideas. Essentially the Northerner is a child of the Enlightenment; and his theology is very much like Tom Paine's; that is, his religion is to do good, and his own mind is his church. It is in tendency a strongly Protestant mentality which insists on judging a thing by its works.

Consequently one coming to the North from a Southern background is forcibly impressed by the Northerner's willingness to receive any good idea, regardless of its provenance. The Northerner considers irrelevant any question as to whether the bearer of the idea has family or position or current recognition; if the idea is cogent, that is enough. For him, it is only necessary that a thought be able to give a good account of itself dialectically. The North has never had much democracy of condition, especially when judged by its own slogans; but it has enjoyed this democracy of thoughts, which has undeniably served as a fountainhead of enterprise and resourcefulness. It makes for a much greater viability of ideas and for tolerance of criticism, since no person is impelled to feel that his status or his character is being assailed when his idea is being criticized.

In the South the bearer of an idea must come vouchsafed and certified. He must be of a good family or hold some public position or represent some important element before he can get a hearing. Who is he to have an important thought? To put the matter in another way, the Southerner expects the idea to come with what the old writers on rhetoric used to call "ethical proof." That is to say, he frankly evaluates the idea against the background of its origin. I scarcely need add that in most situations the "proof" is not ethical at all, but political or worse, since it attempts to rate thought according to some notion of social prestige. This habit has been one of the stifling influences in Southern culture and more than one otherwise loyal son has complained of it.[1]

However, if the South loses in some respects through this providential view of nature and through this unwillingness to judge by abstract determinations, it gains what many would regard as an important compensation. For one of the most noticeable qualities of the Southern people today is the comparative absence of that modern spirit of envy which has so unsettled things in other parts of the world. Of all the peoples of the Western world, probably only the peasant populations of Europe are so little affected by this increasing distemper.

---

[1]George W. Cable, writing to a friend in the North who had offered to get some publicity for his early work, felt impelled to say: "if you love me don't offer *anything* that I *ever* do to *anybody* except on its intrinsic merits. You will excuse me for appearing to suspect such a thing; it's such a common occurrence down here, and therefore—besides all the better reasons—because I am a Southerner—I would like the handful of people that make up my little world to be assured I am nobody's widow."

And since the absence of envy produces a kind of character not much seen since the decay of the feudal order, some account of it may here be in order.

When I affirm that the average Southerner of traditional mentality does not envy, I do not mean that he will not take a better job if it is offered him, or that he will pass up a chance to make a quick fortune, or that he will not admire material success. He will do all these things, and without apology. What I do affirm is that it is not in his character to hate another man because that man has a great deal more of the world's goods than he himself has or is ever likely to have. He is not now and never has been a leveller. The fact that three fourths of the soldiers in Confederate armies owned no slaves and never expected to own any is part of this pattern. If the principle of envy I have mentioned had been abroad, these armies would have dissolved in a matter of months. But the historical fact is that the Confederate armies possessed one of the toughest morales in modern history, a morale which is studied by war colleges today in an effort to learn what made it so impervious to cracking. Something of the pattern endures today. If a rich man lives in a Southern community, he will be a subject of talk, as he would be anywhere, but he will not be an object of envious hatred because fortune has dealt lavishly with him and sparingly with his neighbors. Much contemporary political and economic thought carries the implication that we should pull down our neighbor's house if we cannot have a house at least as fine; but the average Southern proletarian, urban or rural, has never been penetrated with this notion. The poor success of trade unionism in the South is one of the concrete evidences. Trade unionism runs up against both the distrust of analysis and this hesitancy about tampering with a prevailing dispensation. Whereas modern social doctrine encourages a man to question the whole order of society if he does not have as much as somebody else, the typical Southern farmer or millhand tends to regard fortune, like nature, as providential. From his point of view there is nothing written in the original bill of things which says that the substance of the world must be distributed equally. Nor was there anything, before modern advertisers availed themselves of the press and radio, to tell him that he is entitled to the best of everything. That some should have more and others less is, in his view, part of the inscrutable provision. This modern impulse which elevates envy into a principle of social action and which animates much of the class struggle in regions supposedly more advanced is thus completely foreign to his tradition, though now and then he has struck back politically when he felt that he was the victim of sectional political exploitation. For the failure of collectivist doctrine to penetrate the South the Southern Chambers of Commerce may not claim the slightest credit. That opposition was determined long ago, and at a level far deeper than such organizations can reach.

The factors considered thus far go back to the beginnings of Southern history, but it cannot be overlooked that an important part of the Southern philosophy is a philosophy of the South's place in the nation since the Civil War. Southerners have undergone some peculiar experiences which have left them a highly conscious minority within the nation. Everyone remarks the surface manifestations of this status, the self-awareness, defense-mindedness, over-assertiveness, and occasional bad manners. But I feel the need here to push below these surface displays and look at some of the ways in which special conditions have affected profoundly the Southern intellectual and cultural outlook. They have had the effect of giving the Southerner a point of view and a set of values which the remainder of the nation is highly curious about but which he has difficulty in explaining because of the lack of common denominators. A detached account of how he came to his present state may provide some basis of communication.

There occurs in Walter Hines Page's *The Autobiography of Nicholas Worth* a striking figure in which the surviving Confederate brigadiers are likened to ghosts in a stage play. The point of the comparison is that although they have only a ghostly being, they succeed, like a stage ghost, in monopolizing the attention of the audience. What will it do next? what will it say? are the questions it provokes in the minds of the onlookers. Since the Civil War the South as a whole has played this kind of role in the American drama and has held a comparable degree of attention. And it has succeeded in doing this for the same reason as the ghost, if we grant that it possesses a different kind of being from the other actors. That difference of being can be explained through reference to its special history.

If we look at the typical American against the background of his experience, his folklore, and his social aspirations, we are forced to admit that he represents, more than any other type in the world, victorious man. He has surpassed the people of every other country in amassing wealth, in rearing institutions, and in getting his values recognized, for better or for worse, throughout the world. While he is often chided for his complacent belief in progress, it must be confessed that events have conspired to encourage that belief, and to make progress appear the central theme of his history. In all sorts of senses he has never ceased to go forward; and to much of the world America has come to symbolize that future in which man will be invariably successful both in combat with nature and in his struggle with the problems of human organization. This adds up to saying that in the eyes of the world as well as in his own eyes the typical American stands for success unlimited.

But this is the point at which the Southerner ceases to be classifiable as American. He has had to taste a bitter cup which no American is supposed to know anything about, the cup of defeat. Thus in a world where the American is supposed to be uniformly successful, he exists as an anomalous American. Much of the Southerner's nonconformity and intransigence results from the real difficulty of adjusting a psychology which has been nourished upon this experience to the predominating national psychology, which has been nourished upon uninterrupted success.

The effects of this adverse history upon the Southern mentality have never been candidly appraised. For example, it cannot be without significance that the Southerner today is the only involuntary tenant of the American Union. I am not suggesting that there exists at present a mass feeling in favor of political independence, as there did at one time; but the record of American history, which he has to read along with his Northern brother, says that he is where he is as the result of a settlement of force against him. To argue that the resulting condition is economically or otherwise to his advantage is beside this point; the book continues to say that a supreme act of his will was frustrated, and that as a consequence of that defeat he had to accommodate himself to an unwanted circumstance. And that, of course, is the meaning of failure. Therefore in the national legend the typical American owes his position to a virtuous and effective act of his will; but the Southerner owes his to the fact that his will was denied; and this leaves a kind of inequality which no amount of political blandishment can remove entirely. Although there appears today no lively awareness of this frustration, it none the less lies deep in his psychology, a subdued but ingrown reminder that at one time his all was not enough—a reminder, furthermore, that Americans too can fail. Probably this explains why his presence sometimes irks his fellow Americans. He cannot sit in conclave with their unspoiled innocence, for he brings, along with a certain outward exuberance, these sardonic memories.

The comparative poverty which has existed in the South for nearly a hundred years is directly connected with this circumstance; for when the states composing the Confederacy lost the independence which they had asserted, they lost also a large measure of their ability to recover from physical destruction. When a nation is defeated in international war, its opportunities for recovery are enhanced many times if it can only hang on to its political autonomy. It may have to cede territory, to pay indemnity, and to make other sacrifices to expiate its misfortune; but as long as it remains a self-governing unit, it can adapt its internal and external economy to the necessities of the situation. In other words, it can prescribe the medicine that it needs and take it; and it can choose the best conditions for its convalescence. A good example is France after her defeat by Prussia in 1871. But when a nation loses its independence along with the war, its people have to recover on terms set entirely by the enemy, and these will seldom if ever be generous in the sense of promoting a real revival of strength. The South is a clear example of the second situation. After 1865 it not only had to undertake a great task of physical restoration but it also had to undertake this without any real freedom of initiative. It was reduced to being part of a far larger and generally unsympathetic unit called the Union, whose will prevailed in all major policies. The way in which the South was systematically bled in the decades following the war has been set forth by Southern historians, and there is no need to enter into it here. It is enough to point out that a recovery which under favorable conditions might have required ten or fifteen years required more than fifty and actually cannot be regarded as complete yet.

This is substantially what I mean by saying that the South has a different kind of being from the other sections, which gives it something of the interest of the ghost in the play, or something of the ominous presence of the suppliant in a Greek tragedy.

History indeed, as Eliot reminds us in a poem, has many cunningly contrived corridors, and if we will follow this one of defeat and impoverishment, we shall arrive at a view which is better suggested by the ghost or the suppliant in the tragedy than by the studies of sociologists. Let us begin with the touchy matter of education. It has been for many decades a widely received belief that the South is the least educated of the sections; yet there is a true and most important sense in which it is the best or the "most" educated section. I refer here to an education in tragedy, which is the profoundest education of man. The South, as has already been shown, is the only section of the United States which knows through poignant experience that defeat is possible. The ancient states knew it and their sages expressed the truth in memorable sayings; the medieval states knew it, and their writers spoke of the Wheel of Fortune; every state of modern Europe has had to taste some measure of it. Only the victorious American of the North and West has it yet to learn. He may imagine that he knows it from copybook maxims, but that is not knowing it. One must have been through the humiliation and despair, must have felt the impossibility of vindicating oneself before any earthly tribunal to savor the real essence of it. Defeat in war is an unpleasant thing, but truly it is "one of those experiences nobody should be without." Nothing else can bring home so forcibly the truth of the proverb that time and chance happen to us all. The imprint of it upon the mind and character of the South has proved lasting. It is out of this ancestral memory that the South has remained the most militarily inclined of the sections. (To say that defeat in war teaches a people that "force never pays" is fatuous. What it does teach is that "too little force never pays.") It was out of this that its representatives in Congress swung the vote for renewal of conscription in 1941. It is out of this generally that the South serves as a flywheel to the nation as a whole, often slowing down the work of those who would perfect society overnight, yet speeding up those policies which its harder experience has taught it to accept. In this respect the average Southerner may be said to have "a European education." He knows that every great success is poised right on the brink of tragedy; and he knows that those forces which have molded the lives of men for five thousand years cannot be simply waved into abeyance. It may be that his peculiar pride is a perverse outgrowth of this knowledge. He has had to face what the existentialists call "ultimate situations" and he has come through, and it is very difficult to convince him by educators' statistics that he doesn't know anything. Indeed, one of the unfortunate results of this circumstance is a certain contumaciousness toward Northern-endorsed book learning.

This cunningly contrived corridor issues also in the blessing that the South has never had much money. At the risk of presuming on a controversial point, I call this a blessing for the plain reason that it has retarded the spoiling of the South. Everyone recognizes that the possession of wealth, especially if it is long continued, causes men to set their expectations at too high a level. They tend to forget what went into the creation of that wealth; and they begin to assume that this world is naturally a world of comfort and even of surfeit, which is one of the saddest of all distortions of reality. Of course the Southerner has no greater natural immunity to his weakness than any other American; but the situation being what it was, he had to continue working for a living; more than that, he had to work as a primary producer since his only capital (to amount to anything) was the land. From this combination of causes the people of the South have remained predominantly a rural working people. North Carolina, which now stands tenth among the states in total population, stands first in farm population, and other Southern states will show comparable figures. This phase of the South's misfortunes, then, has kept from the Southern people the peculiar degenerative effects of the possession of wealth, and it has kept them in close contact with the natural environment, which can itself be a profound instructor. There is no more eloquent sectional contrast than the fact that whereas the South has the farms, New England has the insurance companies. It has not helped New England to have the insurance companies, except to grow rich; and it has helped the South to have the farms, as can be shown by its biological and imaginative fertility, and by the fortitude of its people. On this last point there is an oblique but interesting commentary in Norman Mailer's *The Naked and the Dead.* General Cummings is addressing Lieutenant Hearn in one of the conversations.

> "After a couple of years of war, there are only two considerations that make a good army: a superior material force and a poor standard of living. Why do you think that a regiment of Southerners is worth two regiments of Easterners?"
> "I don't think they are."
> "Well, it happens to be true. . . . I'm not peddling theories. And the conclusions leave me, as a general officer, in a poor position. We have the highest standard of living in the world and, as one would expect, the worst individual fighting soldiers of any big power. Or at least in their natural state they are. They're comparatively wealthy, they're spoiled, and as Americans they share most of them the peculiar manifestations of our democracy. They have an exaggerated idea of the rights due themselves and no idea at all of the rights due others. It's the reverse of the peasant, and I'll tell you right now it's the peasant who makes the soldier."

Today Southern boys fill up our volunteer armies as the rustics of the Italian peninsula filled up the legions in the days of the Republic.

If the time ever comes to write the definitive history of the Southern people, it may prove impossible to find a better epigraph than the line from *Gerontion*: "Virtues are forced upon us by our impudent crimes."

Before closing this topic of the Southerner's place within the nation I should like to point out a poorly understood source of Southern grievance. This is, more specifically, a circumstance which has kept the North from understanding the South and has kept the South from understanding the North's misunderstanding. The fact is simply that for the North the South is too theatrical to be wholly real; therefore it is "history" and not "real life." The South appears to the North a kind of tableau. It is interesting, even fascinating, to look upon, with its survivals of medievalism, its manners that recall vanished eras, its stark social cleavages, its lost cause, its ballads and sentimental songs. But the very presence of these causes the typical American to view it with the same dubious credulity that one shows toward the exhibit in the glass case of a museum. It is so strange that one cannot conquer the feeling that it must be in some degree fictionized. For this reason mainly the North has never been able to credit the actual suffering which has been a part of the South's story. The tendency is to think that characters so theatrical cannot have suffered any more than the actors who have just presented a stage tragedy. Northerners of the present generation appear to believe, as Warren once put it, that the blood which was shed at Gettysburg and Chickamauga was not real blood at all; it was only tomato ketchup used to make the scene look realistic. That attitude leads to a systematic if unconscious discounting of the facts which make the South what it is today, physically and spiritually.

The Southerner naturally knows that life in his region is quite authentic and has been so from the start, despite certain aspects of pageantry. It may seem picturesque in comparison with lives lived in other regions, but it is paid for in most of the same pains, with a few special ones occasioned by its climate and situation. To work on the land where the temperature reaches 90 degrees in the shade fifty days out of the year, to wrest a living from a soil which was not very fertile to begin with and which has been abused in cultivation, and to move amid the tensions of an almost irremediable race situation do not make a purely idyllic life, whatever the traditional songs of the South may suggest. Temperamentally the Southerner is disinclined to feel sorry for himself; but he is irked to have the solid facts of his history treated as if they were something out of a Gilbert and Sullivan opera; and I believe that the attitude of belligerence which others sometimes sense in him stems from this situation more than from any other.

It should be a welcome sign that contemporary literature, including that written on both sides of the Mason-Dixon line, is doing something to correct this focus. I once heard a Southerner long resident in the Northeast say that he was delighted with "The Little Foxes" because it showed that the South too can have a first-class murderess. The tremendous impression which Miss Mitchell's Scarlett O'Hara made upon the Northern audience is owing to the fact that Scarlett is a type of ruthless entrepreneur which Northerners have met in their own life and can therefore understand and credit. And the dimensions of Mr. Faulkner's world are so unyielding that they have compelled assent in the most reluctant quarters.

If the world continues its present drift toward tension and violence, it is probable that the characteristic Southern qualities will command an increasing premium. While this country was amassing its great wealth, those qualities were in comparative eclipse; but the virtues needed to amass wealth are not the virtues needed to defend it. Such is our ambiguous position today that the possession of the greatest wealth in the world is going to require an amplitude of those qualities developed in the school of poverty and deprivation, and in that of rural living. Important among these "enforced" virtues are fortitude and the ability to do without. But perhaps most important of all is the Southerner's discipline in tragedy. Belief in tragedy is essentially un-American; it is in fact one of the heresies against Americanism; but in the world as a whole this heresy is more widely received than the dogma and is more regularly taught by experience. Just as certainly as the United States grows older, it will have to find accommodation for this ineluctable notion; it is even now embarked upon policies with tremendous possibilities if not promises of tragedy. If we are in for a time of darkness and trouble, the Southern philosophy, because it is not based upon optimism, will have better power to console than the national dogmas.

> It will do good to heart and head
> When your soul is in my soul's stead.

{ 13 }

THE SOUTHERN TRADITION

Many years ago the historian Francis Parkman wrote a passage in one of his narratives which impresses me as full of wisdom and prophecy. After a brilliant characterization of the colonies as they existed on the eve of the Revolution, he said, "The essential antagonism of Virginia and New England was afterwards to become, and to remain, an element of the first influence in American history. Each might have learned much from the other, but neither did so till, at last, the strife of their contending principles shook the continent." If we take Virginia as representing the South and New England as representing the North, as I think we may fairly do, we can say that this situation continues in some degree down to the present. Each section had much to learn from the other: neither was willing to learn anything and that failure produced 100 years ago the greatest tragedy in American history. Today it appears in political friction, social resentment, and misunderstanding of motives despite encouraging signs of growing amity.

This amity will clearly depend upon an appreciation, which Parkman found so sadly lacking, of what each has to offer. You certainly never get anywhere in mutual understanding

New Individualist Review, Vol. III, No. 3 (1964), 7–17.

among peoples or nations by assuming in advance that the other fellow has nothing whatever to offer. We would never think of assuming that in the case of the English or the French or the Chinese, or even the American Indians. But I only report what I have observed if I say that there appears a tendency on the part of a good many Americans to assume that the American South has nothing to offer—nothing worth anybody's considering. That is a proposition in itself, and it needs to be examined in the light of evidence.

My principal theme, therefore, will be those things the South believes it has contributed to this great, rich, and diversified nation and which it feels have some right to survive and to exert their proportionate influence upon our life.

Before I can do this, however, I shall have to say something about what the South is—what makes it a determinate thing, a political, cultural, and social entity, which by the settlement of 1865 is going to be part of the union indefinitely.

It is virtually a truism in American political thinking that the South has been a kind of nation within a nation. You have no doubt learned that "nation" is a hard thing to define in any ultimate sense. But taking the term in the practical, working sense usually employed, we can say that there are a number of evidences of Southern nationalism. The political unity of the section often referred to by the phrase "the solid South" is a fact of considerable notoriety. Its ideological unity, or its community of belief about certain ideas, certain institutions, and certain figures of history is only a little behind the political unity. And the unity of its culture, expressed in its way of life, its speech, its cookery, and its manners, has maintained itself surprisingly in the face of a variety of conditions on the inside and considerable pressure from the outside. I am inclined to think that Southern culture shows a degree of centripetalism, or orientation toward a center, which is characteristic of all high cultures.

In dealing with the factors which have produced this unity of thought and feeling in the South, it seems best to take them in the order of their historical emergence.

The first step toward understanding the peculiarities of the Southern mind and temper is to recognize that the South, as compared with the North, has a European culture—not European in the mature or highly developed sense, but more European than that which grew up north of the Potomac and Ohio rivers, in several respects, even more European than that of New England.

The South never showed the same interest in seceding from European *culture* that the North and West showed. It played an important and valiant part in the Revolution, but this was a political separation. After the Revolution it settled down quite comfortably with its institutions, modelled on eighteenth-century England. A few stirrings of change, I believe, there were in Virginia, but not enough to alter the patterns of a land-owning aristocracy. While Emerson in New England was declaiming, "We have listened too long to the courtly muses of Europe," the South was contentedly reading Sir Walter Scott, not, as Russell Kirk has shrewdly pointed out in his *The Conservative Mind,* just because it liked romance but because in Sir Walter Scott it found the social ideals of Edmund Burke. And Burke is one of the great prophets of conservative society. The European complexion of Southern culture showed itself also in other ways. It showed itself in the preservation of a class society—one might more truly say in the creation of a class society—for very few who settled in the South had any real distinction of family. It appeared in the form of considerable ceremonial in dress and manners. It was manifested in the *code duello,* with all its melancholy consequences. It appeared in the tendency of Southern families who could afford it to send their sons to Europe for their education—even Edgar Allan Poe received some of his schooling in England. And it appeared in a consequential way in their habit of getting their silver, their china, their fine furniture and the other things that ornamented Southern mansions from Europe in exchange for their tobacco, cotton and indigo.

Whether the South was right or wrong in preserving so

much of the European pattern is obviously a question of vast implications which we cannot go into here. But I think it can be set down as one fact in the growing breach between South and North. The South retained an outlook which was characteristically European while the North was developing in a direction away from this—was becoming more American, you might say.

There are evidences of this surviving into the present. A few decades ago when Southern Rhodes scholars first began going to England, some of them were heard to remark that the society they found over there was much like the society they had left behind. England hardly seemed to them a foreign country. This led to attempts by some of them to reassert the close identity of Southern and Western European culture, to which I expect to refer again later.

The second great factor in the molding of Southern unity and self-consciousness was the Civil War. Southerners are sometimes accused of knowing too much about the Civil War, of talking too much about it, of being unwilling to forget it. But there are several reasons why this rent looms very large in the Southerner's memory, and why he has little reluctance in referring to this war, although it was a contest in which he was defeated.

To begin with, Southerners, or the great majority of them, always have believed that their part in this war was an honorable one. Far from regarding themselves as rebels, they felt that they were loyal to the original government, that is to say, they believed that they were fighting to defend the government as it was laid down at Philadelphia in 1787 and as recognized by various state ordinances of ratification. This was a government of restricted power, commissioned to do certain things which the states could not do for themselves, but strictly defined as to its authority. The theory of states' rights was a kind of political distributism which opposed the idea of a powerful centralized government. The Southern theory then as now favored the maximum amount of self-determination by the states and it included, as a kind of final guarantee that states' rights would be respected, the principle of state sovereignty, with its implied right of secession.

In the Southern view, it was the North that was rebelling against this idea which had been accepted by the members of the Constitutional Convention in 1787. Or to put it in another way, the North was staging a revolution, the purpose of which was to do away with this older concept of the American government. The South refused to go along with the revolution, invoked the legal safeguards which it believed to exist, and then prepared to defend itself by force. You may recall that the late historian Charles A. Beard found enough substance in this to call the Civil War "the Second American Revolution" in his *Rise of American Civilization.* Thus in this second American Revolution the Northerners were in the role of patriots, the Southerners in the role of English, if we keep our analogy with the Revolutionary War.

In all great crises of history where you have a legal principle challenged by a moral right, you find people flocking to both standards. The one side says it believes in the duty of upholding the law. The other side says it believes in the imperative necessity of change, even at the expense of revolution. Though the Civil War may not look quite so simple to us now, this is the way many people saw it. A number of years ago, Gerald Johnson wrote an ingenious little book on Southern secession, in which he referred to it as the struggle between the law and the prophets. The South had the law and the North had the prophets, in the form of the abolitionists and also of the advocators, both heard and unheard, of a strong central government, unimpeded by theories of states' rights.

The legal aspects of an issue which has been so long decided can now have only academic interest. But if any of you wish to see a statement of the South's legal position on state sovereignty and secession, the best source is a little book by a man named Bledsoe—A. T. Bledsoe—*Is Davis a Traitor?* Bledsoe was a Kentuckian, and he brought to the task of writing this defense an interesting set of qualifications. He was a lawyer, a professor of mathematics, and for ten years he had been a colleague of Lincoln at the bar of Springfield. Also—and probably this is pertinent to mention, since we are talking here about a metaphysical debate—he had written a book-length refutation of Jonathan Edwards' *Freedom of the Will.* I do not know whether this is true or not, but it has been said that the appearance of *Is Davis a Traitor?* in 1866 was one of the things that made the North decide not to bring Davis to trial. At any rate, the failure to bring Davis to trial was naturally taken by the South as a sign that the North's legal case was too weak to be risked in court.

These are the chief things causing Southerners to feel that, whatever the claims of moral right and wrong, they had the law on their side.

Now we come to the fact of the Civil War itself. It was impossible that a struggle as long and bitter as this should not leave deep scars. Americans, particularly those of the present generation, are prone to forget the magnitude of this civil conflict. The United States lost more men from battle wounds and disease in the Civil War than in any other war of its history, including the Second World War. The battle front stretched from Pennsylvania to New Mexico, and included also the seven seas. A good many of the wars of history have been decided by two or three major battles. In our Civil War at least eighteen battles must be accounted major by reason of the number and resources involved. The minor battles run into scores, and the total number of engagements—somebody once counted them up—is, as I recall, something more than 2200. Of this eighteen major battles you might call five or six "critical" in a sense that, with a more decisive result, they might have ended the war right there or have turned it in favor of the side which eventually lost. I would include in my list of critical battles Shiloh, the Seven Days, Sharpsburg, Gettysburg, and Chickamauga. So you can see it was really a knock-down drag-out fight.

There is a further fact to be noticed in discussing the effect of this war. Nearly the whole of it was fought on Southern soil. With the exception of the Gettysburg campaign, and John Hunt Morgan's raids into Indiana and Ohio, and the small but famous St. Albans raid in Vermont—a group of Confederates in disguise came down from Canada, shot up the little town of St. Albans in Vermont, took the bank deposits and got back across the border—the North was physically untouched. There is a great difference between reading about a war your boys are fighting 500 miles away, and having the war in your midst, with homes being burned, farms being stripped, and your institutions being pulled to pieces. I'll bet any Japanese or German today will testify to this. The war was much more a reality to the people of the South than to those of the North, and it has remained such down to the present.

A natural question to come up at this point is, why should anybody care to remember or write histories about a war which left his country a hollow shell? In order to explain this, I shall have to tell you something else from the Southern credo, something that goes along with this faith in the legal case. It has been a prime factor in preserving Southern morale and in maintaining that united front of the South which I am afraid has been such a vexation to the rest of the country. And the only way I can really tell this is by an anecdote, even though I have to explain the anecdote.

The story goes that a ragged Confederate soldier was trudging his way home from Appomattox. As he was passing through some town, somebody called out to him by way of taunting: "What'll you do if the Yankees get after you?" And his answer was, "They aren't going to bother me. If they do, I'll just whip 'em again." The point of the anecdote, which may need to be explained, is that the answer was at least half serious. It was a settled article of belief with the Southern soldiers—echoed in numberless Confederate reunions—that although they had lost the war, they had won the fighting— that individually they had proved themselves the equal, if not the superior of their adversary, and that the contest had finally been decided by numbers. There is no point in going into the merits of the argument here. But it is easy to see how, right or wrong, it had a great effect in preserving Southern pride, and even in maintaining a spirit of defiance which to this day characterizes a good bit of Southern policy.

It also helps to explain why the South has written so voluminously about the war, and why in libraries today, for example, you can find a biography of practically every Confederate general of any eminence whatever, and sometimes three or four. A quick check of the card files in Harper library reveals ten full-length biographies of William Tecumseh Sherman, but fourteen of Stonewall Jackson, plus biographies of Stoneman, Pleasanton, Grierson, Bedford, Forrest, Stuart, and a definitive biography of Lee by D. S. Freeman; but no definitive biography of Grant. The remark has been made that in the Civil War the North reaped the victory and the South the glory. If you consult the literature of the subject very extensively you find a certain amount of truth in that.

Evidently there was enough substance in the legend to nourish the martial tradition of the South, and to support institutions like VMI, the Citadel and the A & M College of Texas, which do not have counterparts in other sections of the country.

This brings the story down to Reconstruction, which somebody has described as "a chamber of horrors into which no good American would care to look." If that is an exaggeration, it still seems fair to say that this was the most dismal period of our history—a bitter, thirty-year sectional feud in which one side was trying to impose its will on the other, and the other was resisting that imposition with every device of policy, stratagem and chicanery that could be found. We must realize that no people willingly accepts the idea of being reconstructed in the image of another. That is, in fact, the ultimate in humiliation, the suggestion that you must give up your mind, your inherited beliefs and your way of life in favor of that of your invaders. There was a critical period when, if things had been managed a little worse, the South might have turned into a Poland or an Ireland, which is to say a hopelessly alienated and embittered province, willing to carry on a struggle for decades or even centuries to achieve a final self-determination. That was largely forestalled by the wisdom of a few Northern leaders. The work of Lincoln toward reconciliation is well known, but that of Grant, at Appomattox and also later, I think has never been sufficiently appreciated. And the act of Lee in calling for reunion once the verdict of battle had been given was of course of very great influence.

It was an immeasurable calamity that Lincoln was not allowed to live and carry out his words in the lofty and magnanimous spirit which his speeches reflect. He was himself a product of the two sections, a Kentuckian by birth, an Illinoisian by adoption. He understood what had gone into the making of both. As it was, things were done which produced only rancor and made it difficult for either side to believe in the good faith of the other. It is unfortunate but it is true that the Negro was forced to pay a large part of the bill for the follies of Reconstruction.

By all civilized standards the period was dreadful enough. George Fort Milton has called his history covering those years *The Age of Hate.* Claude Bowers has called this *The Tragic Era.* If you desire a detailed account of what the South experienced in these years probably the best source to go to is *Why the Solid South: Reconstruction and Its Results* (ed. Hilary Herbert) by a group of Southern leaders, including a number of governors of states. This is, of course, a Southern view, but it tells you from the inside something about the financial, political, and social chaos that prevailed in those years.

Unquestionably Reconstruction did something to deepen the self-consciousness of the Southern people, to make them feel less American rather than more so. They became the first Americans ever to be subject to invasion, conquest, and military dictation. In estimating the Southern mind it is most important to realize that no other section of America has been through this kind of experience. In fact it is not supposed to be part of the American story. The American presents himself to the world as ever progressing, ever victorious, and irresistible. The American of the South cannot do this. He has tasted what no good American is supposed ever to have tasted, namely the cup of defeat. Of course, that experience is known to practically all the peoples of Europe and of Asia. This circumstance has the effect of making the mentality of the Southerner again a foreign mentality—or a mentality which he shares in respect to this experience with most of the peoples of the world but does not share with the victorious American of the North and West. He is an outsider in his own country. I have often felt that the cynicism and Old-World pessimism which the rest of the country sometimes complains of in the South stems chiefly from this cause. The Southerner is like a person who has lost his innocence in the midst of persons who have not. William A. Percy, going from a plantation on the Mississippi Delta to the Harvard Law School, found that Northern boys were "mentally more disciplined" but "morally more innocent" than Southern boys. His presence is somehow anomalous; he didn't belong.

It is sometimes said, with reference to these facts, that the South is the only section of the nation which knows the meaning of tragedy. I am inclined to accept that observation as true and to feel that important things can be deduced from it. Perhaps there is nothing in the world as truly educative as tragedy. Tragedy is a kind of ultimate. When you have known it, you've known the worst, and probably also you have had a glimpse of the mystery of things. And if this is so, we may infer that there is nothing which educates or matures a man or a people in the way that the experience of tragedy does. Its lessons, though usually indescribable, are poignant and long remembered. A year or so ago I had the temerity to suggest in an article that although the South might not be the best educated section in the United States, it is the most educated—meaning that it has an education in tragedy with which other educations are not to be compared, if you are talking about realities. In this sense, a one-gallus farmer from Georgia, sitting on a rail fence with a straw in his mouth and commenting shrewdly on the ways of God and man—a figure I adopt from John Crowe Ransom—is more educated than say a salesman in Detroit, who has never seen any reason to believe that progress is not self-moving, necessary and eternal. It would seem the very perverseness of human nature for one to be proud of this kind of education. But I do believe it is a factor in the peculiar pride of the Southerner. He has been through it; he knows; the others are still living in their fool's paradise of thinking they can never be defeated. All in all, it has proved difficult to sell the South on the idea that it is ignorant.

In a speech made around the turn of the century, Charles Aycock of North Carolina met the charge of ignorance in a way that is characteristic in its defiance. Speaking on "The Genius of North Carolina Interpreted," he said,

> Illiterate we have been, but ignorant never. Books we have not known, but men we have learned, and God we have sought to find out.
>
> [North Carolina has] nowhere within her borders a man known out of his township ignorant enough to join with the fool in saying "There is no God."

You will note here the distinction made between literacy and knowledge—a distinction which seems to be coming back into vogue. You will observe also the preference of knowledge of men over knowledge of books—this is where our Southern politicians get their wiliness. And you will note finally the strong emphasis upon religiosity.

(It has also been claimed that this tragic awareness perhaps together with the religiosity is responsible for the great literary productiveness of the South today. That is a most interesting thesis to examine, but it is a subject for a different lecture.)

For a preliminary, this has been rather long, but I have felt it essential to present the South as a concrete historical reality. One of the things that has prevented a better understanding between North and South, in my firm belief, is that to the North the South has never seemed quite real. It has seemed like something out of fiction, or out of that department of fiction called romance. So many of its features are violent, picturesque, extravagant. With its survivals of the medieval synthesis, its manners that recall bygone eras, its stark social cleavages, its lost cause, its duels, its mountain flask, its romantic and sentimental songs, it appears more like a realm of fable than a geographical quarter of these United States. Expressed in the refrain of a popular song, "Is It True What They Say About Dixie?" the thought seems to be that the South is a kind of never never land from which the nation draws most of its romance and sentiment, but to which, for this very reason, you do not assign the same weight in the equation as you do to the other sections. Well the sentiment and the romance are there, in considerable measure, but there is a substratum of reality too. People are born and die in the same way as elsewhere: if you prick them, they bleed. The vast majority of them have to work for a living and in a hot climate too. The South also votes in national elections. For this reason, especially, it is important that the nation should see it as a reality and not a fiction, understand it better, both with respect to its likenesses and its differences. (And I certainly would assent to the proposition that the South ought to understand the nation better.) In the foregoing I have tried to present to you something of the peculiar history and formation of the South. In the time remaining I shall try to explain some of the peculiar—in the sense of being fairly distinct in this country—attributes of mind and outlook. It is scarcely necessary to add that these have many connections with that history.

I shall begin by saying something about the attitude toward

nature. This is a matter so basic to one's outlook or philosophy of life that we often tend to overlook it. Yet if we do overlook it, we find there are many things coming later which we cannot straighten out.

Here the attitudes of Southerners and Northerners, taken in their most representative form, differ in an important respect. The Southerner tends to look upon nature as something which is given and something which is finally inscrutable. This is equivalent to saying that he looks upon it as the creation of a Creator. There follows from this attitude an important deduction, which is that man has a duty of veneration toward nature and the natural. Nature is not something to be fought, conquered and changed according to any human whims. To some extent, of course, it has to be used. But what man should seek in regard to nature is not a complete dominion but a *modus vivendi*—that is, a manner of living together, a coming to terms with something that was here before our time and will be here after it. The important corollary of this doctrine, it seems to me, is that man is not the lord of creation, with an omnipotent will, but a part of creation, with limitations, who ought to observe a decent humility in the face of the inscrutable.

The Northern attitude, if I interpret it correctly, goes much further toward making man the center of significance and the master of nature. Nature is frequently spoken of as something to be overcome. And man's well-being is often equated with how extensively he is able to change nature. Nature is sometimes thought of as an impediment to be got out of the way. This attitude has increasingly characterized the thinking of the Western world since the Enlightenment, and here again, some people will say that the South is behind the times, or even that it here is an element of the superstitious in the regard for nature in its originally given form. But however you account for the attitude, you will have to agree that it can have an important bearing upon one's theory of life and conduct. And nowhere is its influence more decisive than in the corollary attitude one takes toward "Progress."

One of the most widely received generalizations in this country is that the South is the "unprogressive section." If it is understood in the terms in which it is made, the charge is true. What is not generally understood, however, is that this failure to keep up with the march of progress is not wholly a matter of comparative poverty, comparative illiteracy, and a hot climate which discourages activity. Some of it is due to a philosophical opposition to Progress as it has been spelled out by industrial civilization. It is an opposition which stems from a different conception of man's proper role in life.

This is the kind of thing one would expect to find in those out-of-the-way countries in Europe called "unspoiled," but it is not the kind of thing one would expect to find in America. Therefore I feel I should tell you a little more about it. Back about 1930, at a time when this nation was passing through an extraordinary sequence of boom, bust, and fizzle, there appeared a collection of essays bearing the title *I'll Take My Stand*. The nature of this title, together with certain things contained, caused many people to view this as a reappearance of the old rebel yell. There were, however, certain differences. For one thing, the yell was this time issuing from academic halls, most of the contributors being affiliated in one way or another with Vanderbilt University. For another, the book did not concentrate upon past grievances, as I am afraid most Southern polemic has done, but rather upon present concerns. Its chief question was, where is industrialism going anyhow, and what are its gifts, once you look them in the mouth? This book has since become famous as "The Agrarian Manifesto." As far as content goes, I think it can fairly be styled a critique of progress, as that word is used in the vocabulary of modern publicity and boosting.

Although the indictment was made with many historical and social applications, the center of it was philosophical; and the chief criticism was that progress propels man into an infinite development. Because it can never define its end, it is activity for the sake of activity, and it is making things so that you will be able to make more things. And regardless of how much of it you have, you are never any nearer your goal because there is no goal. It never sits down to contemplate, and ask, what is the good life? but rather assumes that material acquisition answers all questions. Language something like this was employed by John Crowe Ransom, one of the most eloquent of the spokesmen, in his chapter, "Reconstructed but Unregenerate."

"Progress never defines its ultimate objective but thrusts its victims at once into an infinite series," Mr. Ransom said. And he continued, "Our vast industrial machine, with its laboratory center of experimentation, and its far-flung organs of mass production, is like a Prussianized state which is organized strictly for war and can never consent to peace." "Industrialism," he declared, "is rightfully a menial, of almost miraculous cunning, but no intelligence; it needs to be strongly governed, or it will destroy the economy of the household. Only a community of tough conservative habit can master it." The South, Mr. Ransom felt, was such a community, and he went on to praise it for its stability, its love of established things, its veneration of the past—for all of those qualities which are generally thought to make up Southern backwardness. Mr. Stark Young, the well-known novelist and theatrical critic, defended the ideal of aristocratic indulgence and aristocratic leadership. "We can put one thing in our pipes and smoke it," he wrote, "there will never again be distinction in the South until—somewhat contrary to the doctrine of popular and profitable democracy—it is generally clear that no man worth anything is possessed by the people, or sees the world under a smear of the people's wills and beliefs." There are many other pungent passages which might be quoted, but these should be enough to show that it was a militant book. As you can see, its bias was anti-industrial, anti-scientific, anti-popular. It defended the values of a culture rooted in the soil. Just what the effect was, however, is hard to estimate. But no one conversant with Southern history and culture will deny that it expressed some feelings which survive pretty strongly into the present and which may be found anywhere from the mansions of the *nouveau riche* in Atlanta to the mountain cabins of East Tennessee and Kentucky.

Another cardinal point, touched on here and there in the volume, is the Southerner's attachment to locality. The Southerner is a *local* person—to a degree unknown in other sections of the United States. You might say that he has lived by the principle that it is good for a man to have a local habitation and a name; it is still better when the two are coupled together. In olden days a good many Southerners tried to identify their names and their homes: thus we read in history of John Taylor of Caroline; of Charles Carroll of Carrollton; of Robert Carter of Nomini Hall; of the Careys of Careysbroke; of the Lees of Westmoreland County. With the near liquidation of the old land-owning aristocracy this kind of thing became too feudal and fancy to keep up. Nevertheless, something of it remains in a widespread way still; the Southerner always thinks of himself as being from somewhere, as belonging to some spot of earth. If he is of the lucky few, it may be to an estate or a plantation; if not that, to a county; and if not to a county at least to a state. He is a Virginian, or he is a Georgian in a sense that I have never encountered in the Middle West—though the Indiana Hoosiers may offer a fair approximation. Very often the mention of a name in an introduction will elicit the remark, "That is a Virginia name" or "That's a South Carolina name," whereupon there will occur an extensive genealogical discussion. Often this attachment to a locale will be accompanied by a minute geographical and historical knowledge of the region, a loving awareness of details, of the peculiar physiognomy of the place. Andrew Nelson Lytle once complained in an article that in the world since 1914, nobody has known who he was or where he was from. The South has certainly felt the pressure toward root-lessness and anonymity—which are sometimes named as among the chief causes of modern psychic disorders—but I believe it has resisted the pressure better than most parts of the United States and Europe. It still looks among a man's credentials for where he is from, and not all places, even in the South, are equal. Before a Virginian, a North Carolinian is supposed to stand cap in hand. And faced with the hauteur of an old family of Charleston, South Carolina, even a Virginian may shuffle his feet and look uneasy.

The pride of local attachment is a fact which has two sides; it is a vice and a virtue. It may lead to conceit, complacency, and ignorance of the world outside. It frequently does lead to an exaggerated estimate of the qualities and potentialities of the particular region or province. The nation as a whole is acquainted with it in the case of Texans, who have developed this Southern attribute in an extreme degree. I was teaching out in Texas about the time we were ending the Second World War. A jocular remark that was passed around with relish was: "I know we are going to win the war now. Texas is on our side." It was a fair gibe at Texan conceit.

But on the other side, provincialism is a positive force, which we ought to think about a long while before we sacrifice too much to political abstractionism. In the last analysis, pro-vincialism is your belief in yourself, in your neighborhood, in your reality. It is patriotism without belligerence. Convincing cases have been made to show that all great art is provincial in the sense of reflecting a place, a time, and a *Zeitgeist.* Quite a number of spokesmen have pleaded with the South *not* to give up her provincialism. Henry Watterson, a long-time editor of the Louisville *Courier Journal,* told an audience of Ken-tuckians, "The provincial spirit, which is dismissed from po-lite society in a half-sneering, half-condemnatory way is really one of the forces of human achievement. As a man loses his provincialism he loses, in part, his originality and, in this way, so much of his power as proceeds from his originality." He spoke caustically of "a miserable cosmopolitan frivolity stealing over the strong simple realism of by-gone times." He summed up by asking, "What is life to me if I gain the whole world and lose my province?"

Thirty years later Stark Young, writing in the agrarian manifesto to which I referred earlier, pursued the same theme. "Provincialism that is a mere ramification of some insistent egotism is only less nauseous than the same egotism in its purity . . . without any province to harp on. But provincialism proper is a fine trait. It is akin to a man's interest in his own center, which is the most deeply rooted consideration that he has, the source of his direction, health and soul. . . . People who give up their own land too readily need careful weighing, exactly as do those who are so with their convictions." What often looks like the Southerners' unreasoning loyalty to the South as a place has in this way been given some reasoned defense. Even Solomon said that the eyes of a fool are in the ends of the earth. One gives up the part for the whole only to discover that without parts there is no whole. But I have said enough about the cultural ideal of regionalism. If you would be interested in a book which brings these thoughts together in a systematic treatment, see Donald Davidson's *The Attack on Leviathan.*

Despite what I have said about this love for the particular, which is another name for love of the concrete, the Southern mind is not by habit analytical. In fact the Southern mind has little capacity for analysis and I think one could almost say that it is opposed on principle to analysis. There seems to exist a feeling that you do not get at the truth of a thing—or that you do not get at a truth worth having—by breaking the thing in pieces. This explains undoubtedly why the South has always done so poorly in business and technology, which demand analytical methods. The Southern mind is, on the other hand, synthetic and mythopoeic—it seeks out wholes, representations, symbols. Especially is it mythopoeic, or given to the creation of myths and stories. The American tall tale was a creation of the Southern frontier. And one cannot go into a mountain community in Eastern Kentucky or to a plantation in say, Alabama, and open his ear to the talk of the people without having borne in upon him an amazing wealth and variety of stories—dramatic, intense, sometimes grotesque. As a mine of material for the creative writer there is nothing to compare with it anywhere else in America. I have heard people ask where William Faulkner gets that stuff that goes into his novels—whether he dreams it in nightmares, and so on. No one who had spent any time in Mississippi with his ears open would have to ask that question. He would know to what extent incidents and stories of this kind enter into the imaginative life of Mississippians. This mythopoeic or poetic—in the Aristotelian sense—faculty is surely behind the present flowering of the Southern novel and short story. It has already given us an interesting body of fiction, and it may one day give us a great literature. The South is not so much sleeping as dreaming, and dreams sometimes beget creations!

Finally something must be said about the South's famous conservatism—famous or infamous, depending upon your point of view. It is certainly a significant fact, but it has not gone wholly uncriticized at home. Walter Hines Page, growing up as a young man in North Carolina, spoke bitterly of what he called "an unyielding stability of opinion." Having failed in his effort to do anything with it, he declared that "the only successful rebellion was an immediate departure." He then fled North, to become editor of *The Atlantic Monthly* and eventually our ambassador to Britain during the Wilson Administration. Ellen Glasgow satirized it in her urbane novels of Virginia life. Thomas Wolfe took a few hefty swings at it in his description of old Catawba. And there have been others who have complained of a stifling uniformity of thought on many subjects.

With some of these specific protests I would gladly agree, yet there is perhaps another light in which we can see this "unyielding stability of opinion." Stability has its uses, as every considerate man knows, and it is not too far-fetched to think of the South as the fly-wheel of the American nation. A fly-wheel is defined by the science of mechanics as a large wheel, revolving at a uniform rate, the function of which is to stabilize the speed of the machine, slowing it down if it begins to go too fast and speeding it up if it begins to go too slow. This function it performs through the physical force of inertia. There are certain ways in which the South has acted as a fly-wheel in our society. It has slowed down social change when that started moving rapidly. And, though this will surprise many people, it has speeded up some changes when change was going slowly. Without judging the political wisdom of these matters, I merely point out that without Southern order, the New Deal probably would have foundered. Without Southern votes, the Conscription act would not have been renewed in 1941. Generally speaking the South has always been the free trade section. It is not very romantic or very flattering to be given credit only for inertia. But conservatism is not always a matter of just being behind. Sometimes conservatives are in the lead. I could give you more examples of that if I had time. It requires little gathering up of thread to show that a mind produced by this heritage is diametrically opposed to communism. With its individualism, its belief in personality, its dislike of centralized government, and its religiosity, the South sees in the communist philosophy a combination of all it detests. If that issue comes to a showdown, which I hope does not happen, there will never be any doubt as to where the South stands.

I suspect that a good many of you entertain thoughts of changing the South, of making it just like the rest of the country, of seeing it "wake up." It seems to me that the South has been just on the verge of "waking up" ever since I have been reading things about it. My advice is to be modest in your hopes. The South is one of those entities to which one can apply the French saying, "the more it changes the more it remains the same." Even where you think you are making some headway, you may be only heading into quicksand. It waits until you are far enough in and then sucks you under. It is well to remember that the South is very proud of its past, hard as it has been; it does not want to be made over in anybody else's image, and it has had a century of experience in fighting changes urged on it from the outside. I agree with W. J. Cash that the Southern mind is one of the most intransigent on earth; that is, one of the hardest minds to change. Ridiculing its beliefs has no more effect, as far as I have been able to observe, than ridiculing a person's religious beliefs— and the Southerner's beliefs have been a kind of secular religion with him: that only serves to convince him further that he is right and that you are damned.

Intransigence in itself, however, is not good, of course. No mind ought to be impervious to suggestions and the influence of outside example. Intercommunication and cross fertilization are necessary. I covet a chance to talk someday to a Southern audience on what they need to learn from the North. But these express two-way relationships. It is a peculiar blindness to assume that the factors which have produced you are real, whereas the factors that have produced the other fellow are unreal. Those succeed best who go forward in the spirit of inquiry, seeking to understand the lines of force, and above all, realizing that there is something to be learned wherever complete lives are lived. With this kind of attitude it is possible for Virginia to learn from New England and New England from Virginia with a happy result that Parkman visualized but did not live to see.

THE SOUTH AND THE

AMERICAN UNION

Stretching from the Potomac River across the southeastern quarter of the United States in a broad arc into the plains of Texas is a region known geographically and politically as "the South." That this region has been distinctive by reason of its climate, type of produce, ethnic composition, culture, manners, and speech is known to every citizen of the country. That it existed for four years as an independent, if beleaguered, nation is one of the focal chapters of American history. All the while it has been a challenge, never very well met, to Americans to understand themselves historically.

The chief reason for this is that in the minds of most Americans there exists, like an inarticulate premise, the doctrine of American exceptionalism. This assumption is that the United States is somehow exempt from the past and present fate, as well as from many of the necessities, of other nations. Ours is a special creation, endowed with special immunities. As a kind of millennial state, it is not subject to the trials and divisions that have come upon others through time and history. His-

Rubin and Kilpatrick, eds., *The Lasting South* (1957), 46–68.

tory, it is commonly felt, consists of unpleasant things that happen to other people, and America bade goodbye to the sorrows along with the vices of the Old World.

It must be owned in fairness that two facts lend some plausibility to this seductive notion. One is that the American Union began at a definite point in time. The dates of its origin can be cited by any schoolboy reasonably well up on his books. Its beginning does not have to be traced sketchily in a mist-shrouded antiquity. It became a republic by *fiat*, as it were, and even the documents involved in its creation survive for our inspection.

The second is that this union of States was formed by men who sat down and discussed among themselves principles and ideals before drawing up a form of government. This was, of course, a rational undertaking, which many find more agreeable to remember than the prior fact that the nation owes its existence to the battlefield. The thought of forming a government *de novo* at a definite point in time does therefore encourage the conclusion that here is an exception to history. Our flag-waving orators—and flag-waving historians too—have seldom failed to make special claims for us on the basis of it. The feeling pleases that to be an American carries qualification and exemption.

The Founding Fathers who worked over the problems of government that hot summer of 1787 in Philadelphia, though conscious of their great opportunity, were on the whole realists. They were under no illusion that their creation would be exempt from the trials of history. A great political thinker has written: "The existence of man in political society is historical existence; and a theory of politics, if it penetrates to principles, must at the same time be a theory of history." Most of the State delegates at Philadelphia had read history soberly, and one lesson they had gathered was that evil continuously arises from the nature of man and is capable of perverting the best of institutions to wicked purposes. They desired a government with greater power, yet the problem of restraining that power was never absent from their thoughts. Abuses of power had recently driven them to armed rebellion, and they wanted no more of these. On the other hand, they thought they saw grave dangers in excessive democracy and the anarchy it might produce.

The device which they created out of an awareness of these two perils is, as is well known, a system of checks and balances, whereby any branch of the government, if it took the road to aggrandizement, could be restrained by one or both of the others. As most of the Founding Fathers felt that man needs to be guarded against his own worse impulses, so they believed that government needs to be protected against itself. It was a brilliant conception, which speaks well of their foresight of things, and their realization that the new government would not be exempt from contingencies or the temptations that might dazzle men in future circumstances.

Not everything was taken care of equally well, however. We must remember the heat, the fatigue, the limits of time, the uncertainties, the pressures of private business, and above all a widespread and determined opposition to the structure of union known to be under design. Some sleeping dogs had to be left alone. What about the principle of rebellion, so recently invoked and blessed with success? The Declaration of Independence certainly suggested that the right to rebel was a right inherent in all peoples. Might it not be asserted again sometime? In such case the American revolutionaries might discover that they did but "teach bloody instructions, which, being taught, return to plague the inventor."

What about the true locus of sovereignty in the new nation? The States claimed it, yet the new instrument of government seemed to gather many sovereign powers to itself. Could sovereignty be divided? Was not the idea of a dual sovereignty just a way of deceiving yourself? Of all the questions left unresolved by the new instrument of union, this was to be the most fateful. Yet it was a question too dangerous for this hour, since most of the States were extremely jealous of their rights, and only the most conciliatory attitude could get them to ratify at all. Despite the great influence of Alexander Hamilton, the important State of New York ratified by the slim margin of thirty to twenty-seven and then stated that it did not regard its ratification as irrevocable. Virginia went even further and spelled out in its ordinance of ratification the right to resume the powers thus delegated if Virginia should ever become convinced that they were being abused. North Carolina stayed out for two years until it could be persuaded that its people were not entering a combine that might be perverted to their injury.

When the issue of the scope of Federal power was raised a decade later, in connection with the Alien and Sedition Acts, the famous Kentucky Resolutions, of which Jefferson himself was the author, affirmed that "free government is founded in jealousy, not in confidence; it is jealousy and not confidence which prescribes limited constitutions to bind down those we are obliged to trust with power." It was resolved accordingly that "the several States composing the United States of America are not united on the principle of unlimited submission to the General Government." These words and actions fairly indicate the attitude of the States in subscribing to the compact of union. Had they then been told they were entering a door which could never be opened again, it is questionable whether a single one would have entered.

The Constitution was, especially in its bill of rights, a creation of eighteenth-century classical liberalism, which looked upon the freedom of the individual from state coercion as the highest political object. As John C. Calhoun was to point out later, the constitution of a free state is primarily a *negative* document in the sense that it consists of prohibitions and restraints imposed upon the authority of the state. It is a fixed obstacle to that government by confidence, to echo the language of the Kentucky Resolutions, under which so much oppression in the Old World had been possible. The ways in which men seek power over other men are almost infinitely various and subtle, and it was felt that if the new government were left to judge the extent of its own powers, there could be no way of forestalling eventual tyranny. The true aim of a constitution, from the standpoint of classical liberalism, is not to create empowerments, but to "bind down the powers of men to do mischief." Several, if not most, of the States desired to preserve some form of veto in case that power should exceed its prescribed bounds.

In essence, what the Founders established was a federal republic of limited delegated powers. How limited those powers were was the subject of diverse interpretations. But even in the North at this time Senator Maclay of Pennsylvania could write in his Journal for March 22, 1790: "Is it to be expected that a federal law passed directly against the sense of a whole State will ever be executed in that State?" Now it is necessary to follow some of the great historic forces that turned these questions of freedom and organization into concrete issues.

Even at the time of the Revolution there was an awareness of important differences between North and South. The leaders of that movement did their best to keep them in the background, but they were often mentioned privately. These differences were not merely in economic life, but also in what may be designated as "regime," or general way of life. Historical realism shows that people living side by side do not necessarily grow to resemble one another. They may grow apart, and this the North and South did rather rapidly after the second war with Great Britain.

Many attempts have been made to characterize the Northern and Southern minds; few of them satisfy our perceptions. I am inclined to think that no account of the mind of the South can be valid unless it stresses the extent to which the Southerner is classical man. Even in the South of today one can find surviving large segments of the classical-Christian-medieval synthesis. It was not unusual for a Southerner of the upper class to steep himself in Roman history and name his sons after Roman generals. Here the Greek Revival in architecture had its inception; and here, in the region influenced by Charleston, the idea of Greek democracy was not only practiced but articulated in theory, as Vernon Parrington demonstrated in his great work on American culture. Here law was an exalted profession, and the Ciceronian ideal of rhetoric was admired. The fact that the Southerner stayed wedded to the idea of classical liberalism in government, with its fixed limitations of power, may be taken as further evidence of his classical spirit.

The Southern world-outlook was much like that which Spengler describes as the Apollonian. It knew nothing of infinite progressions but rather loved fixed limits in all things; it rejected the idea of ceaseless becoming in favor of "simple accepted statuesque becomeness." It saw little point in restless striving, but desired a permanent settlement, a coming to terms with nature, a recognition of what is in its self-sustaining form. The Apollonian feeling, as Spengler remarks, is of a world of "coexistent individual things," and it is tolerant as a matter of course. Other things are because they have to be; one marks their nature and their limits and learns to get along with them. The desire to dominate and to proselytize is foreign to it. As Spengler further adds, "there are no Classical world-improvers." From this comes the Southern kind of tolerance, which has always impressed me as fundamentally different from the Northern kind. It is expressed in the Southerner's easy-going ways and his willingness to let things grow where they sprout. He accepts the irremediability of a certain amount of evil and tries to fence it around instead of trying to stamp it out and thereby spreading it. His is a classical acknowledgment of tragedy and of the limits of power.

This mentality is by nature incompatible with its great rival, the Faustian. Faustian man is essentially a restless striver, a yearner after the infinite, a hater of stasis, a man who is unhappy unless he feels that he is making the world over. He may talk much of tolerance, but for him tolerance is an exponent of power. His tolerance tolerates only the dogmatic idea of tolerance, as anyone can discover for himself by getting to know the modern humanitarian liberal. For different opinions and ways of life he has not respect, but hostility or contemptuous indifference, until the day when they can be brought around to conform with his own. Spengler describes such men as torn with the pain of "seeing men be other than they would have them be and the utterly un-Classical desire to devote their life to their reformation." It happened that Southern tolerance, standing up for the right to coexistence of its way of life, collided at many points with the Faustian desire to remove all impediments to its activity and make over things in its own image. Under the banner first of reform and then of progress, the North challenged the right to continue of a civilization based on the Classical ideal of fixity and stability. Bruce Catton gives a characteristic expression to this Faustian urge when he writes in an article on the Civil War that "America would cease to have room . . . for a feudal plantation economy below the Ohio, veneered with chivalry and thin romance and living in an outworn dream. . . ."

This Southern philosophy of life, which the North has generally regarded as a stumbling block in the road of progress, may be characterized more directly with reference to three things: the creation, the nature of man, and the ends of living.

To most Southerners the term "creation" comes with its literal meaning. The world is something created for man, but certainly not by him. He can understand some of its intermediate principles and relations, but its ultimate secrets are forever beyond him. He is granted some dominion over it, but not an unlimited one, since that would be setting him on a level with the Creator. Basically nature is right in being as it is. Change for its own sake is not good, and many of nature's dispositions are best left as they are. He has a degree of reverence for the natural order of things and he suspects *hubris* in a desire to change that order radically.

Toward man the Southerner takes an attitude inculcated by orthodox religion and by tragedy also. Man is a mixture of good and evil, and he can never be perfected in this life. The notion of his natural goodness is a delusive theory which will blow up any social order that is predicated upon it. Far from being a vessel of divinity, as the New England Transcendentalists taught, he is a container of cussedness. It is fatuity to suppose that his every impulse is good, for many of his impulses are anti-social and some of them are suicidal. He needs to be protected against himself by the teachings of religion, by law, and by custom. The Southerner has always been *conservative* in his view of man in the sense that he has been pessimistic. Yet this kind of pessimism, just because it refuses to fret over optimistic impossibilities, leaves large room for *joie de vivre.* Laughter and good humor have always been native to the region, with the Negro joining in rather freely.

The South's attitude toward the ends of living has deeply influenced its mores and institutions. In the eyes of its energetic neighbor to the north it has never been sufficiently up and doing. But there is a profound difference between accepting your place and your role and working out the most practicable regimen of enjoyments, and conceiving life as an unceasing struggle which has as its object the reordering of everything. "Southern inefficiency" is a notorious phrase, but then "efficiency" is a term out of science and business. If you set little store by science and business, you will not be much influenced by the rhetorical force of "efficiency." True, life cannot be lived without some sense of making progress, but progress may occur through intensification and elaboration; and the art of living in the South remains a rather complex thing. The saying of John Peale Bishop is worth recalling, that the South excelled in two things which the French deem essential to civilization: a code of manners and a native cuisine. Both are apt to suffer when life is regarded as a means to something else. Efficiency and charm are mortal enemies, and Southern charm indubitably derives from a carelessness about the efficient aspects of life.

One further fact is of great consequence: the South has maintained, generally speaking, a social rather than a business civilization; one can scarcely imagine a Southerner's saying, as Calvin Coolidge once said, that "the business of America is business." This means that the claims of business have usually had to yield precedence to what has been considered socially desirable or important. It probably would have been "good business," in one sense, for the South to have maintained a nonsegregated school system: It might have cost less; but financial considerations have been powerless against social objections. Likewise the Southerner has often been chided for asking "Who are you?" rather than "What can you do?" But in a world that spins on an axis of social relations, who you are is more important than your efficiency rating. For the Southerner, things tend to derive their reality and their importance from social, not business life, where personality counts, and manners are a deference to personality.

In one of the novels of F. Hopkinson Smith there occurs the story of an old Virginia gentleman who lived on a decayed plantation. Whenever visitors came, he insisted on directing the conversation to the past glories of the ancestral hall. On one occasion he mentioned, purely incidentally, that there were coal outcroppings on the estate. This led to the discovery of extensive coal deposits, which eventually launched the old gentleman into prosperity. But he had not thought the matter of coal worth discussing beside what one ancestor had done at Williamsburg and another at Yorktown. His was a world of human relations. The relative incapacity for business of the Southerner has cost him sadly in this acquisitive world. The choice involves, of course, the contentious subject of the order of values.

While these attitudes were growing deep-rooted in the South, the North was developing in a different direction. Its world outlook traces back fairly clearly to the Reformation and the Puritan Revolution. Especially was the Puritan mentality influential upon the North. A reformist type of mind, it was indifferent toward tradition, inclined to be suspicious of the arts and graces as snares set by the Evil One, and proudly conscious of a duty to make the world over. This Northern or "Yankee" mind, which has been received by the world as the typical American mind, is excellently shaped and disciplined for success in the practical sphere. It focuses sharply, knows how to keep feeling under restraint; it is shrewd in estimating practical consequences. There has never been such a mind for getting things done.

But as always in this ambiguous world, positive qualities carry liabilities in their train, and this mind does not always impress others favorably. To some it seems too insistent on the explicit, too lacking in depths and psychic recesses, too deprived of what might be called resonance. To some it appears like a house kept in perfect neatness and order, but lacking in charm. When the Southerner or the European or the Latin American communicates with this dust-free, unencumbered mind, he finds that things which are significant to him strike no response. Especially is this true of matters of sentiment, and he finds shocking the relegation of sentiment to a kind of Sunday-morning observance. The tendency seems to be to think scientifically and hence abstractly in the interest of manipulation rather than concretely out of respect or pleasure in contemplation. Local attachments seem drag-weights, and allegiance is given, as Tocqueville pointed out, to something large and grandiose. States' rights do not mean much unless you have learned to know and to prize the special contours of your State.

Nowhere has the Northern mind more clearly embraced the Faustian concept than in the idea of progress. There is the constant outreaching, the denial of limits, the willingness to dissolve all into endless instrumental activity, to which even some American philosophers have supplied theoretical support. Hence the incessant urge to be doing, to be transforming, to effect some external change between yesterday and today. The mood of the Americans, another French critic of a century ago remarked, is that of an army on the march. The language of conquest fills the air. They will "master nature"; they will "attack problems"; they will "control energy"; they will "overcome space and time." The endlessness of progress in these terms is the most generally accepted dogma. And thus enchanted by the concept of an infinite expansion, they reject the classical philosophy as too constricting.

The Southerner, to sum up the contrast, has tended to live in the finite, balanced, and proportional world which Classical man conceived. In Cicero and Horace he has found congenial counsellors about human life. The idea of stasis is not abhorrent to him, because it affords a ground for the identity of things. Life is not simply a linear progression, but a drama, with rise and fall. Happiness may exist as much in contemplation as in activity. Experience alone is not good; it has to be accompanied by the human commentary. From this, I believe, has come the South's great fertility in myth and anecdote. It is not so much a sleeping South as a dreaming one, and out of dreams come creations that affect the imagination.

In this way two civilizations of quite different impulse grew up in the United States. Was it inevitable that one should make war on the other and offer it the alternative of being "reconstructed" or perishing? It was not inevitable if you believe that the coexistence of unlike beings is possible. Diversity is a rule of nature, and it would be ideal if the cultures of the world would practice a doctrine of live and let live. It would also be ideal if empires and large nations would consent to a separation of their parts in times of irreconcilable difference. When personalities begin to clash in a household, it is often best for one party to remove and set up an independent establishment of its own. This is what the Americans did in 1775; and the British, taught by this painful experience and others, have since recognized the right to withdraw from the Empire. The Soviet Union has written the principle of secession into its constitution. But the Americans of the North and West have generally viewed the idea as scandalous—or perhaps as blasphemous against the notion of the perfected millennial state.

The events leading up to the historical separation of the two sections are too well known to need detailed review. Economic and political disagreements arose to accentuate the underlying differences. The first issue to poison the relations between North and South following the "Era of Good Feeling" was the tariff. It is unquestionable that the protective tariff has worked great injury to the South from that date until, as one might say, the South was partly transformed into an image of the North through industrialization. For the interest of the South as a region producing agricultural surpluses has historically lain in free trade. The South sent abroad rice, indigo, cotton, and tobacco and took in exchange the manufactured products of Europe. The North began to use the Federal Union to put an artificially high price upon manufactured goods in order to help its industries. The South was thereby forced into the position of selling cheap and buying dear. All this meant that the agrarian way of livelihood, characterized by Jefferson as the most innocent form of vocation, could not be continued except under penalty of a heavy tax. As Abbott Lawrence of Massachusetts wrote to Daniel Webster regarding the tariff of 1828: "This bill if adopted as amended will keep the South and West in debt to New England for the next hundred years." If the South had ever been able to save and fuse what was taken from it by the protective tariff system, it could have afforded a Harvard and a Yale, with a few Amhersts, Dartmouths, and Williamses thrown in for good measure.

There was of course the curse of slavery. During the Civil War one ingenious Northern general pronounced the Negroes to be "contrabands." Contrabands they may well have been from the beginning, and I have often wondered why the sellers of this article were not held more reprehensible than the users, as is true of those who peddle cocaine. A large number of these hapless slaves were brought to America in New England bottoms, and more than one fortune in Newport and New Bedford owes its origin to profits in black flesh. The facts could be represented thus: New England sold the slaves to the South, then later declared their possession immoral and confiscated the holding. The morality of the case was less clear to the Southerners than to the agitators of Boston, and even Lincoln, if we may judge by his less political utterances, tended to believe in the common guilt of the nation.

Alienation of the sections was widened by mutual attacks upon character. Some of these reached an extreme of violence which one would hardly associate with Victorian America. A few were the products of reformist agitators giving way to their feelings, but an appreciable number seem to have been the work of the new journalism, which finds it profitable to stir up strife by assailing character, even if the character is that of a straw man. The South, which had more than its share of pride, retorted with frantic boast and foolish word. It certainly went out of its way to wound Northern vanity. It charged the North with having the deadly virtues of the middle class while claiming for itself the virtues of the chivalric age. On the whole, the South did not have a clear picture of itself or its resources. Being long on the defensive and seeing the tide running against it, the South created a number of phantasms which were to serve it ill. This is what that dour North Carolinian Hinton Helper tried to point out in his *The Impending Crisis.*

Whether the grievances of these States were sufficient to justify a withdrawal from the Union has been argued long and voluminously. Political separations of this kind, as Jefferson observed in the Declaration of Independence, should not be undertaken for light and transient causes. On the other hand, as Calhoun was later to argue, making the Federal government the sole judge and umpire of its authority would be setting up an engine of government from which there would be no kind of appeal. To take the position that every State remained forever a member of the Union, whether it liked it or not and whether it suffered by the association or not, certainly involved grave assumptions of political authority. There is at least as much idealism in the statement of Lee that "a Union held together by bayonets has no charms for me" as in the claim that the Union is forever indivisible. The Southern position goes back, in political theory, to the principle that there are some matters on which a majority cannot override a minority.

The South has always maintained that in this great quarrel it had the law on its side. Its case for the legality of secession rested upon an interpretation of the Constitution in the light of its creation. This contended that the Federal Union was a compact of limited, delegated authority, to which the States voluntarily acceded between 1787 and 1789. The *Federalist Papers* had referred to the States as "distinct and independent sovereigns." Madison, writing in the *Federalist No. 39*, had said: "The proposed government cannot be deemed a NATIONAL one; since its jurisdiction extends to certain enumerated objects only, and leaves to the several States a residuary and inviolable sovereignty over all other objects." These expressions became common currency of the discussion. It would be cynical to assume that this was mere bait, held out to catch reluctant fish which thereafter would be permanently hooked. Surmises of the kind, however, could have been in the minds of New York, Virginia, and other cautious signers. Later one of the textbooks on political science taught at West Point—and this has important bearing upon the decisions of Southern officers in 1861—was William Rawle's *View of the Constitution of the United States,* which accepted the doctrine of State sovereignty.

Legally, secession was seen by the Southern States simply as a repeal of the ordinances of ratification they had adopted 70 years earlier. In the Southern continuum, 70 years is nothing. When South Carolina voted 120 to 0 to rescind her rat- ification, she was repealing in her sovereign capacity what she had enacted in her sovereign capacity. The enactment of secession was not treason under any written law. It might have been treason to a concept, but that is an extra-legal matter, and the concept was not the South's. When Bruce Catton struggles to characterize the heinousness of secession, he can only soar upon wings of metaphor and call it "a wanton laying of hands upon the Ark of the Covenant."

For an American political leader, Abraham Lincoln has a remarkable record of consistency, but on this matter he was not consistent. Speaking in the House of Representatives on January 12, 1848, he made as good a case for the right of secession as the most ardent Southern separatist could have wished for. With reference to Texas and the incidents which had led to the Mexican War, he said:

> Any people anywhere, being inclined and having the power, have the *right* to rise up, and shake off the existing government, and form a new one that suits them better. This is a most valuable—a most sacred right—a right, which we hope and believe is to lib- erate the world. Nor is this right confined to cases in which the whole people of an existing government, may choose to exercise it. Any portion of such people that *can, may* revolutionize, and make their *own*, of so much territory as they inhabit.

But thirteen years later, when faced with a concrete instance of this, he saw secession in an entirely opposite way. Then a portion of a people of a government, having their own terri- tory, revolutionized and set up a government of their own. He countered their claim of right to do this by saying that he had taken an oath to support the Constitution, and that further- more every nation has an inherent duty to protect its integrity. The objections to this position, as the South saw them, were that the Constitution was silent on the question of secession, and that the right to revolution was a right inherent in the people if the American Revolution had any ideological basis. It was not without reason that Southerners in 1861 said, "I am no more frightened by the word 'rebel' than were my forefathers in 1775."

During the War, the western counties of the State of Virginia, having been for decades at odds politically with the remainder of the State, withdrew and set up a State of their own. The Federal government showed no compunction about the legality of this secession, for West Virginia was admitted as an independent State in 1863 and has never been "reconstructed" into Virginia. In this instance Lincoln seems to have reversed himself again and to have upheld the right to revolutionize which he had emphasized in his speech on the Mexican War. It begins to look like a matter of whose ox is gored.

Another case in point is the treatment of Jefferson Davis. The passions of the victorious side demanded that he be arrested and tried for treason, and he spent about two years in prison at Fortress Monroe. But when the task of getting up the prosecution was undertaken, it was realized that there was no law under which he could be convicted—this, it should be added, was a pre-Nuremberg doubt, which troubled men in a day when nations were unwilling to invent *ex post facto* law by which to hang defeated enemies. Acquittal would have been a great embarrassment to the victors, who had no desire to lose in court what they had won in war. Therefore Davis, instead of being hanged on a sour apple tree, went free with no other penalty than disqualification for office-holding, which was provided by the newly enacted Fourteenth Amendment.

Thus the South has remained convinced that whatever the differing moral views of slavery and secession, it had the law on its side as the law had come down from 1787. From the standpoint of these considerations, perhaps the best description of the terrible conflict which ensued is that of Gerald Johnson, who called it a war between "the Law and the Prophets." On the side of the South was the law, with its promise of respect for the sovereignty of the States and its recognition of slavery. It was with reference to this that Alexander Stephens, vice-president of the Confederacy, was to entitle his apologia *A Constitutional View of the Late War Between the States.* On the side of the North were the prophets of emancipation, industrialization, and nationalization. Of these the most potent was nationalization, and it should be remembered that Lincoln professed his willingness to preserve slavery if by so doing he might preserve the Union.

The potency contained in the cry "Union" at this time must always be of curious interest to students of political psychology. "Union" became in the North the paramount slogan of the War, and the popular term of opprobrium applied to Confederates was not "slaveholders," but "secesh." Middle Westerners in particular favored "saving the Union," sometimes to the exclusion of all other issues involved. What was there to make the idea of union sacred?

Considered in its essence, union is an instrumentality of power. This fact appears in the common saying that "in union there is strength." But what is this strength wanted for? Unless it has some clearly understood applicability, the mere preservation of union is a means without an end. And because one of the prime purposes of the idealistic founders of the nation was to check the growth of a centralized, autonomous power, the things that have been done in the name of "Union" might lead one to say that it is the darling of the foes rather than of the friends of the American experiment in free government. H. L. Mencken once observed that there are, of course, advantages in union, but that they usually go to the wrong people. They usually go to the ones whose real interest is in power and the wielding of it over other men. The instrumentality of union, with its united strength and its subordination of the parts, is an irresistible temptation to the power-hungry of every generation. The strength of union may first be exercised in the name of freedom, but once it has been made monopolistic and unassailable, it will, if history teaches anything, be used for other purposes.

One cannot feign surprise, therefore, that thirty years after the great struggle to consolidate and unionize American power, the nation embarked on its career of imperialism. The new nationalism enabled Theodore Roosevelt, than whom there was no more staunch advocate of union, to strut and bluster and intimidate our weaker neighbors. Ultimately it launched America upon its career of world imperialism, whose results are now being seen in indefinite military conscription, mountainous debt, restriction of dissent, and other abridgements of classical liberty. We must be "unified" at home so that we can be strong abroad—indeed, there are now those who would outlaw party division over foreign policy. But why does one have to be strong abroad? From the clear perspective which the Founding Fathers seem to have enjoyed, Charles Pinckney of South Carolina observed: "Conquest or superiority among other powers is not, or ought not ever to be, the object of republican systems." But this was not the view of those who were to make use of the great consolidation effected by the Civil War.

To the mass of soldiers in blue and to the Northern civilians, "Union" seems to have been a kind of mystique—a vague attitude against which political and metaphysical demonstrations of reserved rights had no power to make an impression. "Union" was hypostatized and bowed down to, and the question of whether separation does not have some advantages also was ruled out as not in keeping with the times. The material fact is that under this potent cry the union of the United States was shifted in 1865 from a basis of voluntary consent to one of force.

When the Joint Committee on Reconstruction presented its report in 1866, it opened with a terse description. "They [the Southern States] were in a state of utter exhaustion, having protracted their struggle against Federal authority until all hope of successful resistance had ceased, and layed down their arms only because there was no longer any power to use them. The people of those States were left bankrupt in their public finances and shorn of the private wealth which had before given them power and influence."

This might appear a situation dire enough, yet the South still had to face about a dozen years of having its bones picked. To make real what went on during the years of so-called "Reconstruction" demands the pen of a novelist, and it is regrettable in a way that this chapter of our national history has not received more attention from creative writers. Lincoln had taken the view that the States were really never out of the Union, and had mentioned that if in any Southern State ten per cent of the population—surely a curious fraction, but perhaps the best that could be hoped for—were found "loyal," that State might resume its standing and function within the Union. But this was, as Professor E. Merton Coulter has pointed out, a conservative solution, and no such thing was in the minds of the Radical Junto which took over after Lincoln's death. They saw their chance "not only to remake Southerners in many respects that had no direct relationship to the war; they would also remake the Union by not only degrading the Southern States but in the process also depriving all States of much of their power and bestowing it upon the central government. Here was the fruition of a growth in extremism evident in the North long before the war broke out, but now made easy by that war's having been fought."

Under their program the Southern States were to be held in the Union as far as the purposes of rule and exploitation went, but kept out of the Union as far as rights and the ability to protest effectively were concerned. This was a method of having the States and eating them too, and it was highly profitable both politically and financially.

The invading army was in control. Down from the North swarmed carpetbaggers looking for a good thing, and up popped scalawags ready to assist them. The Negro, who, it must be admitted, behaved considerably better than circumstances might have warranted, was a useful auxiliary. State governments were set up consisting of outsiders with various axes to grind, the scum of the local populace, and the misled and eventually victimized freedmen. There ensued a carnival of debauchery, corruption, and political buffoonery such as no other modern nation has witnessed. In a hundred ways, kangaroo legislation robbed the stricken people not only of their present but of their future substance also. Over the whole affair hangs an aura of unreality, so that even the most cynical might question how this was possible after a hundred years of American traditions. The best verdict on Reconstruction was written by Richard Harvey Cain, a Negro editor of Charleston: "When the smoke and fighting is over, the Negroes have nothing gained, the whites have nothing left, while the jackals have all the booty." It is proof of the public morality which existed in the Southern people as a whole that these States were eventually able to recover, instead of sinking permanently to the level of the worst mismanaged Latin American countries.

William A. Dunning, the Columbia professor of history, expressed admiration for the way in which Reconstruction was carried out against "a hostile white population, a hostile executive at Washington, a doubtful if not decidedly hostile Supreme Court, a divided Northern sentiment with regard to Negro suffrage, and an active and skillfully directed Democratic Party." On the same principle one might express admiration for the way in which the South managed to preserve some remnants of its civilization against an invading army and an alien and partly disaffected race, with a government in which it was not represented claiming authority over it. Some of the means, for example the Ku Klux Klan, were irregular, but essentially it was the political genius of Jefferson, of Washington, of Madison, and of Pinckney expressing itself in times of trouble and oppression.

The nightmare of Reconstruction ended in 1877, after the South, in a frank "deal" to get rid of the occupying forces, decided not to contest the election whereby the Republican Hayes had fraudulently won over Tilden. But it was another twenty years before the South was able to struggle back to its feet economically, and it was even longer before it could begin the establishment of an adequate school system. There was no Marshall Plan for the Southern States. Instead, the South's economic disadvantage was prolonged, if not intensified, by even higher protective tariffs and by its contributions to national pensions for a clamorous GAR.

The era of Reconstruction is thus an indelible memory in Southern minds. In effect the period was a forging process which hardened the South's determination not to be assimilated into the national pattern, but to preserve her character and autonomy in all ways that could not be prevented. The palpable unfairness of the era even brought recruits to the South's side, for Kentucky, which had been divided during the war, turned pro-Southern and Democratic in politics as soon as it saw the uses that were being made of the victory. If, as President Edwin Alderman of the University of Virginia wrote, "under the play of great historic forces this region developed so strong a sense of unity in itself as to issue in a claim of separate nationality, which it was willing to defend in a great war," it seems equally true that its experience during the great upheaval confirmed the feeling that it was in spirit and needs a separate nation. It might be viewed as an American Ireland, Poland, or Armenia, not indeed unified by a different religious allegiance from its invader, but different in its way of life, different in the values it ascribed to things by reason of its world outlook, and made more different after the war by its necessary confrontation of the tragic view, which success and optimism were holding in abeyance in the North. The South has in a way made a religion of its history, or its suffering, and any sign of waning faith or laxness of spirit may be met by a reminder of how this leader endured and that one died, in the manner of saints and saviors. It has, in fact, its hierarchy of saints, and the number of public tributes offered up to Lee and Jackson must run to untold thousands. Being a Southerner is definitely a spiritual condition, like being a Catholic or a Jew; and members of the group can recognize one another by signs which are eloquent to them, though too small to be noticed by an outsider.

There are some who will say that this is talk of old, unhappy, far-off things, and battles long ago. But a nation is made what it is by its past; there is no identity without historicity. And the South, far from being ashamed of its past, as a good many outsiders seem to assume, is proud of it just because that past is a story of resistance to many things urged or forced upon it from the outside. If these things are added together, they will be seen to comprise rather completely what is known as modernism or "progress." In the political field the South has resisted nationalization and centralization of authority, sometimes with cannon and musket, and sometimes with political maneuver, as in the case of the States' Rights Party of 1948. In the economic and financial field, there has been an instinctive opposition to industrialism; and if the spirit is not very conspicuous now, it has flourished strongly enough in the past to warn the South against mechanization and standardization. Southerners owe a debt of gratitude to Russell Kirk, who comes from Michigan, for pointing out that "Despite its faults of head and heart, the South—alone among the civilized communities of the nineteenth century—had hardihood sufficient for an appeal to arms against the iron new order, which, a vague instinct whispered to most Southerners, was inimical to the sort of humanity they knew." The historic South has been indeed "unprogressive," but defiantly so and on principle.

Pragmatists have never been able to convince the South that religion is just another one of the cylinders of the engine that produces "progress." The South retains a belief that religion is the expression of man's poetic, tragic, and metaphysical intuitions of life, and that as such religion is tied neither to science nor utility. Hence the South's famous fundamentalism and literalism, the footwashings of the primitive Baptists, the doctrinal rigor of Southern Presbyterians. Believing in the necessity of man's redemption, the people—especially country people—typically like preachers who preach hell fire and damnation better than those who put their faith in psychiatry and socialism. The preference is essentially for the older religiousness, such as one finds before the age of rationalism.

By the same token, the South has never lost sight of the fact that society means structuring and differentiation, and that "society" and "mass" are antithetical terms. It has never fallen for a simple equalitarianism, nor has it embraced the sentimentalism that anyone on the bottom *ipso facto* belongs on top. Its classes have gotten along together with surprisingly little envy because they have been fused into a society by a vision which has kept subordinated the matter of varying degrees of success in the pursuit of money. Because the mass looks with hatred upon any sign of the structuring of society, the South has been viewed with special venom by Socialist and Communist radicals, past and present. One of their prime goals is to break down the South's historic social structure and replace it with a mass condition reflecting only materialist objectives.

These facts and others which could be cited mean that the South remains a great stronghold of humanism, perhaps the greatest left in the Western World. It has opposed by word and deed the kind of future portended by George Orwell's *1984*. In doing so it has developed considerable toughness and resourcefulness, and it has never run from a fight. Its people still have no desire to be pulled in and made to conform to a regimented mass state, by which homes that look like homes, whether in Tidewater or in the Blue Ridge, must give way to the ant-colonies of public housing, and the traditional courtesy of a region must change into "public relations."

Today the South is faced with fresh assaults upon its regime and its order of values. All the while it has known that what grudging respect it has obtained from the North has come because the South has maintained the standards of white civilization. It knows that if it were to accept without reservation the dictates of the Supreme Court, it might be turned into something like those "mixed sections" found in large Northern cities. Such sections are there spoken of in whispers, and those who have the money flee as from the plague when they find a neighborhood beginning to "go." The South cannot learn these facts from Northern newspapers and journals, which maintain a curious attitude of unreality upon the subject. But it notes the behavior of Northerners who come South to live; it learns of the plummeting of Northern real estate values where "integration" is on the march; and if a Southerner happens to journey North, he finds the hotels and resorts conspicuously unmixed. As Bishop Hugh McCandless of New York's Protestant Episcopal Church of the Epiphany recently admitted: "What the North generally has done is to accept the social conventions of the South, while condemning the reasons for those conventions." Naturally the Southerner wonders from what area of the Northern consciousness the great outcry against segregation comes.

For such reasons, the Supreme Court's decretal has to it the look of a second installment of Reconstruction. As the first was inspired by vengeance, so this looks inspired by a desire to impeach the South and to impose upon it conditions which have generally proved impossible even where the obstacles were far less. The South knows that in wide areas a forced integration would produce tensions fatal to the success of education. It believes that the advice of Booker T. Washington to the Negro, though not the easiest, is still the best. Let the Negroes cultivate excellence. When they create something that the world desires, the world will come and ask to have it, and will have to accept it on the Negroes' terms. That is the way other races have raised themselves, and it is the only permanent way. The South's decision to resist the new forward motion of the centralizing and regimenting impulse has won it support in the North among those who see the issue of authority as transcending this particular application.

The question of whether the South deserves separate nationality will today be dismissed as academic. It has not forgotten its tremendous sacrifices in the bid for independence, as its innumerable Confederate monuments, its continuing Confederate pensions, and its odes to the Confederate dead testify. And with the United States insisting on independence for this and that country halfway around the world—independence for Czechoslovakia, independence for Indo-China, independence for Korea, independence for Israel—it has certainly been handsome of the South not to raise the question of its own independence again. But putting this aside as one of those considerations which may be logical but are politically fantastic, let us turn to the role of the South in the future of the Union.

Many years ago a Southern speaker in a eulogy of George Washington predicted that at some distant date the nation would again need to look for such a man for its salvation. He based this upon a prophecy that one day the nation would arrive at such an embittered tangle of animosities, brought on by the clashing of pressure groups, the contradictions of opportunistic policy, and the blindness of relativist doctrines that it could no longer save itself by ordinary means. There would be no recourse but to turn to a man of pure, disinterested, and unshakable character to lead it out of the impasse produced by snarling self-interest and the obscuring of principles.

Washington is in many ways the prototype of the Southerner. His image adorned the Great Seal of the Confederacy; he has been, with Lee, the beau ideal of the conservative section.

Broadening this somewhat, I am inclined to believe seriously that the nation may one day have to look to the South for leadership as it once looked to the Virginia planter and soldier. If the future of the world shapes up as a gigantic battle between communism and freedom, there is not the slightest doubt as to where the South will stand. It will stand in the forefront of those who oppose the degrading of man to a purely material being, and it will continue to fight those who presume to direct the individual "for his own good" from some central seat of authority. On this matter, its record is perfectly clear. The South has opposed scientific materialism while the rest of the nation mocked it for being old-fashioned. If it has had little use for evolution, neither has it had any for Marxism. It has maintained a respect for personality while other sections were tending to relegate personality to the museum of antiquities. It has proved its conviction that when principles are at stake, economics is nowhere. Though it believes in coexistence, as I tried to show earlier, it is quick to scent the kind of aggressor that makes coexistence impossible—and hence, I think, its readiness to arm in 1940–41. By all the standards that apply, the South has earned the moral right to lead the nation in the present and coming battle against communism, and perhaps also in the more general renascence of the human way of life. The stone which the builders have so persistently rejected may become the headstone of the building. This would not be a new thing in history, and the present trend of events indicates to me that it is in the making.

One quality of the Southerner has a special relevance here. Over most of the free world today one sees an alarming loss of confidence in self in the upper or guiding classes. They seem weary of the past, disillusioned by the forces that created them, pessimistic about their future. Even a suicidal motif appears, and they are found subsidizing and even fighting for those forces which would avowedly destroy them. They go in for "liberalism," for socialism, even for communism; and if they think of resistance at all, it is usually in terms of appeasement. They seem ready for extinction by the first rude barbarian who says, "I will."

To this the South is an exception. The reverses to which the

Southerner has been subjected and the great enginery of propaganda which has been directed against him have never been able to break his belief in himself. His self-confidence, sometimes irritating to those who lack it, comes from a knowledge that he stands in a central human tradition, and that the virtues which stem from this, though they may sometimes pass out of fashion, are never out of season. About certain matters he has an "unyielding stability of opinion," often complained of, but a priceless asset when the foundations of things are being threatened.

It may be that after a long period of trouble and hardship, brought on in my opinion by being more sinned against than sinning, this unyielding Southerner will emerge as a providential instrument for the saving of this nation. With pragmatists and relativists giving away the free world bit by bit, his willingness to fight with an intransigent patriotism may be the one thing that can save the day from the darkness gathering in Eastern Europe and Asia. If that time should come, the nation as a whole would understand the spirit that marched with Lee and Jackson and charged with Pickett.

INDEX

The typeface for the text of this book is *Baskerville.* Its creator, John Baskerville (1706–1775), broke with tradition to reflect in his type the rounder, yet more sharply cut lettering of eighteenth-century stone inscriptions and copy books. The type foreshadows modern design in such novel characteristics as the increase in contrast between thick and thin strokes and the shifting of stress from the diagonal to the vertical strokes. Realizing that this new style of letter would be most effective if cleanly printed on smooth paper with genuinely black ink, he built his own presses, developed a method of hot-pressing the printed sheet to a smooth, glossy finish, and experimented with special inks. However, Baskerville did not enter into general commercial use in England until 1923.

Book design by Hermann Strohbach, New York, New York
Editorial service and index by Harkavy Publishing Service,
New York, New York
Typography by Typoservice Corporation, Indianapolis, Indiana
Printed and bound by Worzalla Publishing Company,
Stevens Point, Wisconsin